NORTHUMBERLAND FROM THE AIR

NORTHUMBERLAND FROM THE AIR

STAN BECKENSALL

TEMPUS

First published 2008

Tempus Publishing
The History Press Ltd.
Cirencester Road, Chalford,
Stroud, Gloucestershire, GL6 8PE
www.thehistorypress.co.uk

Tempus Publishing is an imprint of The History Press Ltd.

British Library Cataloguing in Publication Data.
A catalogue record for this book is available from the British Library.

ISBN 978 0 7524 4688 2

Typesetting and origination by The History Press Ltd.
Printed in Great Britain

CONTENTS

Wings pulse through air to gain height.
Wings tilt imperceptibly,
Plane the currents of rough wind
Until I rise above pale scattered clouds
To hold earth locked in my sharp eye.
Posed in clear blue
My mind delights in sweep of brown and green below,
I swoon into cool rush,
Mind alert and body tuned,
Warmed with joy of all my being.

Stan Beckensall

ACKNOWLEDGEMENTS

I have taken most of the photographs myself, and am grateful to the pilots of light aircraft and microlights who took me, especially Jim Martin (now flying the Northumberland Air Ambulance helicopter).

I am most grateful to Marion Clark, Matthew Hutchinson and Gordon Tinsley for their contributions, and to *The Hexham Courant* and the Museum of Antiquities, University of Newcastle (NUM) for allowing me to print their copyright pictures. For the Blawearie coverage, I thank the Royal Air Force for taking the pictures with my camera, an aged Nikon left to me by the Scottish antiquarian Ronald Morris when he died; I still use this camera for slide film. Ronald would have been amused to learn that in September 2007, a roll of film was blown out of the camera by a gust of wind as I was loading it during a microlight flight.

I am indebted again to Marc Johnstone for the map of places featured in the book.

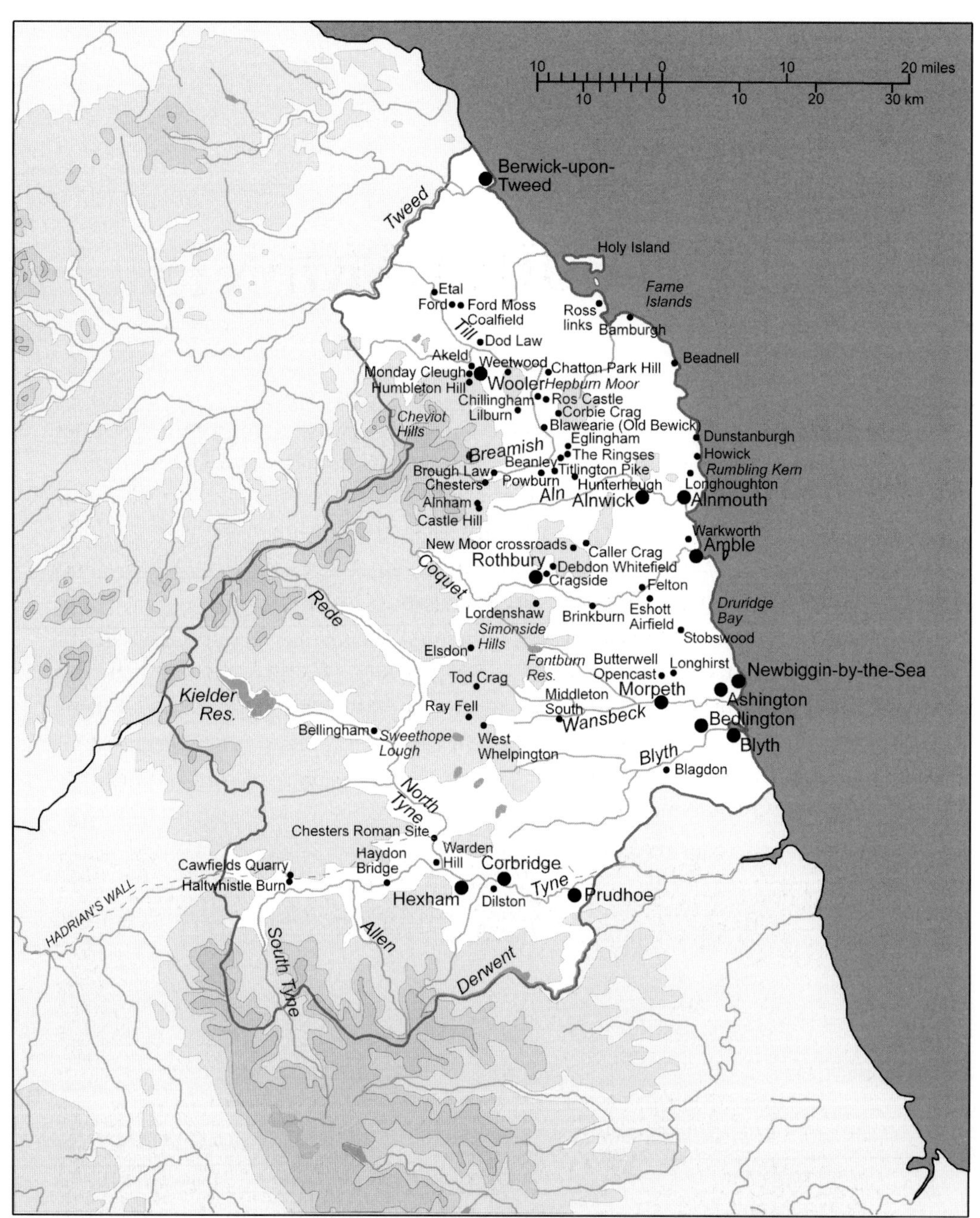

Map of the sites mentioned in the text (Marc Johnstone).

1

INTRODUCTION

As Northumberland is a county from which many sites give extensive views over the countryside, it is possible to get very good views not only from the air, but from hilltops and hillsides. In both cases it is possible to see everything in perspective, so that a place is not just isolated as one feature but part of a much larger whole. Parts of the county have recently been systematically photographed from the air, expensively and accurately as part of a programme of recording and discovery, so can my own photographs or those of other people contribute anything to the picture? The answer is yes, because, as in all photographs, the time of the year, the angle of the sun and other factors are going to make a great difference to how we see things. All air photographs have something to add to the archive, including those of the casual pleasure-flight passenger from a variety of aircraft or the weekend pilot.

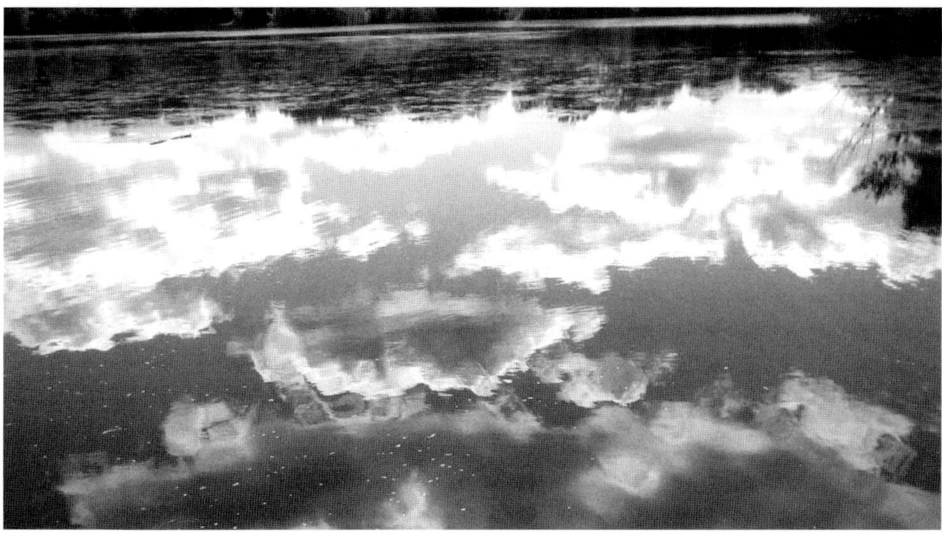

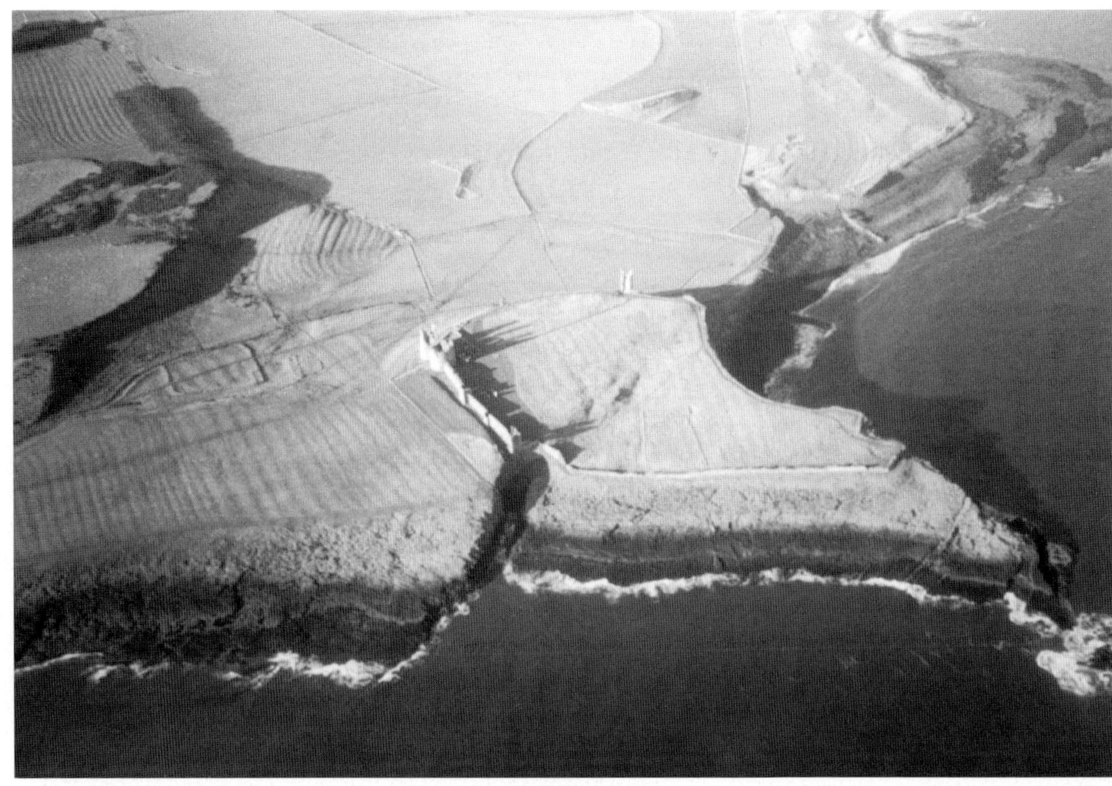

1 Dunstanburgh Castle (Marion Clark).

The photograph here was taken on a pleasure flight from Newcastle airport, and captures not only the structure of the castle, but also the rig and furrow ploughing that covers much of the landscape, not often seen. It also highlights a rectangular structure within the castle because the sun is so low in the sky.

It shows not only how the castle site has used the steep cliffs and the narrow inlet as natural fortifications; it also illustrates how land is used for different purposes. The silted-up harbour above the castle was taken into cultivation for cereal crops (indicated by rig and furrow) and by small, walled enclosures. Towards the top right the area has been converted into a golf course.

The steep cliffs are home to abundant birdlife and are streaked with their droppings.

Much of the coastal plain provided not only good agricultural land, but was an easy route to the north and to ports.

Dunstanburgh Castle is one of many different kinds of fortification in this book. Sited on an outcrop of volcanic whinstone (dolerite) its position was already strong. The walls enclosing a large area reinforce that position, with heavy concentration on the gateway which was built at the weakest point – the approach from the south. This gateway became the main living accommodation from the early 1300s, and then was strengthened by John of Gaunt towards the end of that century. Its name means 'a fortification on a stone hill'.

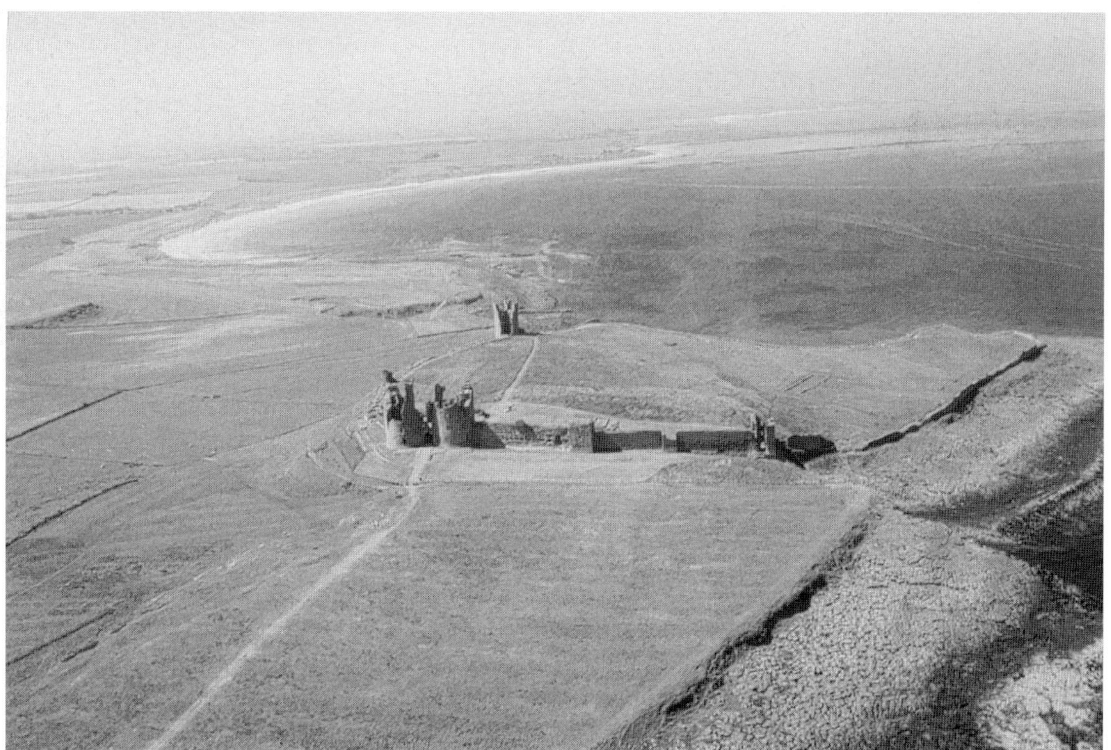

2 Dunstanburgh (SB).

The second photograph, taken from the south, adds detail by showing the castle in relation to Embleton Bay. The castle, unlike Alnwick or Warkworth, remained pretty well unchanged as it soon lost its importance.

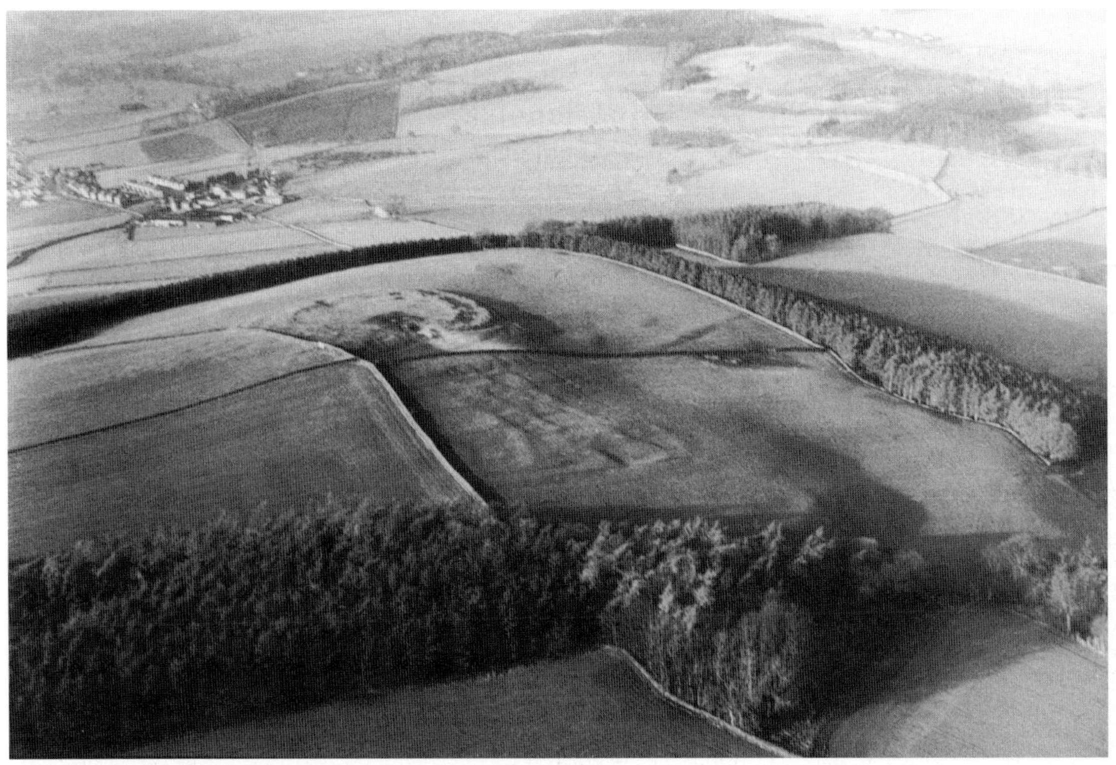

Above & opposite 3 & 4 Warden Hill.

These photos are taken over Warden Hill from a light aircraft in February, from an open cockpit. The flight took in much of the Tyne valley, including Hexham and Hadrian's Wall, passing over Warden Hill. Whereas the hillfort is well known and its walls and ditches are easily seen from the ground, the low light conditions revealed several other unrecorded features, such as grassed-over field walls, small house sites outside the main enclosure and a remarkable number of different kinds of enclosure to the east (right). This shows how the site has been used over a long period, with parts of the walls being dug into and extensions added. Although I plotted the features on a map as best I could as a guide to further study, the history of this site will be better understood with the aid of a geophysical survey that gives a picture of what lies below the surface and, ultimately, by selective excavations. Until then, we do not know the purpose or date of many of these features. It is also clear from the picture why the settlement is there: it is on a hill which dominates the view in many directions. The village of Fourstones and the Tyne valley are visible, with the sandstone and whinstone scarps beyond. What is not visible is the assumed line of the early Roman Antonine frontier, the road called the Stanegate, which runs from

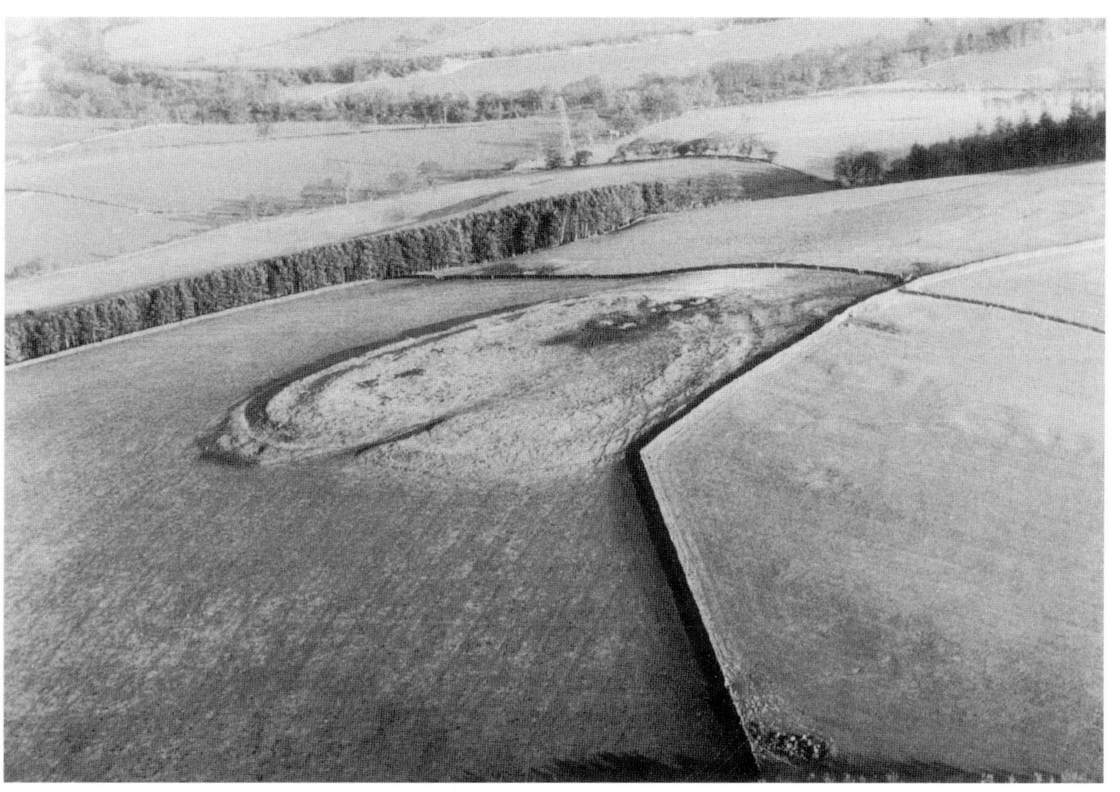

east to west to the north of the hill, behind the later Hadrian's Wall and vallum; it is buried. The whole hill has enormous historic interest, from Middle Stone Age times onwards, with a possible Neolithic long barrow, terraces that may be as early as prehistoric and an early castle site with a possible motte. The hill enclosure is probably of Iron Age date, with a use in Romano-British times, and it was later used as a stock enclosure, though we do not know when. The name Warden Hill, first recorded in use in 1175, comes from the Old English *weard-dun* and means 'a look-out hill'.

A third example (overleaf) of the interesting features that can best be seen from the air, shows the gravel deposits at Powburn, just off the main road north to Scotland.

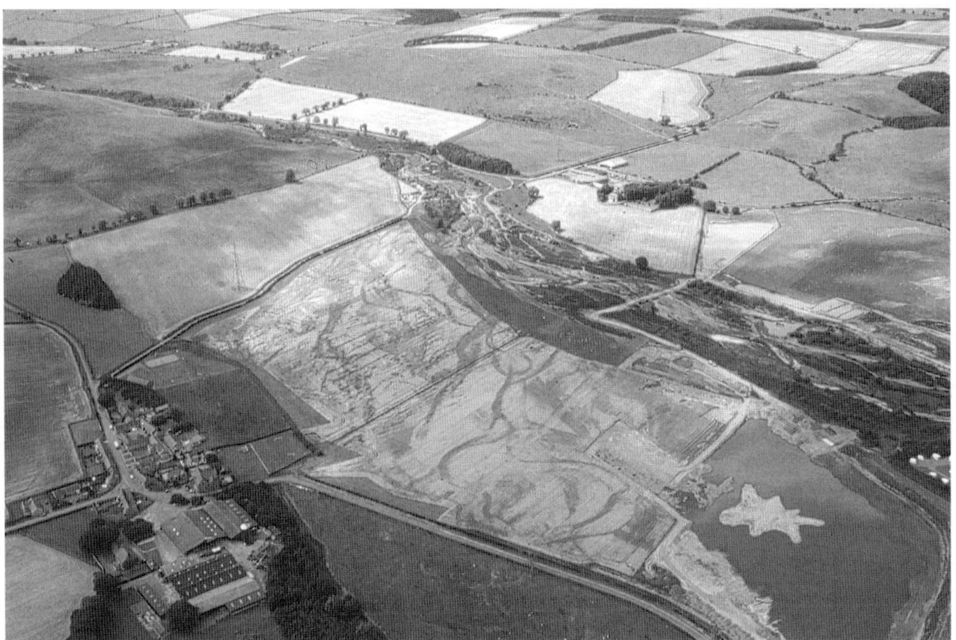

5 Powburn.

At the centre of the picture are sand and gravel deposits that have either been left behind by sheets of ice or eroded more recently from the hills. Ice sheets from the north covered most of the low ground during the Ice Age and when the ice melted it left behind debris that can be as thick as 30 metres. At Powburn a temporary lake was formed and its overflow cut a deep channel through solid rock to the south of the village, where the abandoned railway and the A697 road run.

The name Powburn, first recorded in 1868, refers to the pools seen along the stream today, as the element 'poll' means a pit or pool. The gravel is extracted commercially; the workings and artificial pond are seen here. A proposed extension of the industry into the Ingram valley was recently blocked, and the workings are now exploiting deposits to the east, towards Beanley. Powburn is the place where the River Breamish, unlike the other county rivers, makes a sharp turn north; it is renamed as the River Till at Old Bewick, cuts through the Fell Sandstone at Weetwood Bridge, then joins the Tweed via the Milfield Plain.

The village, though small, has one of the few petrol stations and cafes and inns on the main road, its buildings ending at the place where the road enters the glacial meltwater channel.

Although the largest part of this picture is taken up with gravel deposits, the fields around are ideal for agriculture. Gravel soils were usually well-drained and provided some of the earliest settlement sites in Britain.

2

THE VALUE OF AERIAL PHOTOGRAPHY

As an aid to understanding the past and how things have changed, aerial photography is relatively recent. Its value is thought to have begun with a photograph taken of Stonehenge in 1906 from a balloon, and with the rapid development of military and commercial use of air space it has accelerated. It has its own specialised techniques, mainly developed during the Second World War when military intelligence was crucial to the success of the war effort. There is now a National Mapping Programme for recording and interpretation, all to common standards. High altitude and satellite photography are not so useful in revealing details found in low-altitude imaging. Much of Northumberland has been photographed at low altitude, but these techniques and results demand a different kind of expertise and do not fall within the scope of this book.

The value of aerial photography is shown in this pictorial record of an excavation and in a survey of its surrounding landscape.

A SEQUENCE OF EVENTS RECORDED IN AN EXCAVATION

The year 1984 saw the beginning of the excavation of the Blawearie Cairns, Old Bewick Moor, directed by the author, initiated by the Northumberland County Education Committee. Most of the workforce was from High Schools and many of the volunteers were accommodated at the field centre nearby. Other local volunteers travelled to the site daily. The report is published in the *Proceedings of the Prehistoric Society*. These aerial photographs show what a valuable resource it is to have a sequence of pictures taken during the excavation and after the site had been reinstated in 1988.

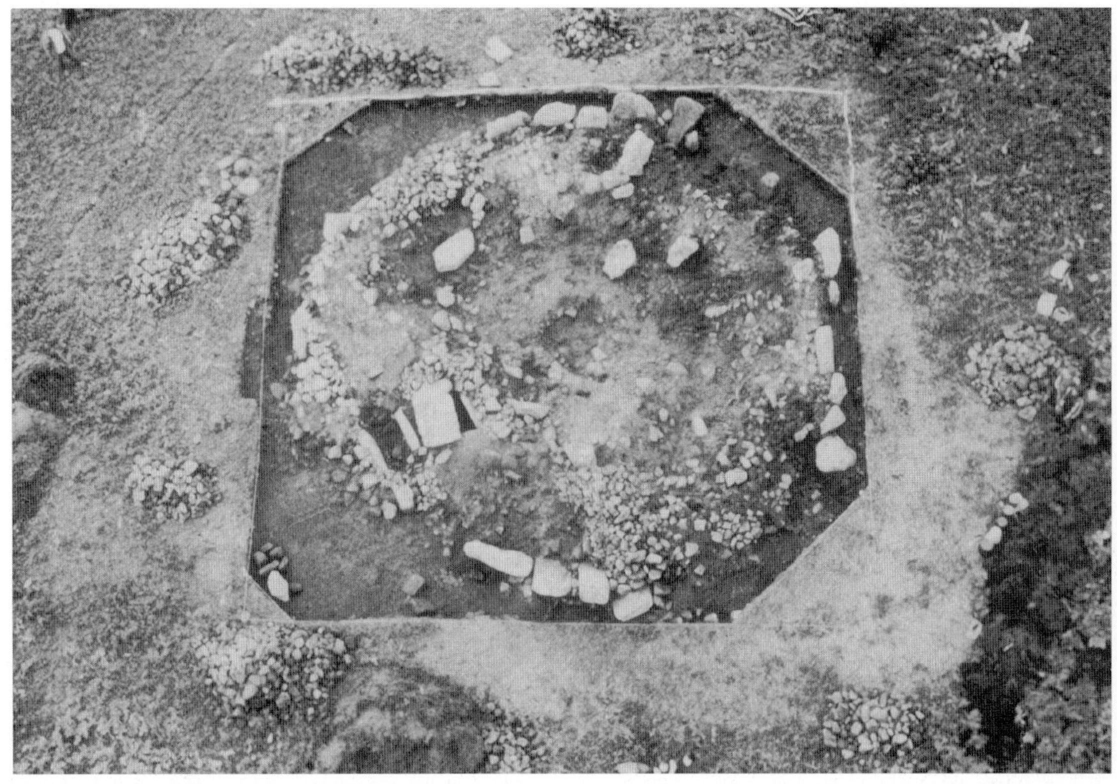

6 Blawearie 1: 1984.

The 12m diameter cairn has been superficially cleared of vegetation. Loose stones have been recorded and piled outside the 'cut'. The main features are now visible – a roughly circular area formed by an interrupted enclosure of standing stones. Three cists are visible, one with its capstone completely covering it (top left). There is a hole in the centre and some scattered large stones. Much of the disturbance to the site was made by Canon Greenwell's men in the nineteenth century during a rapid dig using workmen.

During our clearance a necklace of amber beads was found near the large cist with its lid moved slightly to one side. After our clearance, the loose stones were replaced on the cairn to help protect it, ready for the next season's dig.

The soil is thin and acidic, providing a habitat for heather, with extensive intrusions of bracken. Below this top soil is a bright yellow sand/clay which was dug through when the standing stones and cists were inserted.

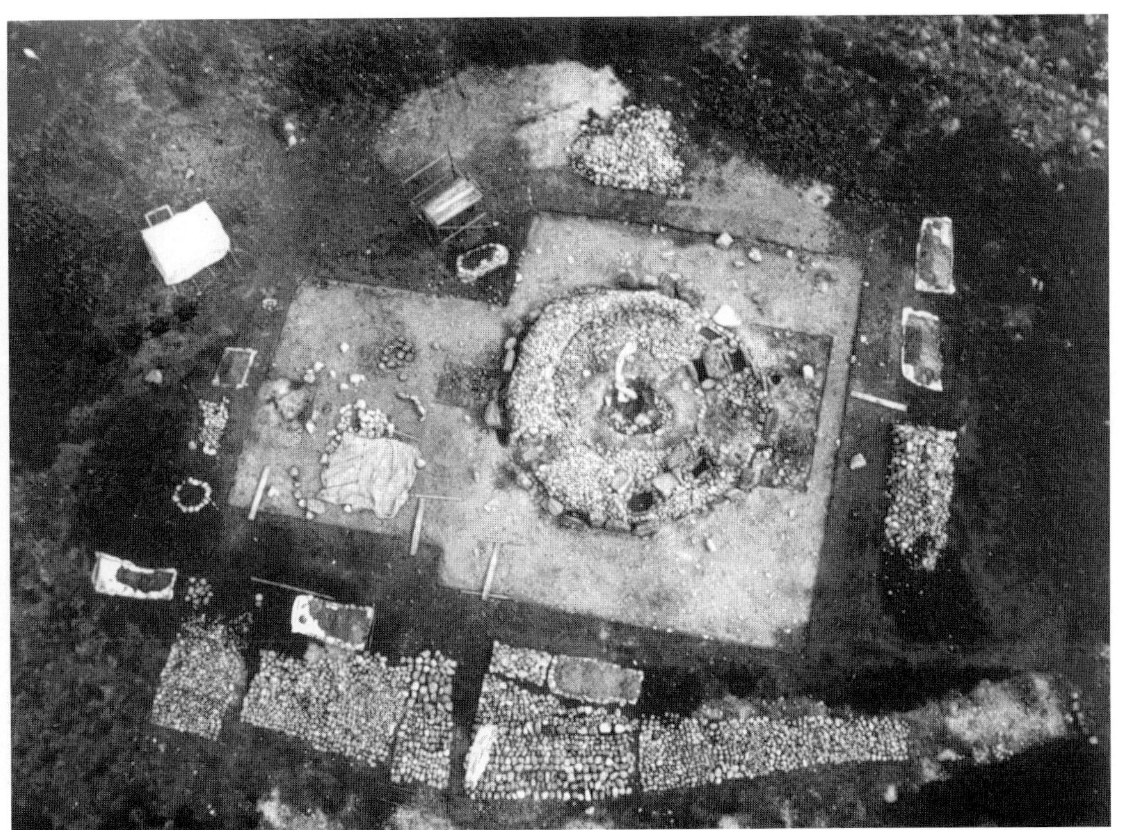

7 Blawearie 2: 1987.

This shows a considerable development in the planning and excavation of the site. The 'cut' has been extended to include smaller cairns, which we did not know about when the dig started. This shows the large cairn to be part of a cemetery, and more cairns were found to the south, recorded, but not excavated. Two more cists have been revealed, and two cremations in small pits. The socket holes of missing kerb stones have been located.

All these features show up as dark areas within the excavated site, and to the right within the 'sondage' cut there is a small black hole which was full of cinders and the remains of human cremation.

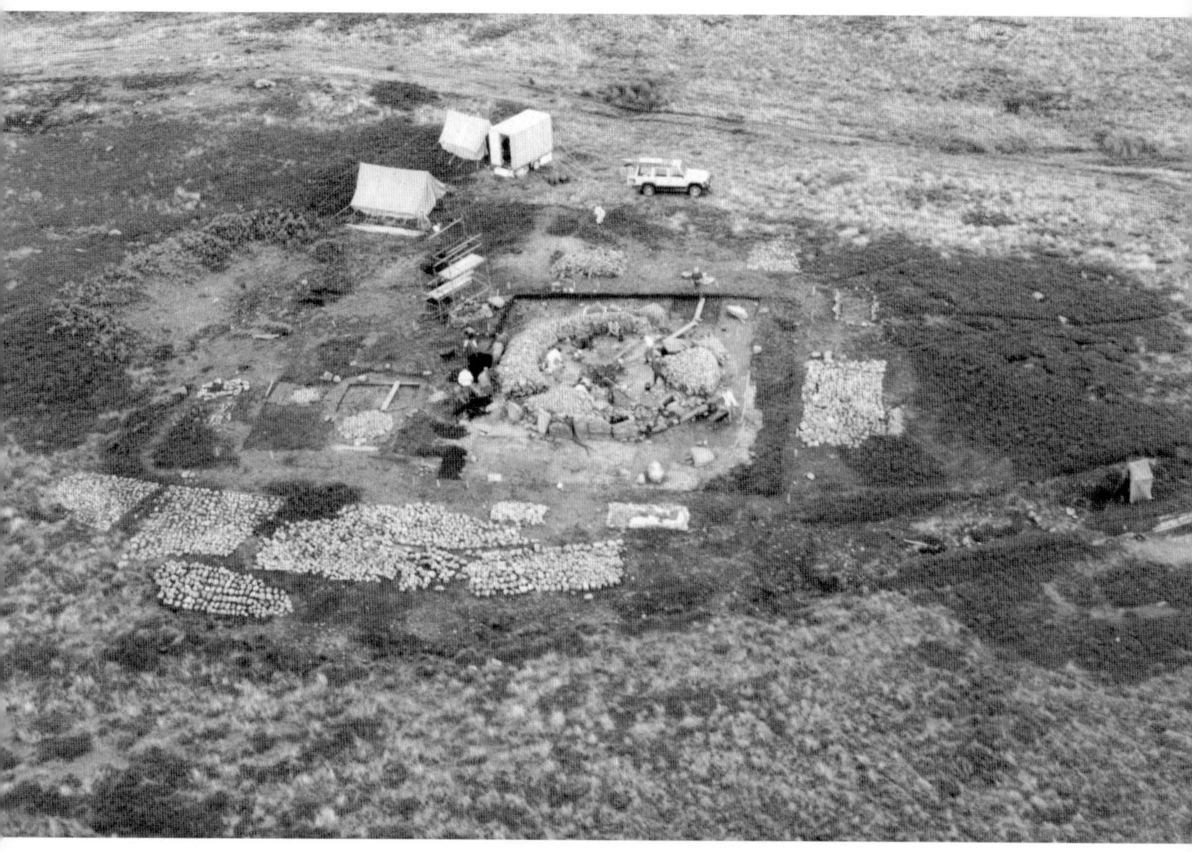

8 Blawearie 3: 1988.

The excavation is entering its final stage. Soil is being replaced where that part of the excavation has finished whilst the centre is completed. The excavated stones at the bottom of the picture and soil on polystyrene sheets are to be used to rebuild and consolidate the cairn. The site office, a caravan, tents for equipment and a platform for photography are clearly seen. The small cairns to the left are surrounded by turf so that the edges will remain visible.

It is clear from this picture how systematic excavation has to be so that nothing is missed and everything can be accurately recorded both on site and in the site office.

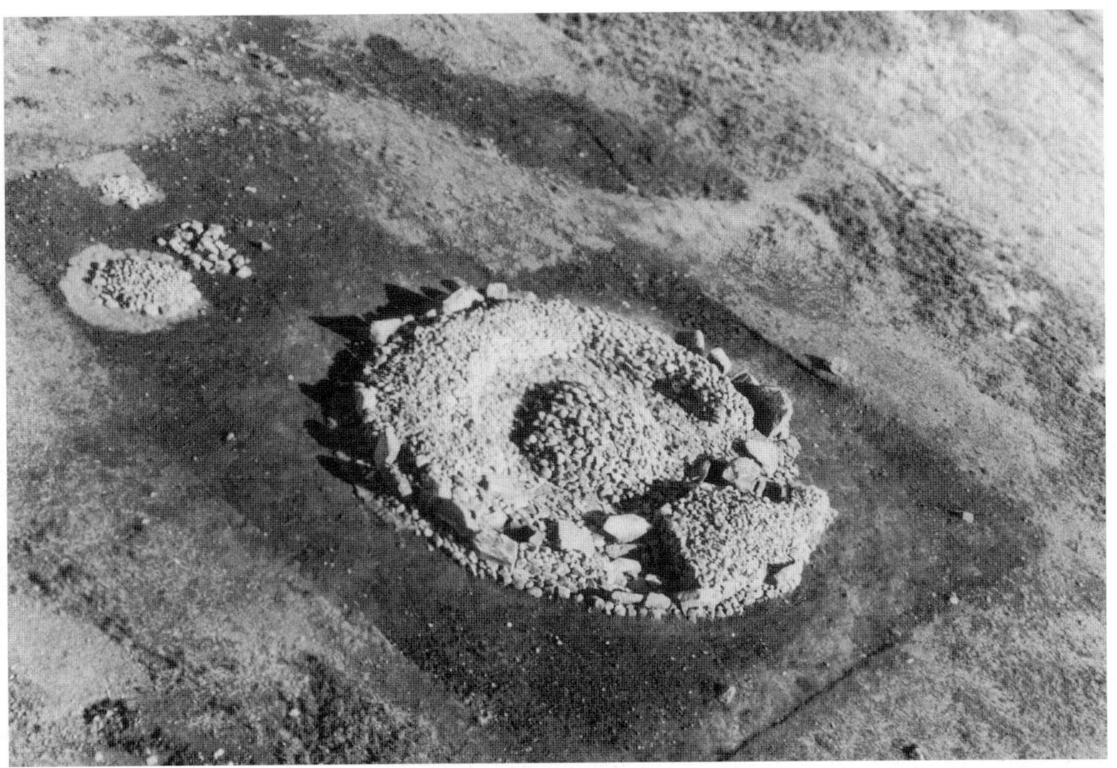

9 Blawearie 4.

The site has been completely reinstated. The surrounding soil has been raked and is left to whatever chooses to colonise it. Small cobbles around the outside of the large cairn echo the support given originally to the large kerb stones. A path around the centre of the mound enables people to walk around inside and view the four cists that are left open, without clambering all over it.

Since this picture was taken, the site has reverted to heather, and although it is frequently visited no damage has been done. It is rare for the public to be able to share a site like this in such detail, as most cairns are scarcely visible.

The dark colour of the excavated soil is partly the result of our leaving bracken root, which spreads out extensively and deeply each winter, mixed with the returned soil.

A WIDER VIEW OF THE AREA

The general area where the cairns are sited is part of the Fell Sandstone scarpland, with its scarp to the west and its dip slope to the North Sea coast in the east. The scarps form prominent features as they run from north to south, then swing round to the south-west, on to the Simonside Hills, forming the edge of an upturned basin with the Cheviot Hills at its core.

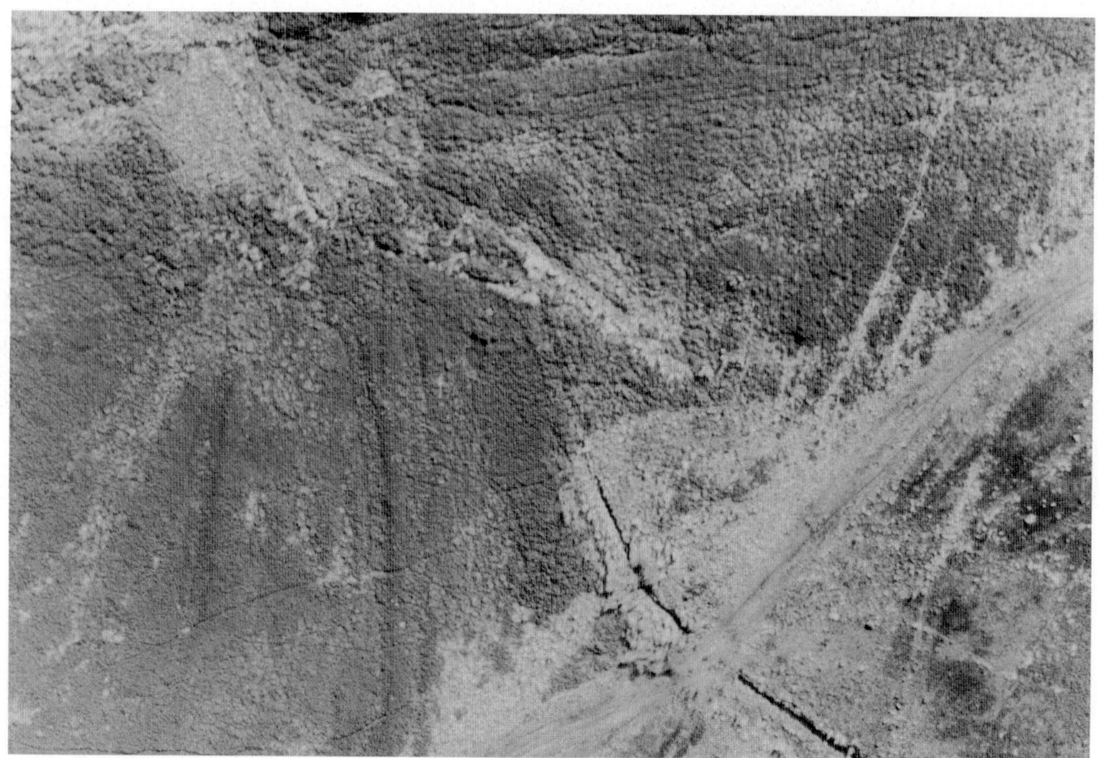

10 Trackways.

Trackways across Old Bewick moor are etched into the landscape by quarry vehicles, and by army manoeuvres during the Second World War. A track built in the 1850s and later reinforced by prisoners of war in the 1940s leads from the village to Blawearie, a now-ruined house.

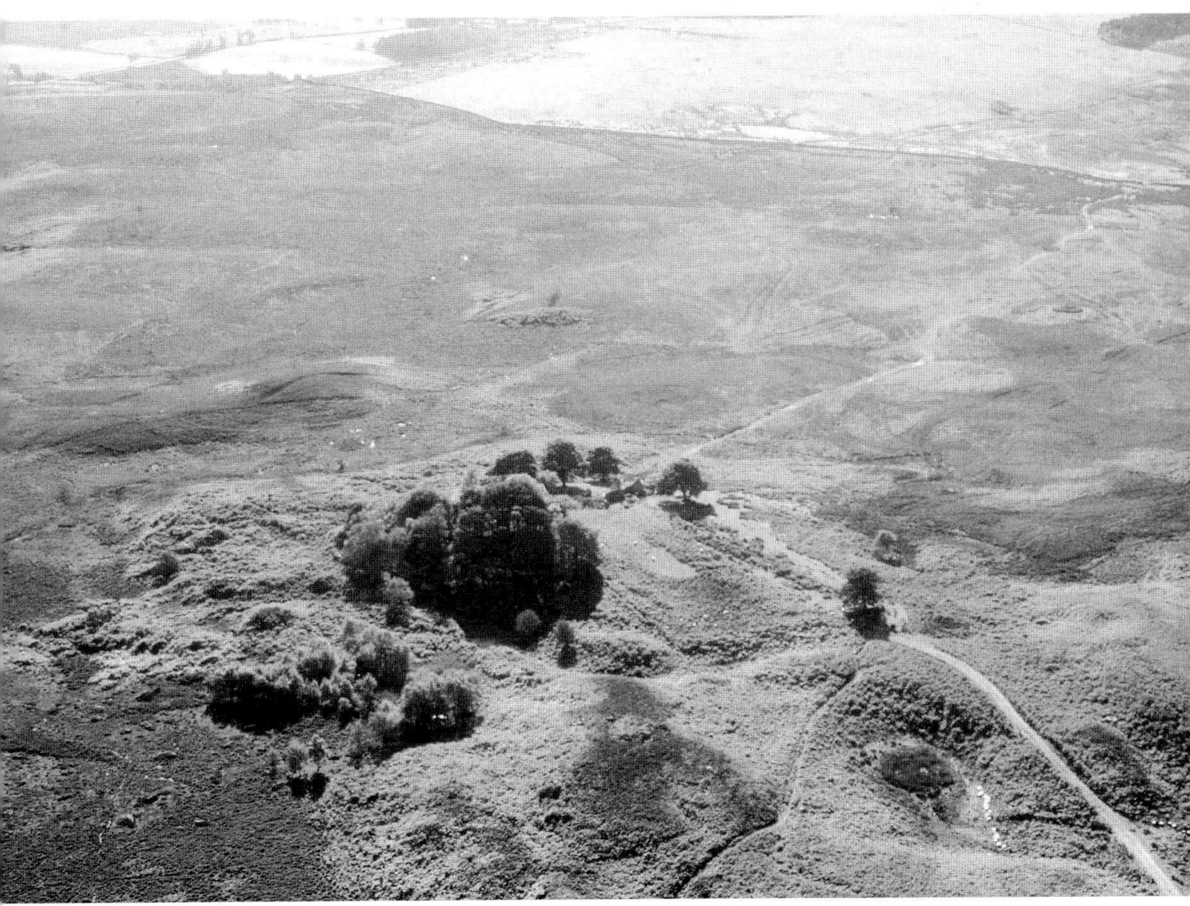

11 Blawearie house.

This is a central place in the landscape, built around 200 years ago as a private and isolated house. Like an oasis in the moorland wilderness, the clusters of trees were deliberately planted, showing that a similar woodland could have existed there in prehistoric times too. The rock outcrops where the house is situated have been quarried for stone, and its garden uses both that and cobble as walls.

To the right of a small line of trees, a trackway leads towards Old Bewick village, and to its right is the faint circle of the excavated cairn. When the track reaches a wall, the land above has been cleared of heather and planted with grass. This field leads up to a double hillfort.

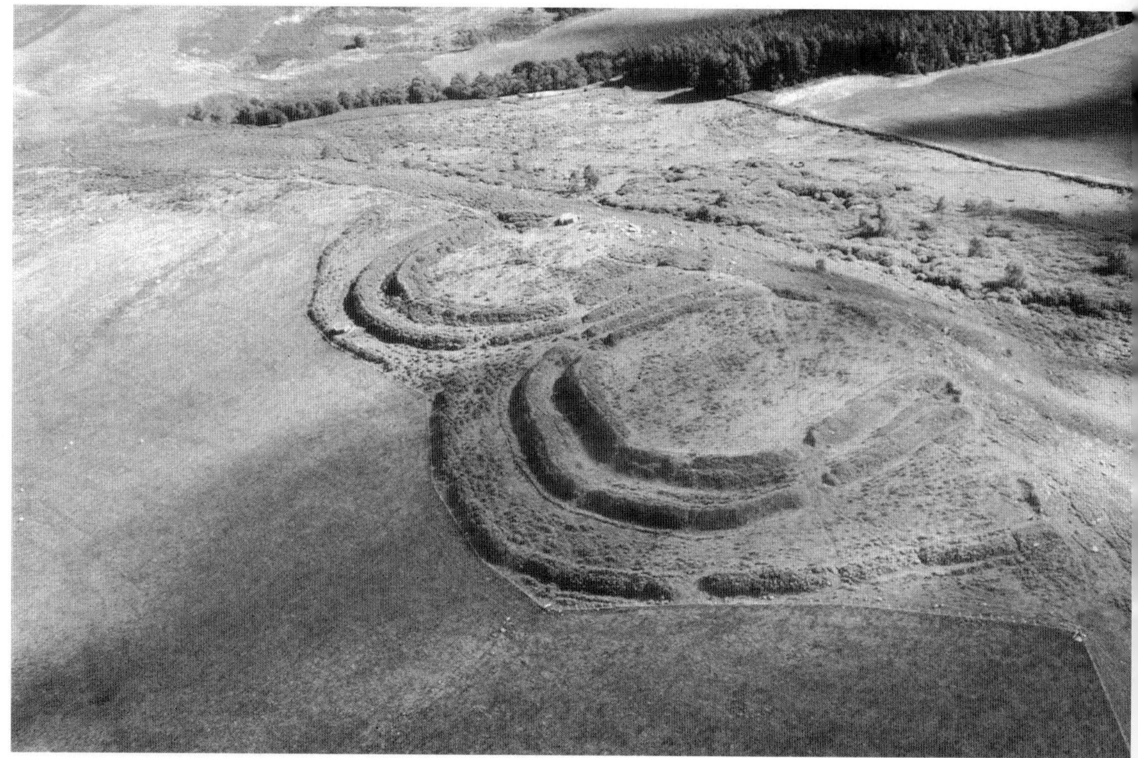

12 Double hillfort and prehistoric rock-art site.

Built on the edge of the scarp, ditches and concentric walls of the enclosure lead to the scarp edge. In the grassed field there is faint evidence of an additional wall and ditch. There are wartime pillboxes within the enclosure walls and a hollow caused by millstone extraction, also used as a temporary pond. The field was only recently reclaimed from heather. Within the field on the far side is a large prominent slab of ice-dumped sandstone that was decorated with elaborate cup-and-ring marks over 4000 years ago.

The adjoining enclosures are built to take advantage of the steep scarp slope (above), but when or why one was added to the other is not known. More enclosed space was obviously needed; the three ramparts and ditches would have contained an area for stock, and there are faint round-houses from pre-Roman times.

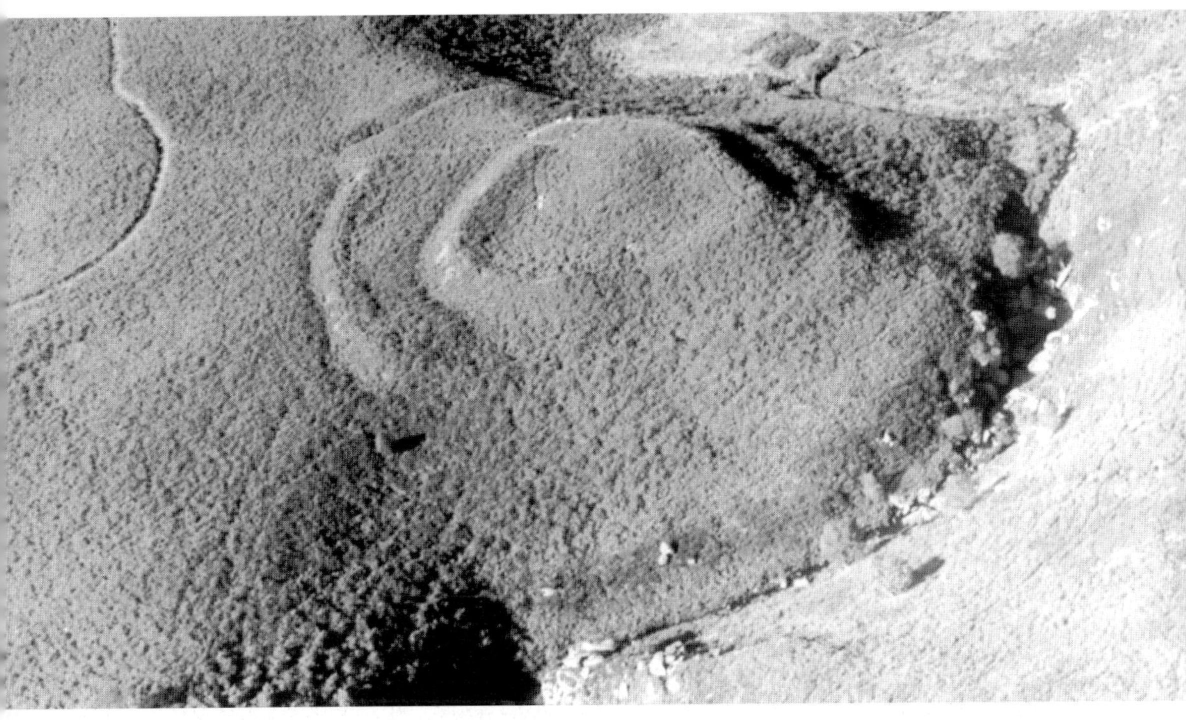

13 Corbie Crags hillfort.

An impressive, though small, ditched and walled area has an extension enclosed by a steep outer rampart, probably used as an animal enclosure in prehistoric times. The nature of the soil would not allow much arable farming to take place here, but it would have been ideal for hunting and pasturing animals. The site is located on the steep edge of the Harehope Burn. A 'corby' is a crow.

We do not know what its relationship is to the enclosures illustrated previously, or whether they were both in use at the same time. Excavation might answer that.

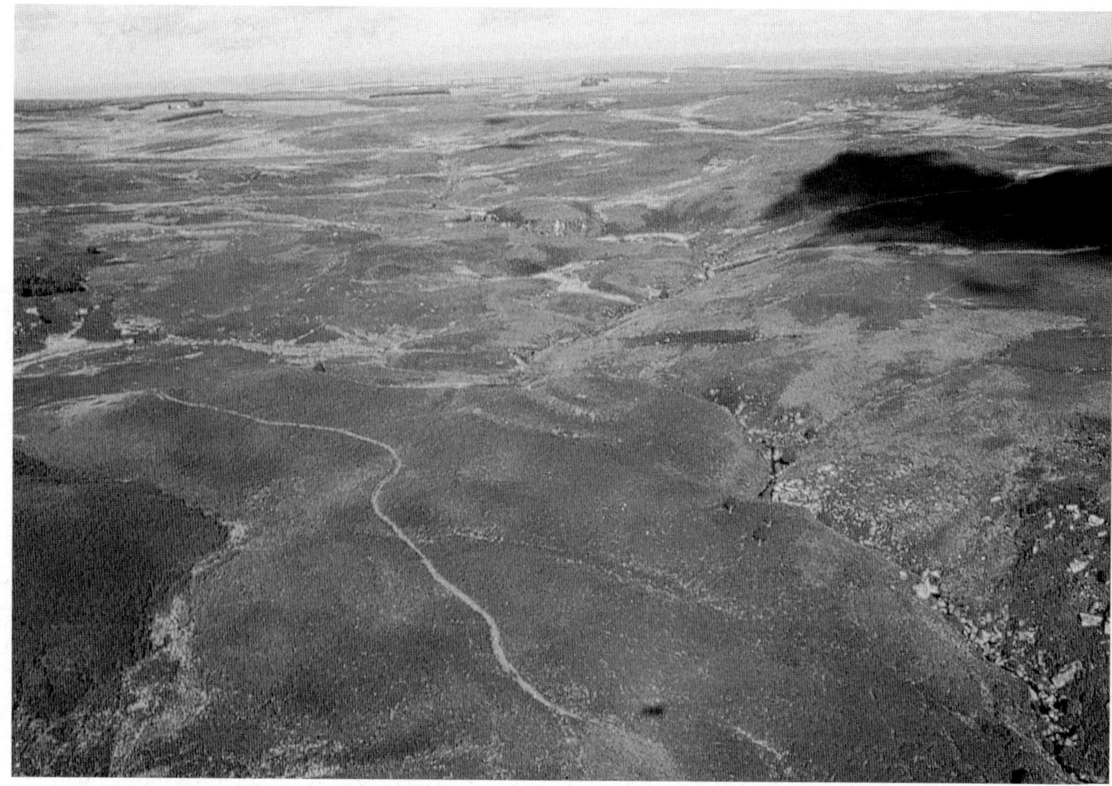

14 Hepburn Moor, fields and moorland.

This view shows the division between uncultivated wasteland (moor) and more recent clearance for pasture. It includes the site of the pre-Roman enclosure on the crag above the Harehope Burn, seen in detail in the preceding photograph.

North of Blawearie the land rises to a continuation of the steep scarp edge that continues as a ridge to overlook Chillingham Castle. The name Hepburn means 'the high burial mounds'.

This kind of landscape was not good agricultural land, as the soil is thin and sour. It would have supported light woodland and have been used for animal pasture and hunting.

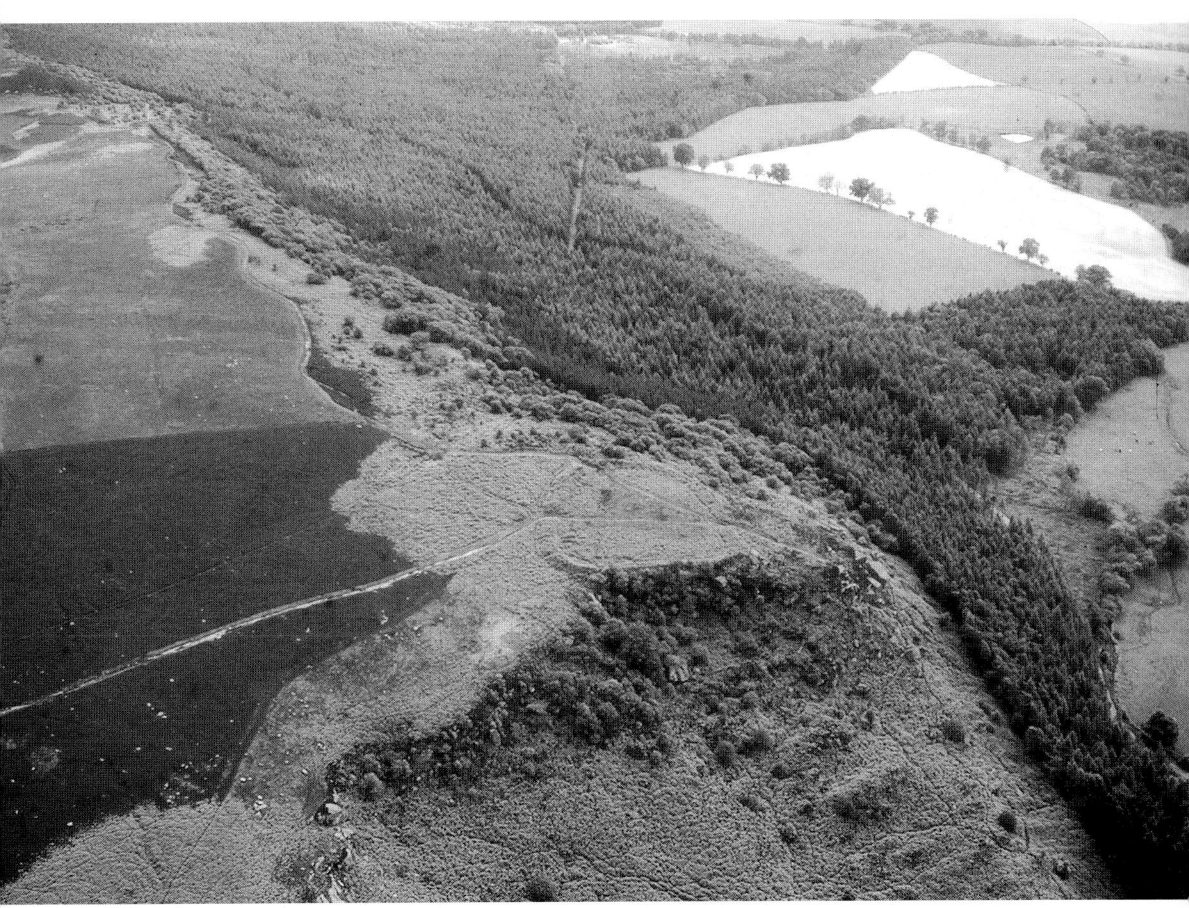

15 Hepburn Hill.

Further north along this scarp is a distinct prehistoric enclosure overlooking Hepburn Wood, planted since 1940. The photograph emphasises the cutting edge of the scarp and the contrast with the lowland farmland. It overlooks the Till valley and the Cheviot Hills to the west. Above the edge of the scarp is a flattish area, at the end of which is a prehistoric enclosure and an abandoned farmstead. Heather is in bloom. Below the scarp are harvested fields, leading to Chillingham to the right.

There is great contrast between the thin soils on the scarp and the arable fields on the more fertile glacial deposits below. The wood on the scarp slope was planted after the Second World War.

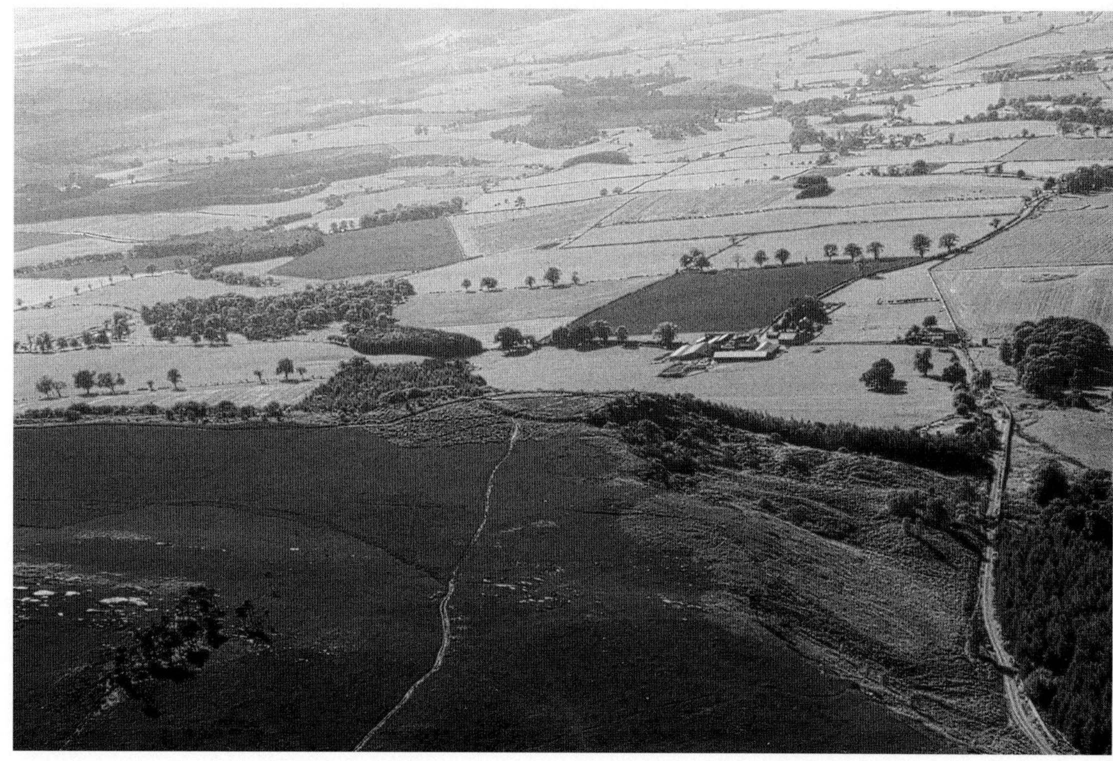

16 Hepburn Hill.

The north end of Hepburn Moor, looking south-west across a fertile valley through which flows the River Till (renamed at Old Bewick, before which it was the Breamish).

We see that the area is stone-free, used as rough pasture, before the scarp plunges to the lowland with its more fertile soils, used for crops and pasture.

The small road to the right leads to Hepburn Cottage, turns a sharp corner to Hepburn Farm, and then travels on to Chatton via Chillingham. To the right of this small road is the Chillingham estate.

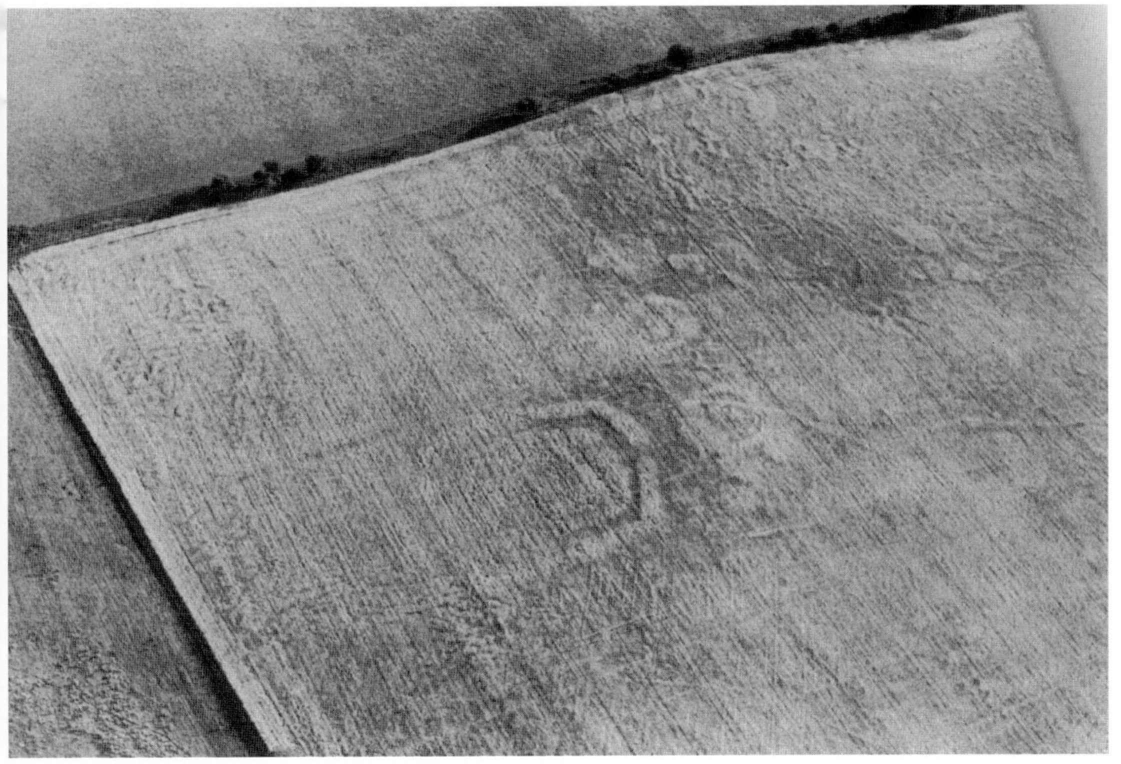

17 West Bewick Bridge (NUM).

We have turned south below the scarp to the fertile land bordering the River Breamish/Till to pick out a pre-Roman enclosure and the circles of possible prehistoric burial cairns. We can see these things because the crop-marks have defined where old ditches were dug. Although everything has been ploughed out, the varying depth of soil caused by digging into the subsoil has caused crops to grow more richly where there is a greater depth of soil.

Many similar sites have been recorded as a result of recent aerial photography; in this particular area, as we follow the River Till to the Milfield Plain, there are Anglo-Saxon house sites, sunk in small rectangles in the ground. The same revelation of 'crop-marks' led to the discovery of the Anglo-Saxon palaces of Yeavering and Maelmin.

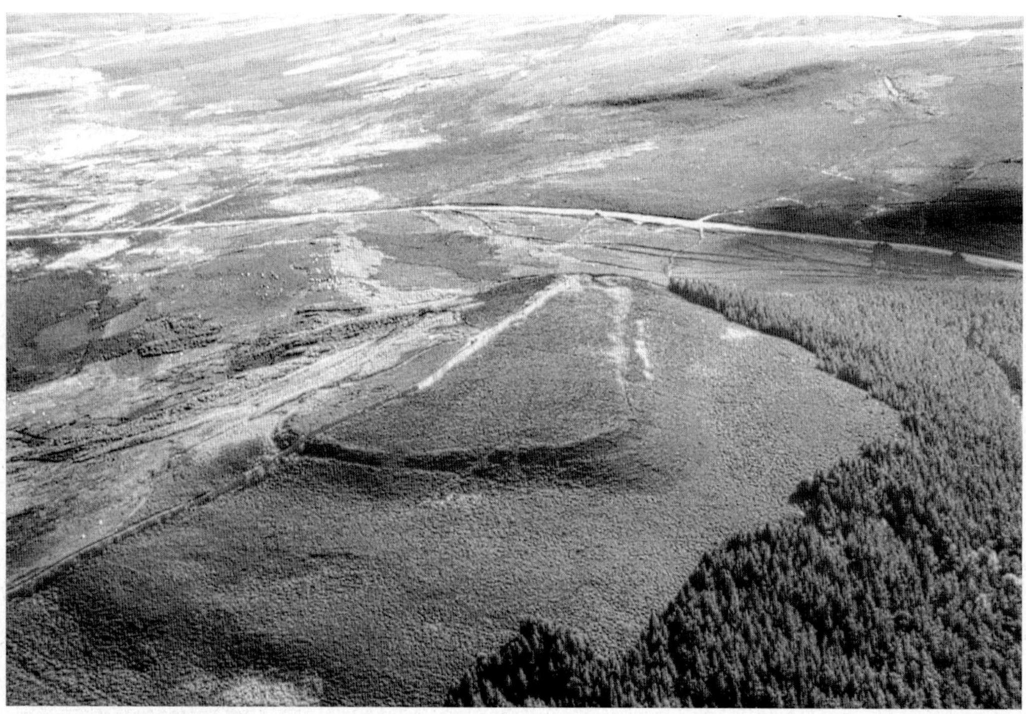

18 Ros Castle.

We fly now north-east over land already covered to the prominent natural hump in the sandstone that is the site of another pre-Roman enclosure (see also *colour plate 21*). Ros means either a moor or a hillock, and here it is both. The elongated walled and ditched enclosure is named 'castle', as many similar sites are, not because it is a stone building, but because it is fortified. Half planted with trees, it now belongs to the National Trust. Around it is one of the most open landscapes in the county, with very few buildings, but there are traces of mineral extraction and lime kilns.

The enclosure takes advantage of the contours, which it follows – hence the unusual shape. It has not been investigated archaeologically, but one assumes that it was an enclosure for livestock and people. Below it runs a minor, gated road to the A1 and to Hepburn Farm.

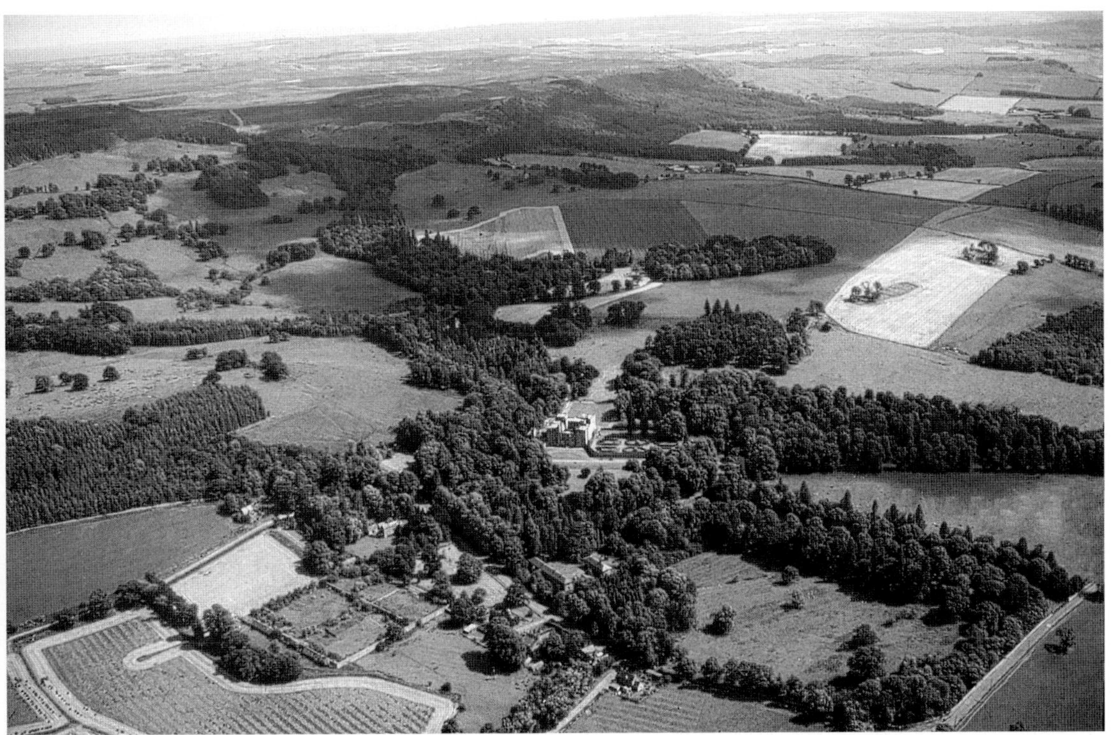

19 Chillingham.

To emphasise the contrast with the rough moorland scenery of Northumberland, this view of Chillingham over to the west shows the castle within its carefully-managed, orderly estate. At the top of the picture is the edge of Hepburn leading to Old Bewick Hill (far right). Scarpland has given way to a valley through which ice has moved, shaped and deposited material that has made it fertile. The richer the land, the greater the risk to ancient features, as the land is constantly ploughed and re-ordered. Chillingham is named after Ceofel, an Anglian settler.

It is not surprising that what has been recorded so far contains so many ancient sites. They survive because people's needs change, as climate changes and as soil fertility declines. However, the demands of a new age led to the establishment of mining, quarrying and forestry, which have destroyed sites perhaps as extensively as modern arable farming. We have already seen all these processes at work in this limited area.

The spotlight now turns on the coastal plain.

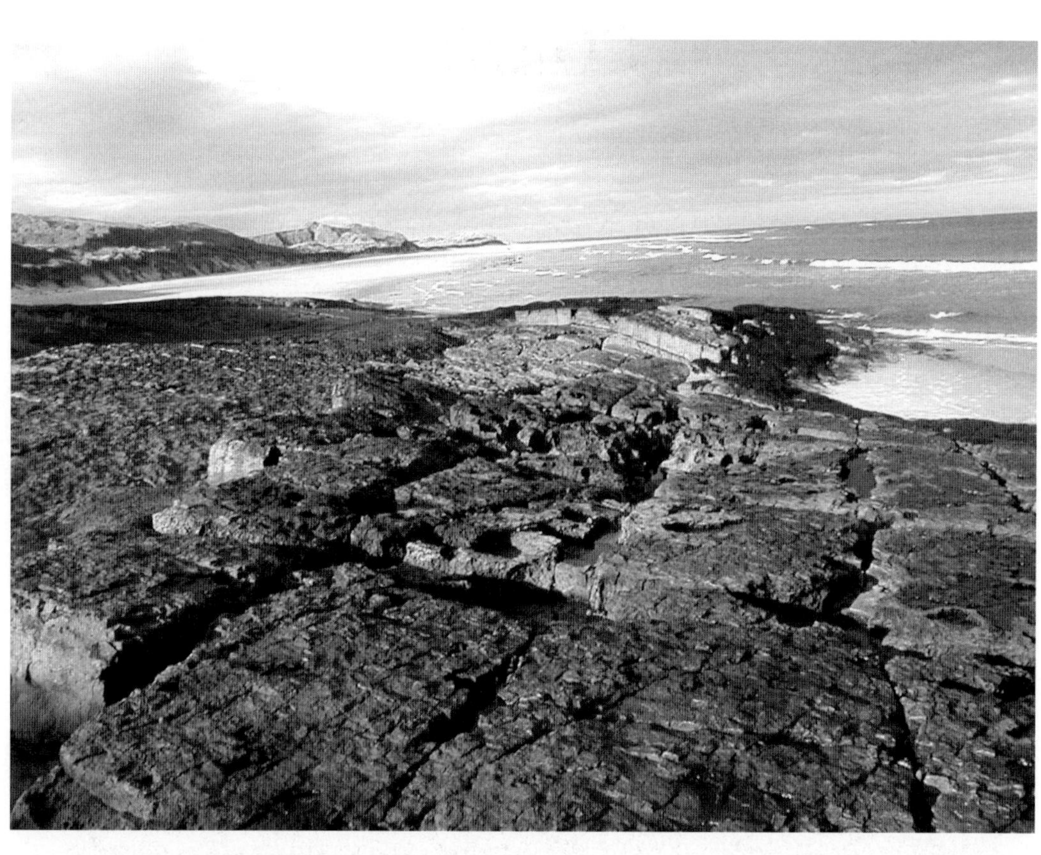

3

COAST

The Northumberland coastline is long, stretching in a line from just north of Berwick-upon-Tweed to the north of Tynemouth. There is a great variety of scenery, including impressive, beautiful stretches of sand, curving bays, river estuaries and outcrops of whinstone. There are also parts that bear witness to an industrial past, with dumped waste particularly from coal mining. There are few islands, with Holy Island, the Farnes and Coquet Island being the main ones.

Historically, the coast was the main route into Scotland; its soils form a fertile belt that contrasts with some of the rougher upland pastures of the interior. Today the A1 and the main railway from Newcastle to Edinburgh follow it.

There are some castles and other strongholds along the strand, such as Dunstanburgh Castle, Warkworth, Bamburgh and Berwick and some large estates.

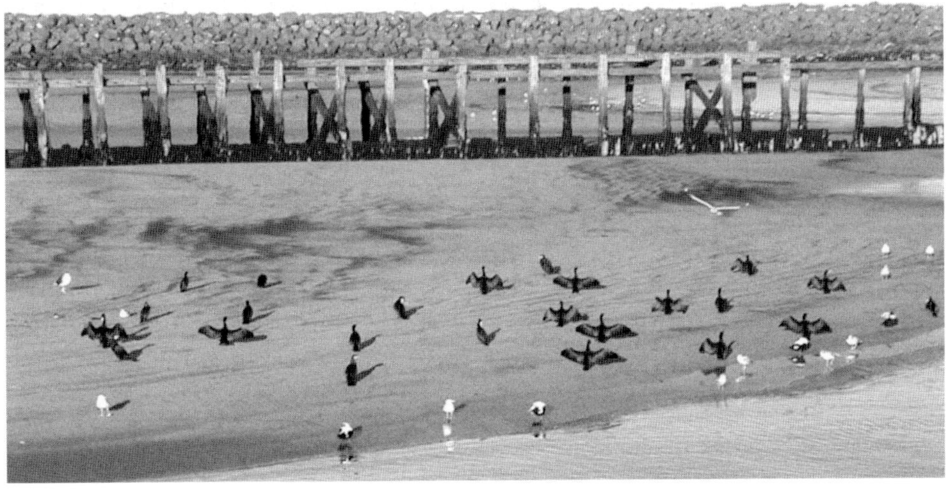

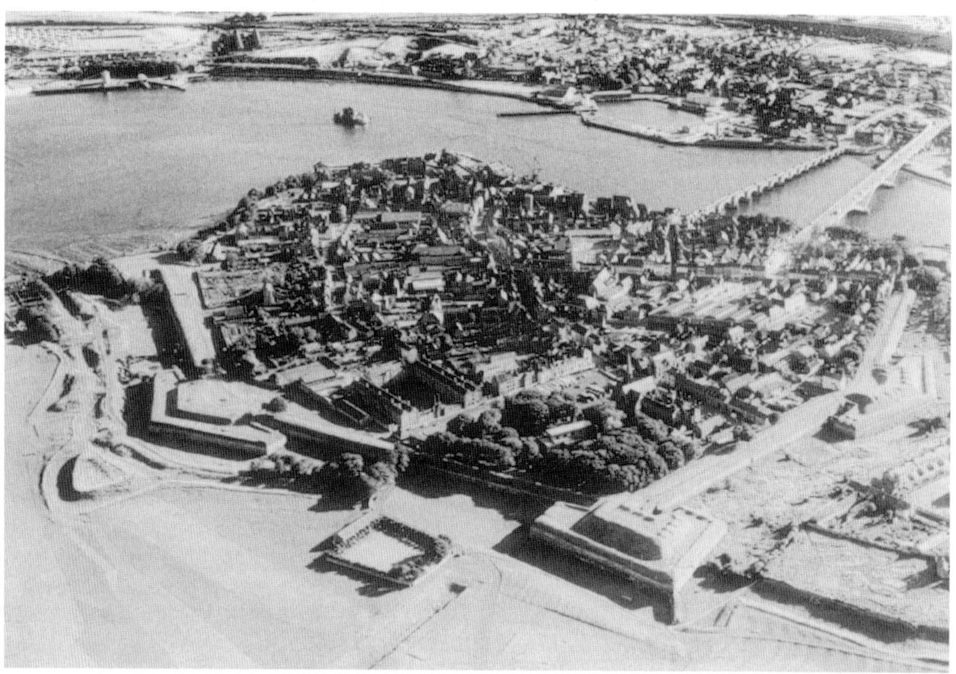

20 Berwick from the north (NUM).

The view is from the north. The Elizabethan defensive wall (bottom) has protruding bastions, beginning with an unfinished one called Meg's Mount by the river (right), then the Cumberland Bastion, Brass Bastion, Windmill Bastion and King's Mount. These face a ditch to the north and east with a counterscarp. Ancient rig and furrow ploughing is seen below the wall to the right.

Much of the town is walled by defences that were the height of military strategy in the sixteenth century, although by the time they were completed the need for such fortifications against the Scots had diminished. They now provide an attractive parapet walkway round the town. The town's layout as a fortress concentrates the main walls to the north and east, as the other approaches were more easily defended. The town centre has fine, attractive buildings. Outside are the housing and industrial developments that have allowed its preservation, since the town is no longer an important garrison site. The Tweed is still famous for its salmon fishing and for the swans that occupy the estuary. Berwick's name comes from the Old English *bere-wic* meaning a barley farm.

The road and medieval bridge cross the river to the right, from the settlement of Tweedmouth on the opposite side, where an artificially-enclosed dock is visible, opened in 1876, and still in use. Tweedmouth and Spittle (named after the Hospital of St Bartholomew in the thirteenth century) are now part of Berwick-upon-Tweed. Top left is a grain mill and a disused brewery and maltings.

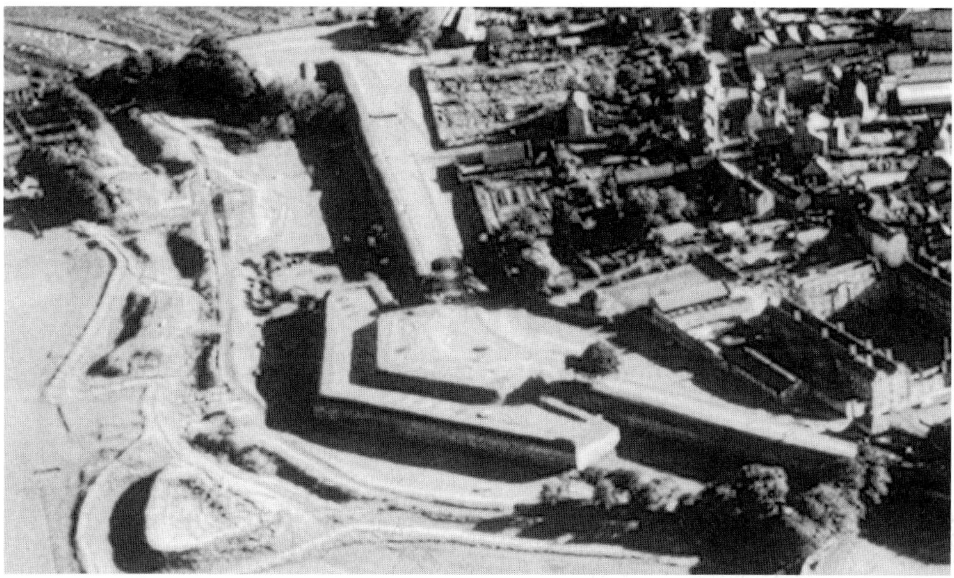

21 Berwick: an enlarged section of the defences (NUM).

The close-up features the Windmill Bastion, lower left, which is complete and well-preserved, with flankers on either side – recesses for cannons that could cover an assault along the wall. It had stone and concrete gun emplacements added more recently. Notice the additional bulwark earthworks in the direction of the point, and others running along the left edge of the picture, on the medieval circuit. The barracks are to the lower right, built as a walled enclosure. The parapet running to the river estuary encloses a powder magazine and allotments, behind which Ravensdowne runs as one of Berwick's parallel planned streets.

What cannot be appreciated easily from the air are the different levels on which these buildings stand, or their quality – for Berwick is a very attractive town, viewed so admirably from its walls.

Berwick has always hovered between England and Scotland, changing ownership many times. Today there is still a strong feeling that it is Scottish rather than English, reinforced by some advantages such as the absence of tuition fees for students.

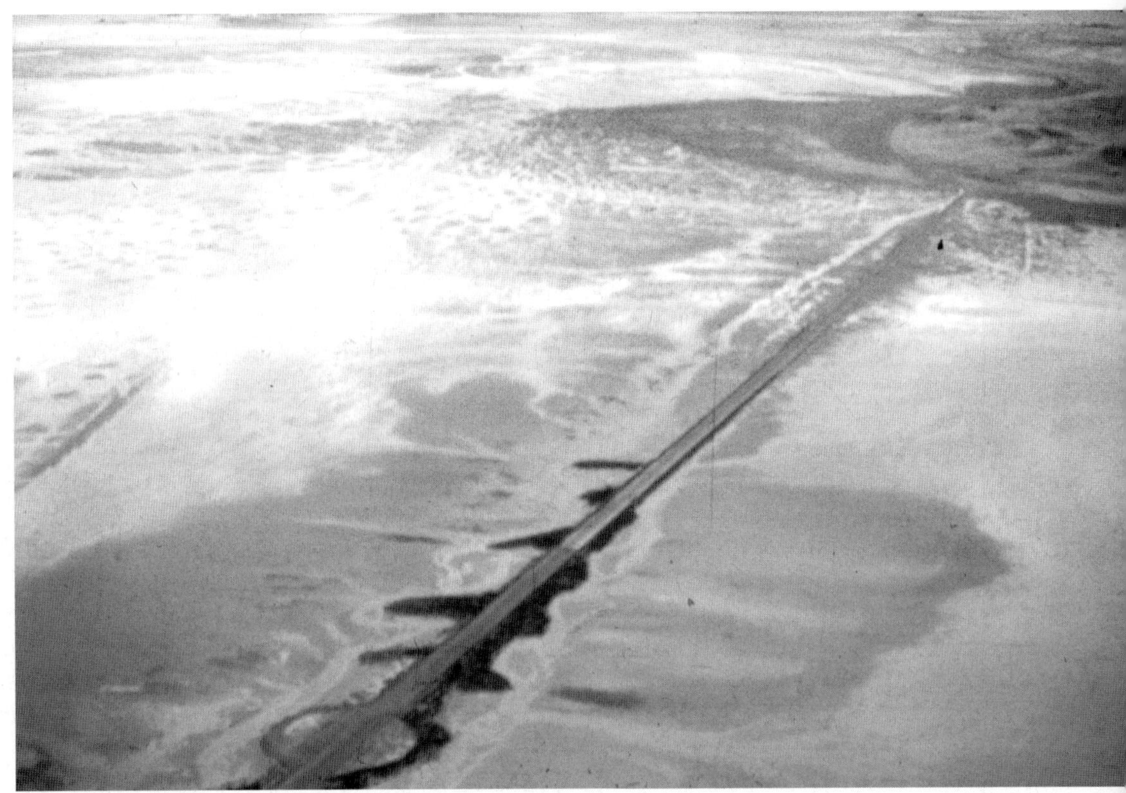

22a) Holy Island.

Lindisfarne, or Holy Island as it became, is one of the greatest centres in the history of early Northumbrian Christianity. Here we see the value of the causeway, where high tide cuts off the island from the mainland and thus afforded the monks some seclusion.

Outcrops of limestone in the north and north-west of the island were exploited industrially from an early date. The Priory and parish church lie on the site of an earlier monastic settlement, with the modern village once serving a largely fishing community, attached to it. The island, with its dominant castle on a whinstone outcrop, is visible for miles around.

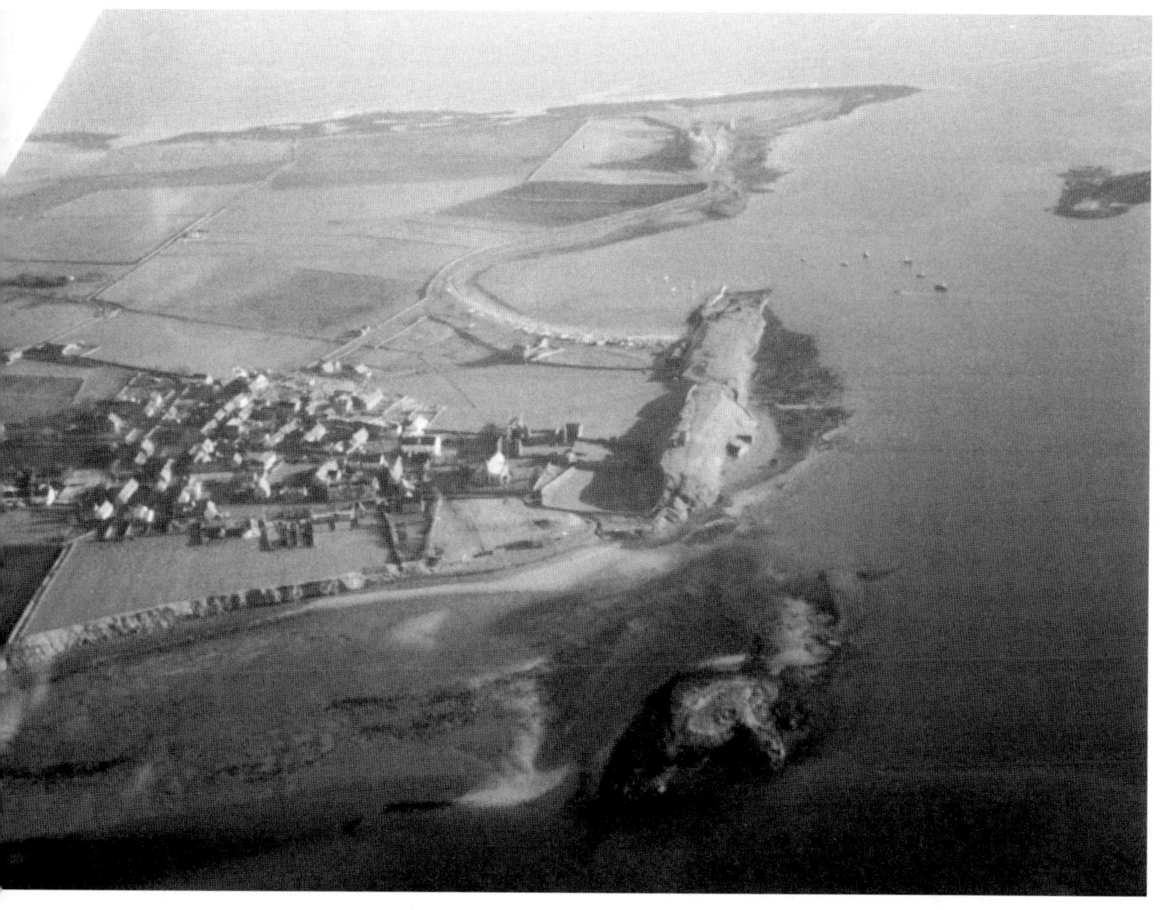

22b) Holy Island. The view is of the village (including the Priory) and the harbour.

To the right of the settlement is a raised platform-like outcrop of whinstone, which outcrops again on the other side of the curved harbour bay, forming a natural mound for the castle.

This small island has fame far beyond its size, for it was here the early Anglo-Saxon monastery that became a springboard for missions and a workshop for the production of the famous Lindisfarne Gospels was located. It remains a potent pilgrimage destination.

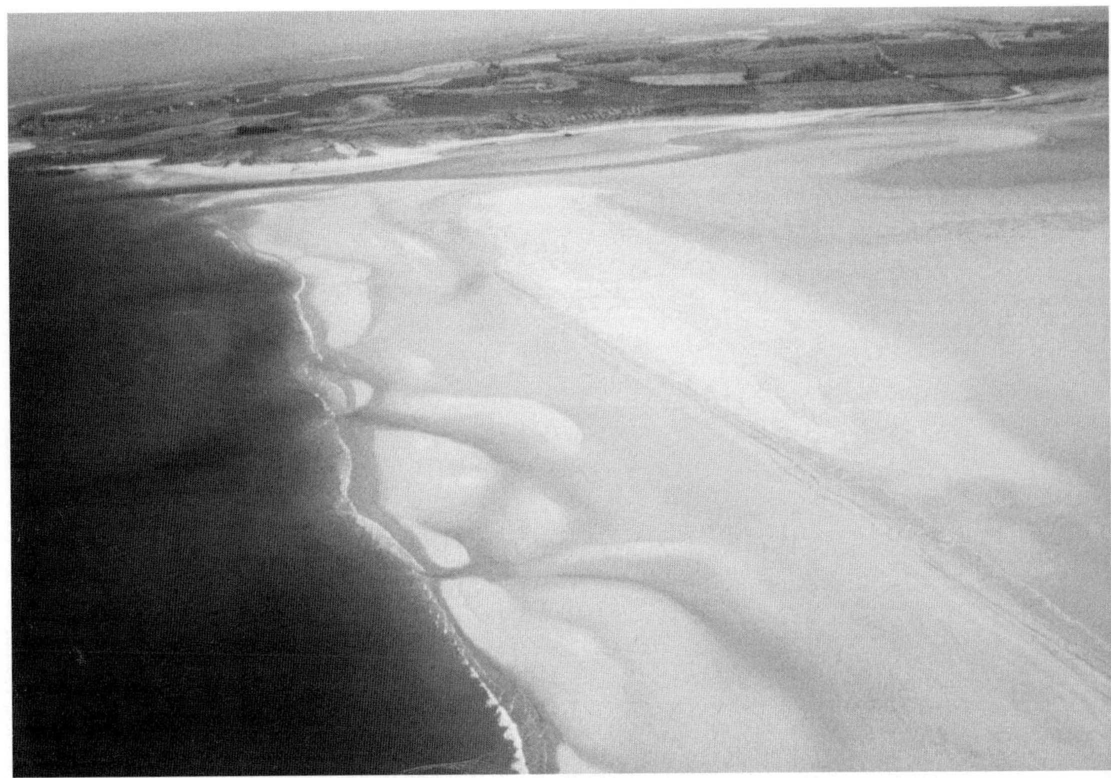

23 Ross Links.

Taken from the north, this stretch of sand is one of the finest in Britain. It flanks the estuary of the Waren Burn (named after alder trees) around which the tidal flow attracts thousands of sea birds to feed there. The dunes further inland were home to some of the earliest people to live in Northumberland over 8000 years ago. South of the river (top) is Spindlestone and the land leading to Bamburgh Castle.

Opposite 24 Bamburgh (Gordon Tinsley).

Bebba, after whom the fortification is named, was the wife of King Aethelfrith of Bernicia. The fortress is perched on an outcrop of whinstone that rises vertically over sandstone, and would have been served by a fine harbour. The village lies further inland, marked by its ancient church. The settlement was crucial to early British history, as a major capital, but now its castle is largely a splendid rebuilding by the industrial magnate, Lord Armstrong of Cragside, and its village largely geared to tourism. Ongoing excavations are revealing more of its complex history each year.

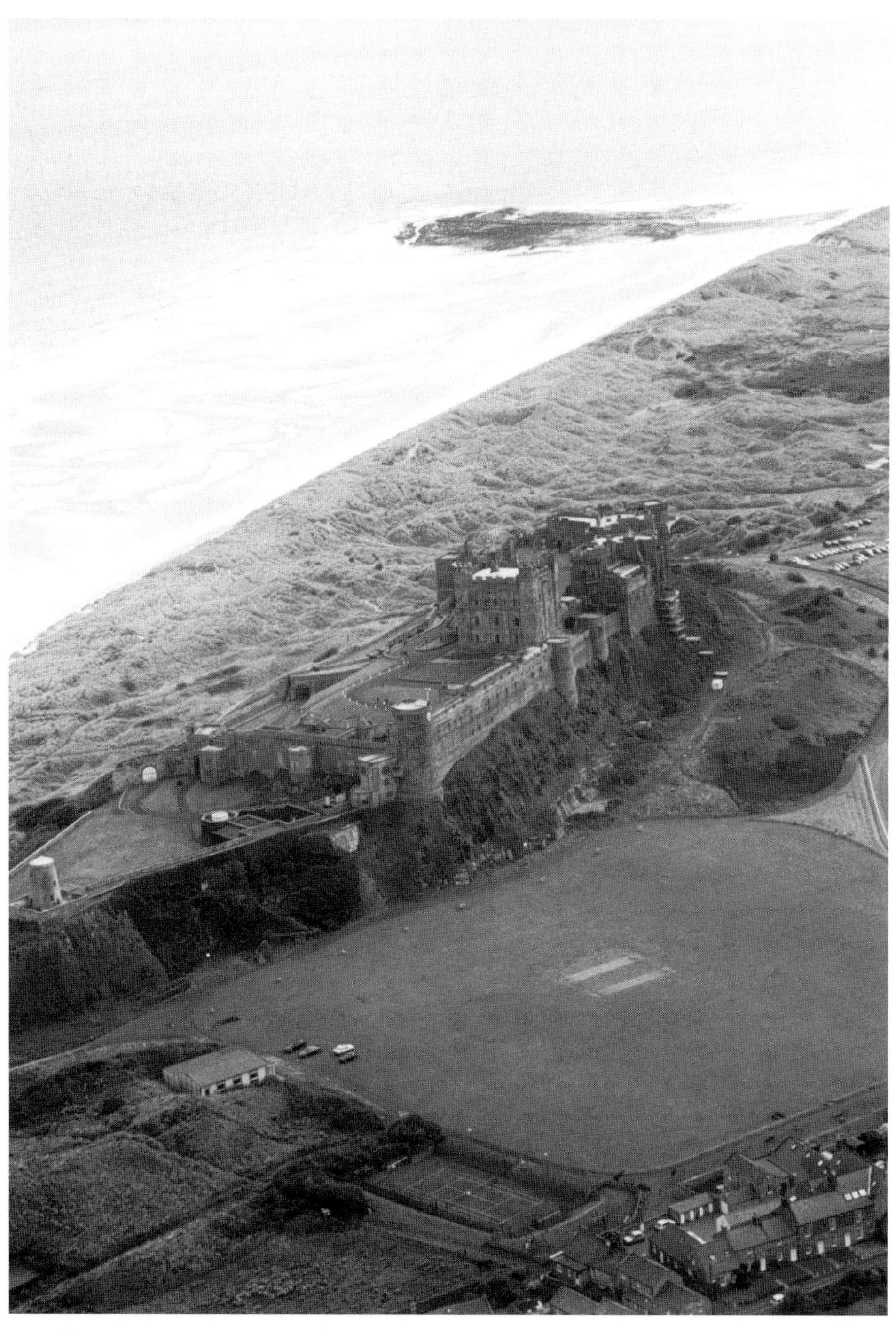

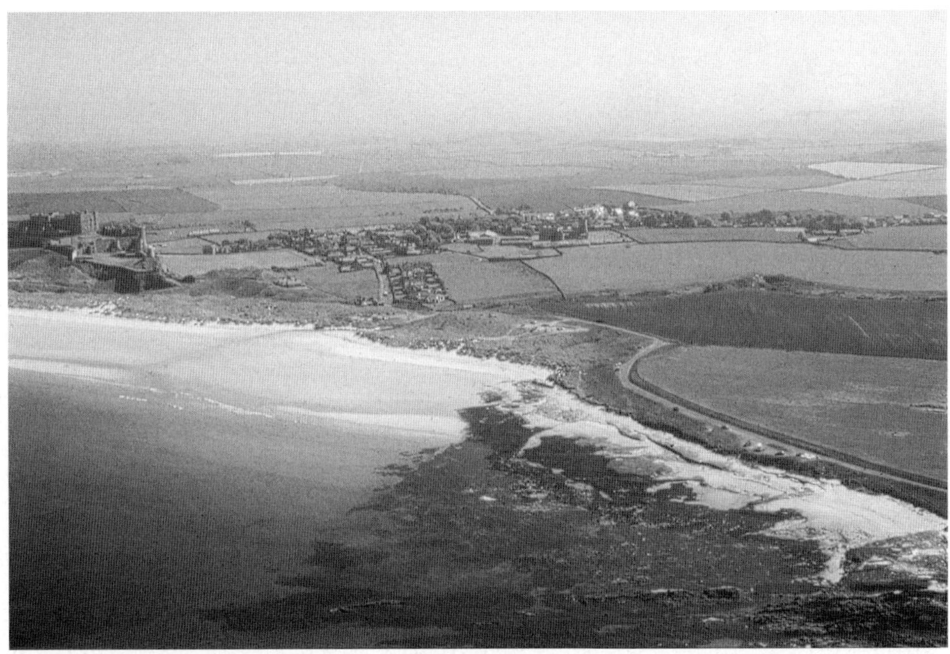

25 Bamburgh Castle with Ross Links and Budle Bay in the foreground.

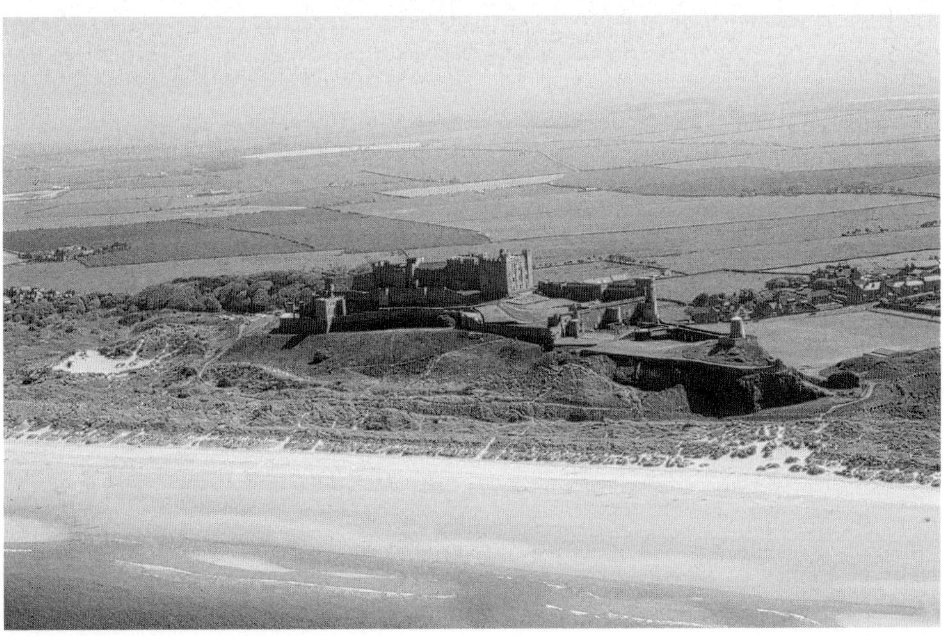

26 Bamburgh Castle from the sea.

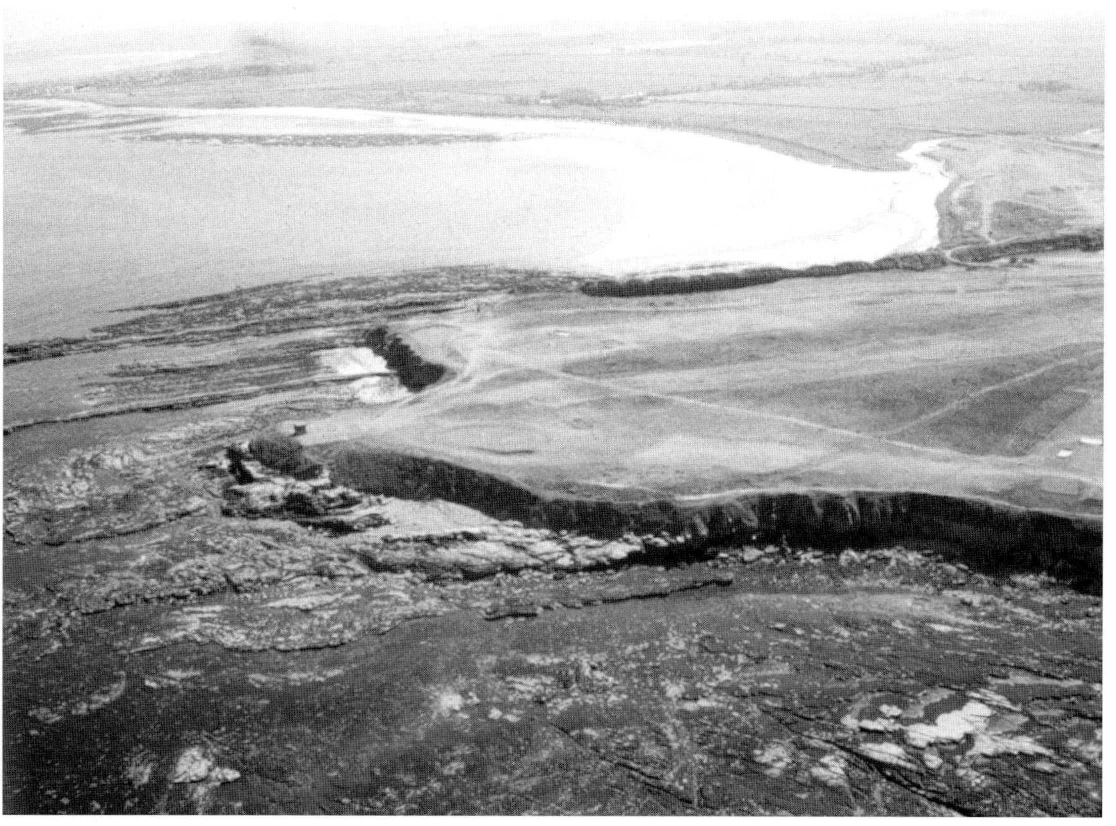

27 The coast south of Beadnell.

The character of the coast changes as we leave Bamburgh, as Seahouses is dominated by a large caravan site, although the old harbour and disused limekilns are still attractive.

The pattern is repeated at Beadnell, although large parts of the coast remain unspoilt, as shown in the picture.

Here we are looking southwards. The general strike of the sedimentary rocks (limestone, sandstone, shale and coal) can be seen as parallel lines running out to sea.

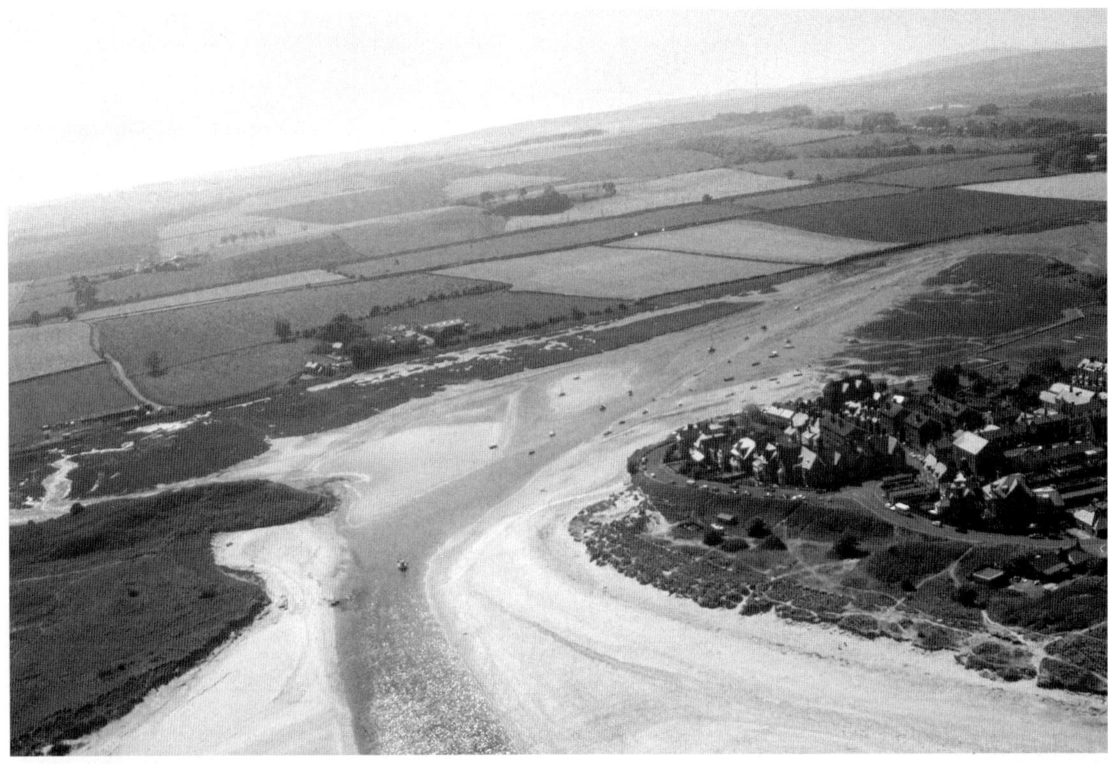

28 Alnmouth.

Alnmouth used to be a flourishing harbour, exporting grain, as it lies at the end of the 'Corn Road' from Hexham. The river changed its course, and the pictures show where it now runs. To the north is a hill, below which is one of England's earliest golf courses. The village, especially the terrace called Louvaine, is a particularly attractive view from the mainline railway to the west.

It remains a popular resort for visitors to the seaside, many of them local day-trippers. It still has a railway station on the main Newcastle-Edinburgh line, and was once connected by rail to Alnwick. Plans have often been proposed to re-open this line.

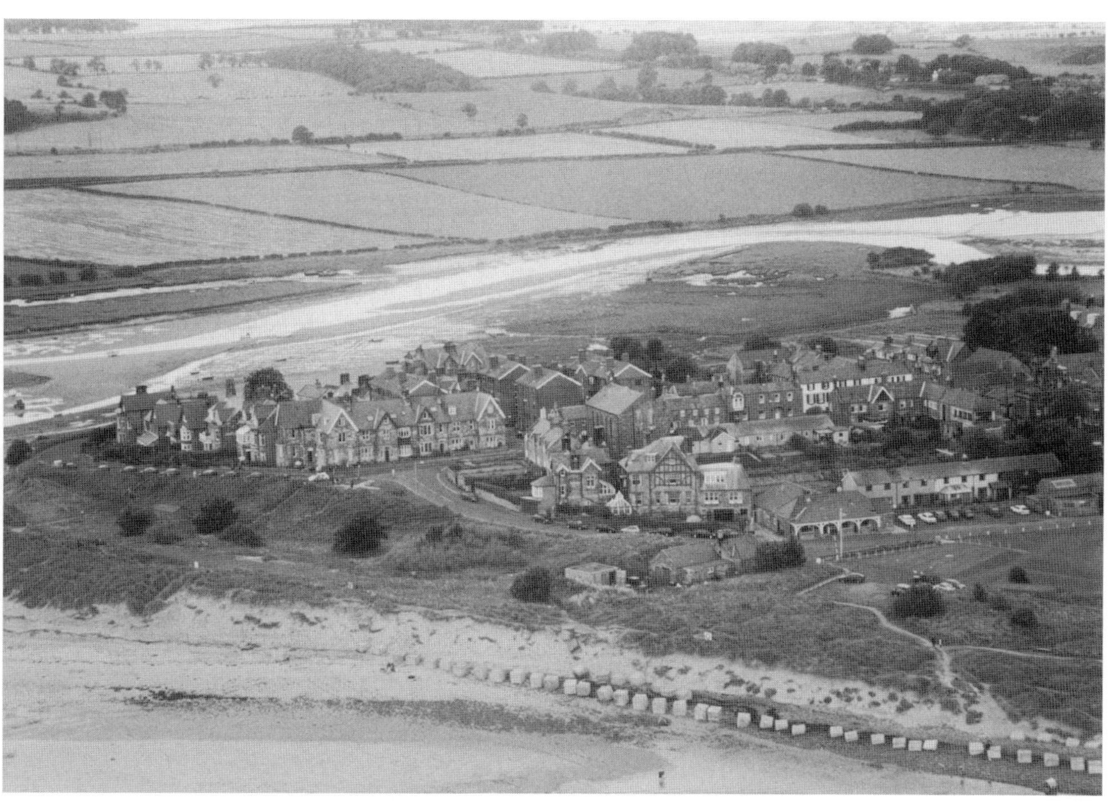

29 Alnmouth (Gordon Tinsley).

The village lies between the River Aln and the coast, with a regular pattern of fields and railway line at the top. The coast has anti-invasion concrete blocks still in a row. The golf club-house and course lie above these. The village is a mixture of mostly recent buildings, those to the left with pointed gables.

There is very little left of any great age in the village, although to the south there are the remains of an ancient church, abandoned when the river changed course. Some Saxon carved stone was found there, now in Newcastle museum.

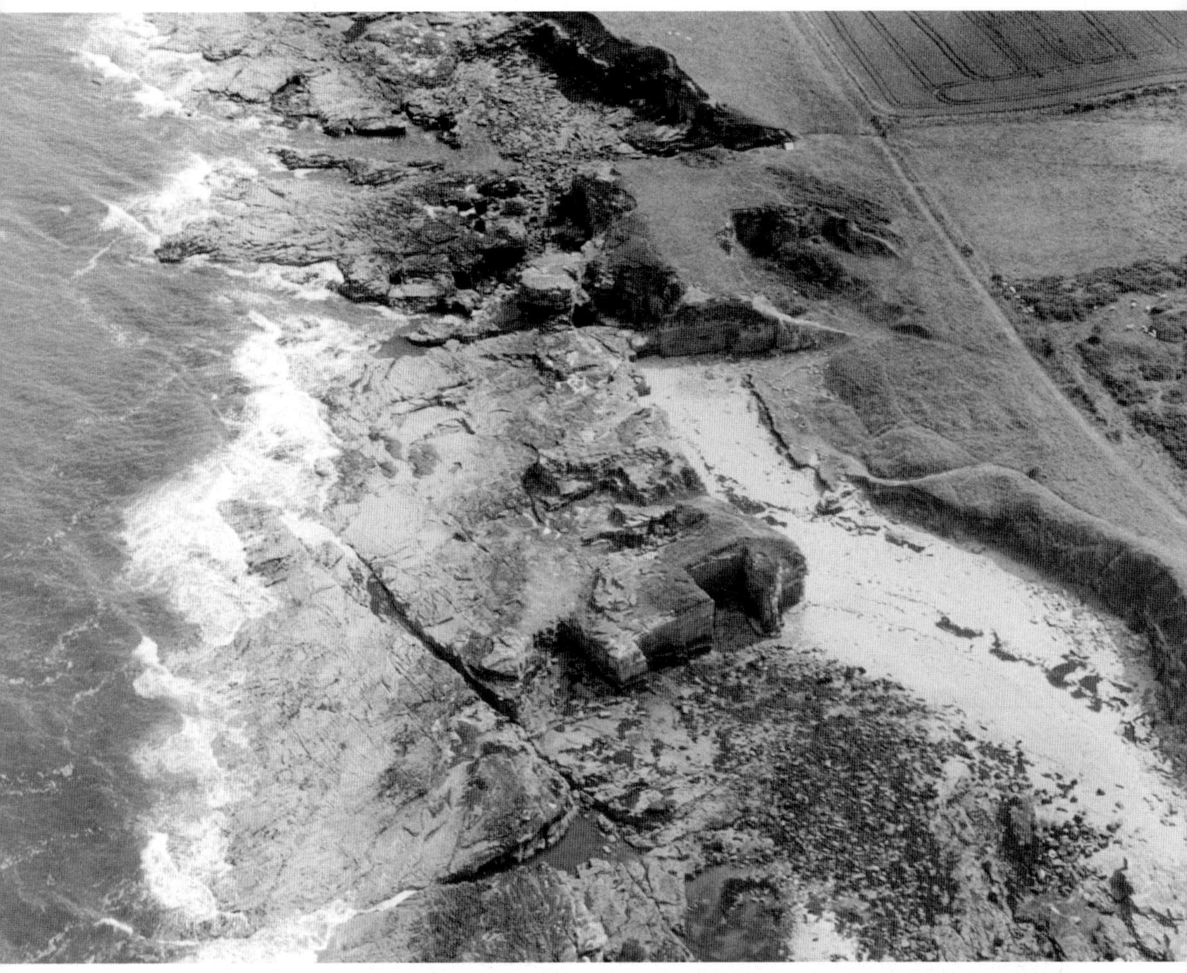

30 Rumbling Kern.

At Howick, south of Craster the coast displays a variety of rock formations, including a gap through which the sea pounds; indeed the name derives from the water churning and rumbling through the rocks. Here we see that some of the sandstone has been quarried away, leaving a secluded sandy beach. The cultivated field above has one of the earliest excavated house sites in Britain, from Middle Stone Age times. Since it was built the sea has crumbled away much of the cliff. Further inland is a later prehistoric enclosure. Although the variety of rock formations is apparent from the air, they are even more exciting from the ground.

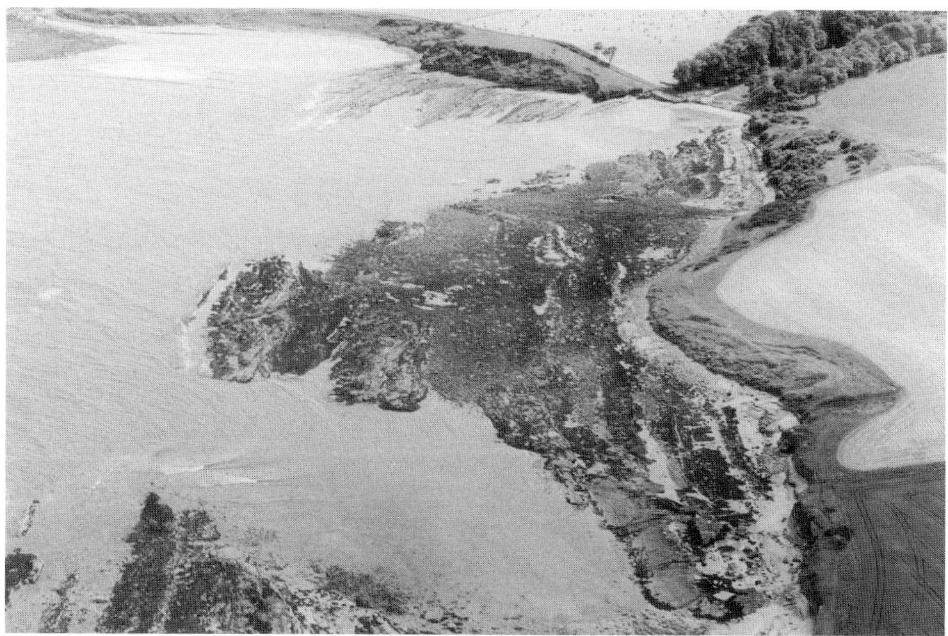

31 Further south.

A fine bay of silver sand provides yet another beauty spot along this coast, which is accessible by a coastal path.

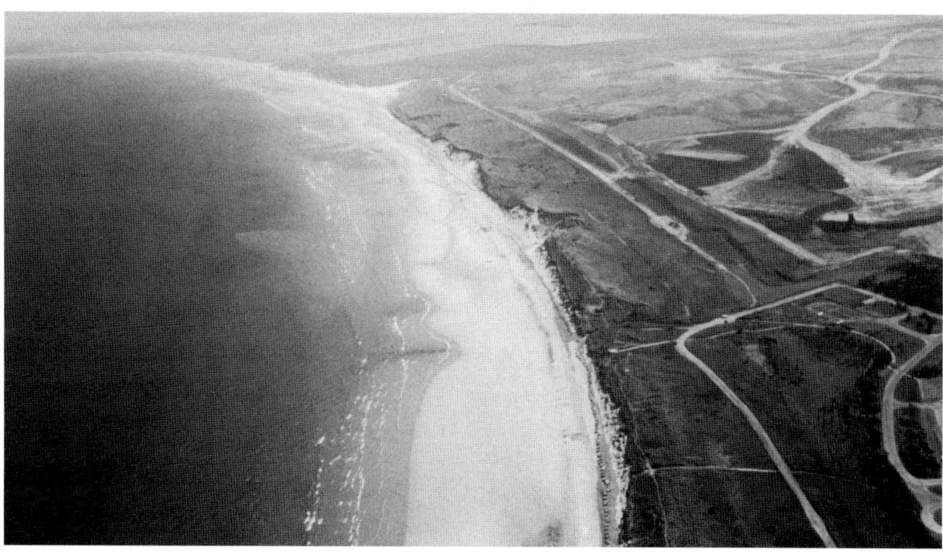

32 Druridge Bay.

This part of the coast is in the coal-mining area and was also used for extensive removal of sand until local protests put a stop to it.

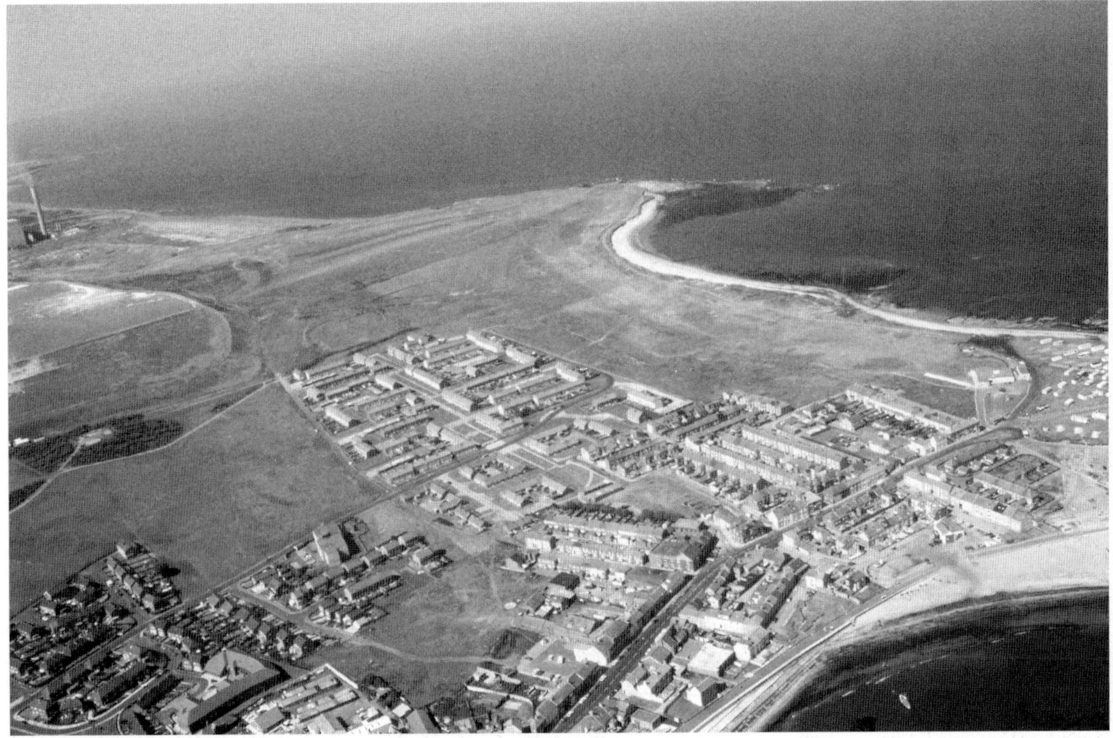

33 Newbiggin-by-the-Sea.

There are many Newbiggins in Northumberland, as the name means simply a new building. Flints found in the area date its earliest use to about 8000 years ago, but the most interesting old building is its church, built on a headland like many early monastic foundations. The bulk of the settlement owes much to the popularity of seaside holidays for workers in the nineteenth century onwards, before cheap air travel and higher pay led to its desertion.

The picture shows industrial use to the north of the town. In a recent revival of the beach, sand was imported from Lincolnshire.

Consciousness of the cost of our 'carbon footprints' and disillusionment with the hassle of air travel may lead to a revival of Newbiggin as a resort.

BLYTH

Blyth (the river name meaning 'gentle, merry, pleasant') was known as *Snoc de Bliemue* in 1130, which places the settlement on projecting land at the mouth of the river. What we see today is late nineteenth- and early twentieth-century development, made possible by coal and railways, with the proximity of a good harbour and a shipbuilding industry. Many eighteenth-century buildings were destroyed in a general clear-up that did not honour listed buildings, leaving very little of earlier architectural note.

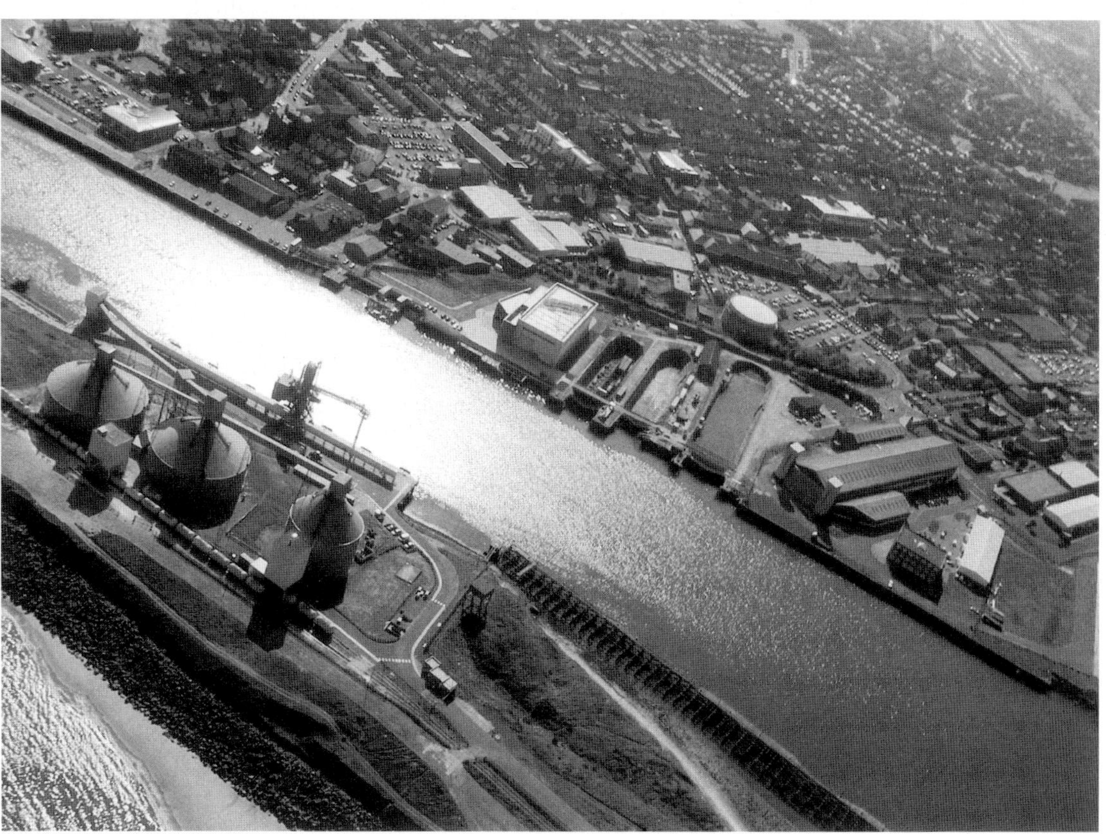

34 The harbour.

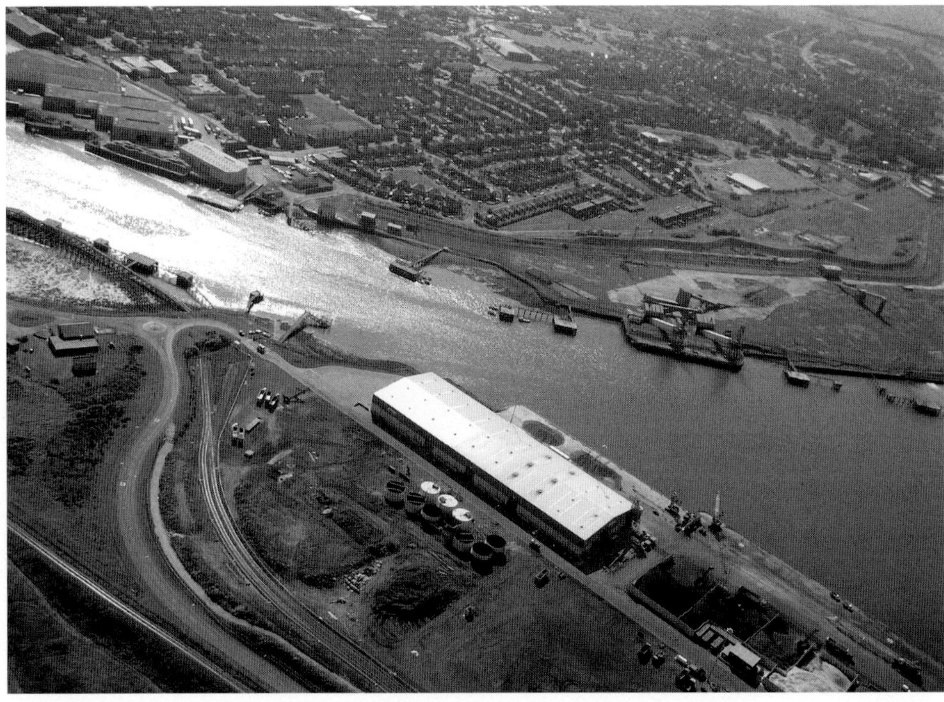

35 The town from the east, with the river to the right.

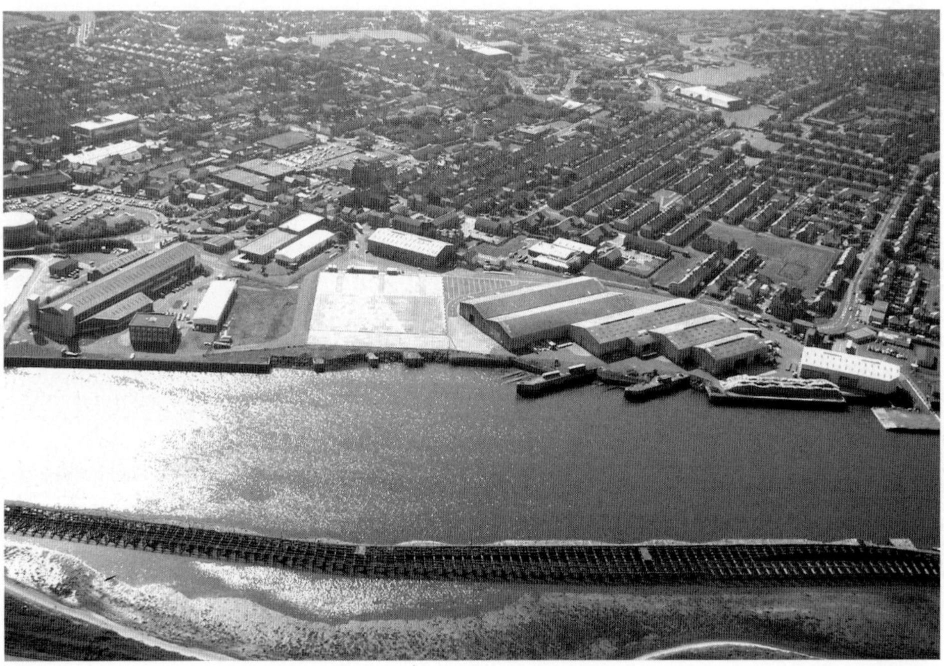

36 Blyth harbour and the eastern part of the town.

THE FARNE ISLANDS

The Farne Islands are important as a breeding site and sanctuary for birds. Historically, the islands provided an additional retreat for the monks, especially for St Cuthbert. They are made of the volcanic rock, whinstone.

The photographs (Gordon Tinsley, 1998) first show the Farnes from the east coast, then two views are given of the site where St Cuthbert built his cell. Since then the site has developed to include walled gardens, and there is rig and furrow where ploughing has taken place. The name was Farne in 730, and like one of the elements in Lindisfarne, this may mean that it was settled by people from afar.

The other fairly large island (not illustrated), is Coquet Island.

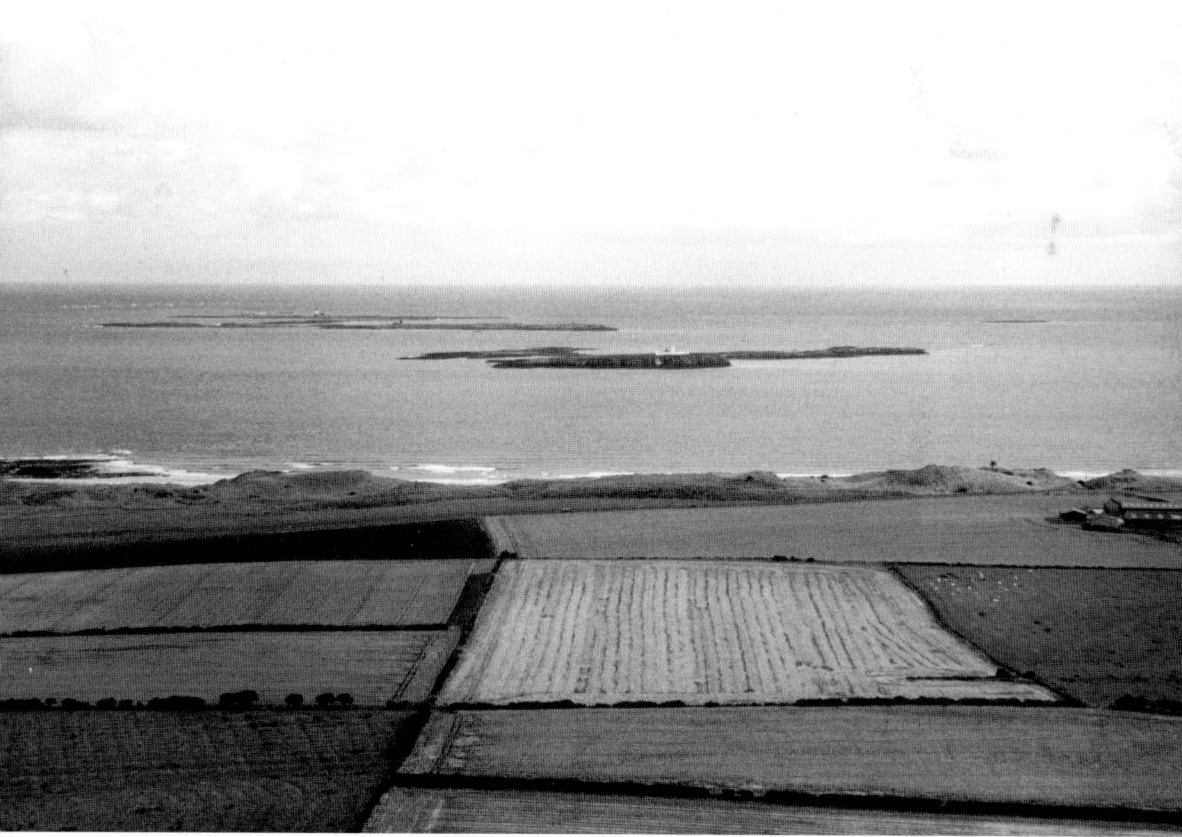

37 The Farne islands from the coast (Gordon Tinsley).

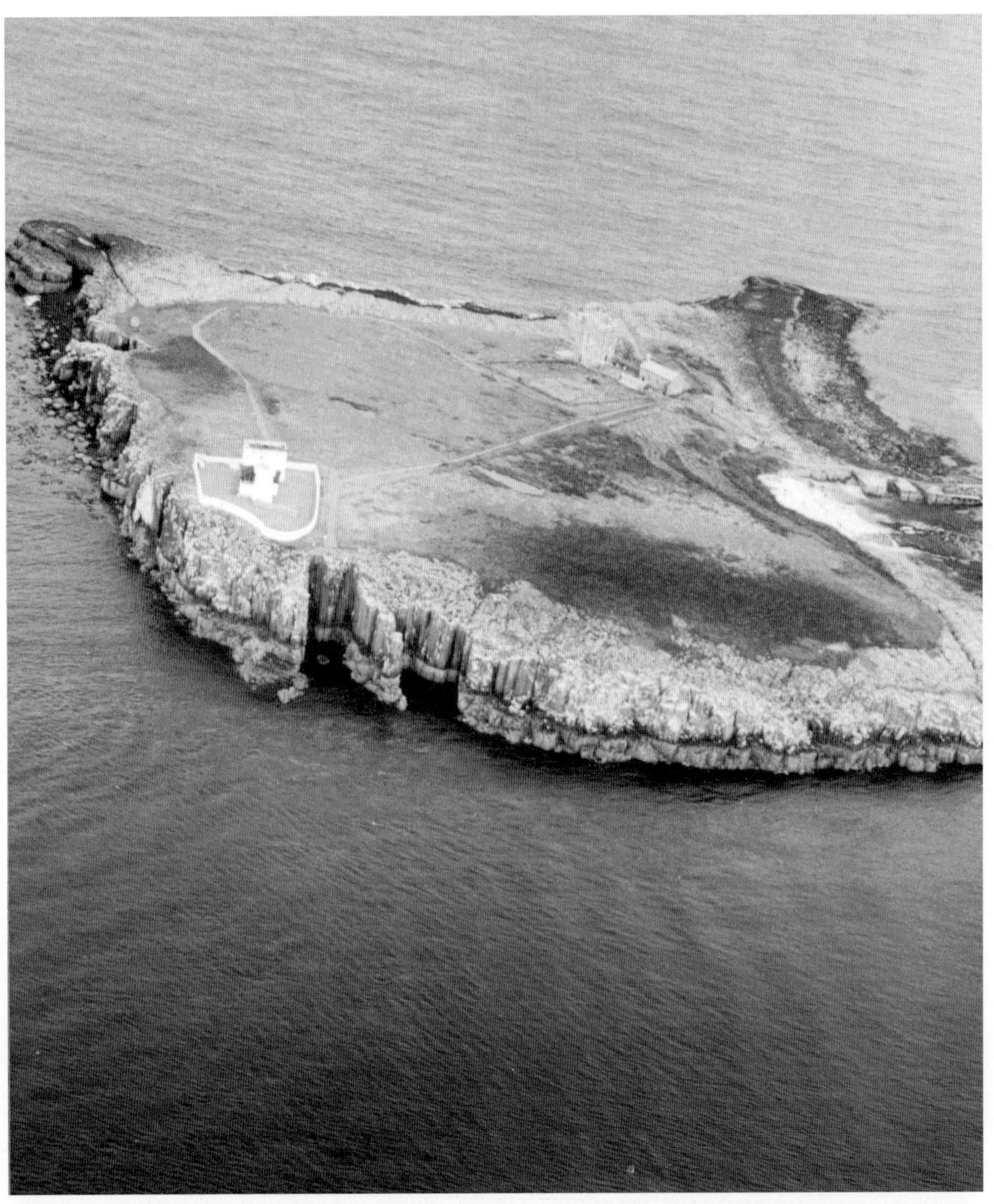

38 The Inner Farne, with its lighthouse, chapel and tower (Gordon Tinsley).

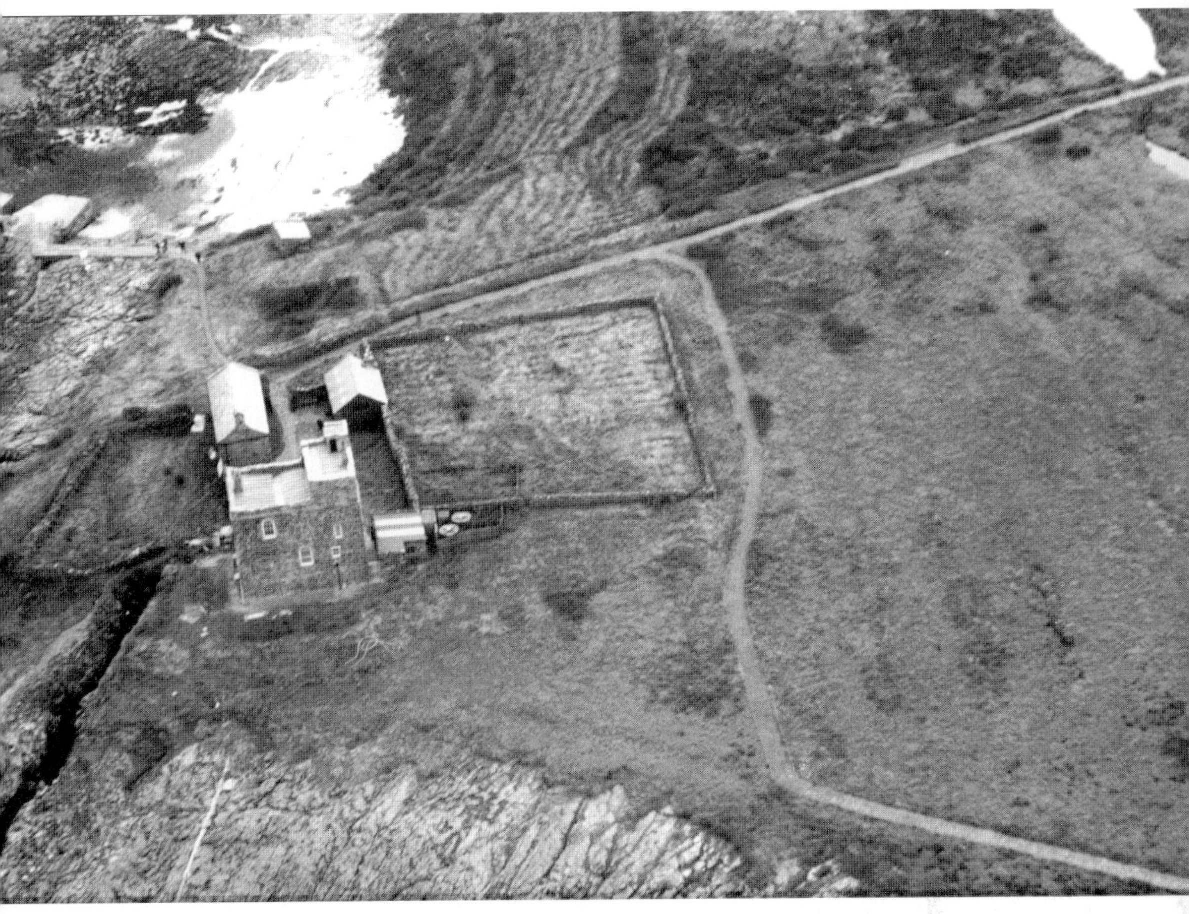

39 St Cuthbert's Chapel (Gordon Tinsley).

There are many areas of the coast that have been transformed from their original industrial role, greatly helped by the beauty of the sea and the rocks and sand of the coastline. Parks which are maturing each year have been created for visitors, such as that at Hauxley, south of Amble. The coast therefore, as a result of much human intervention, presents us with natural features and man-made ones in great variety.

St Cuthbert is perhaps the most famous of the early Northumbrian saints. He lived a life of simplicity, choosing the Farne Islands as an additional island retreat, surrounding his cell with a wall that cut out the view of everything but the sky. His pet name is 'Cuddy'. Eider ducks are known as 'Cuddy's ducks'.

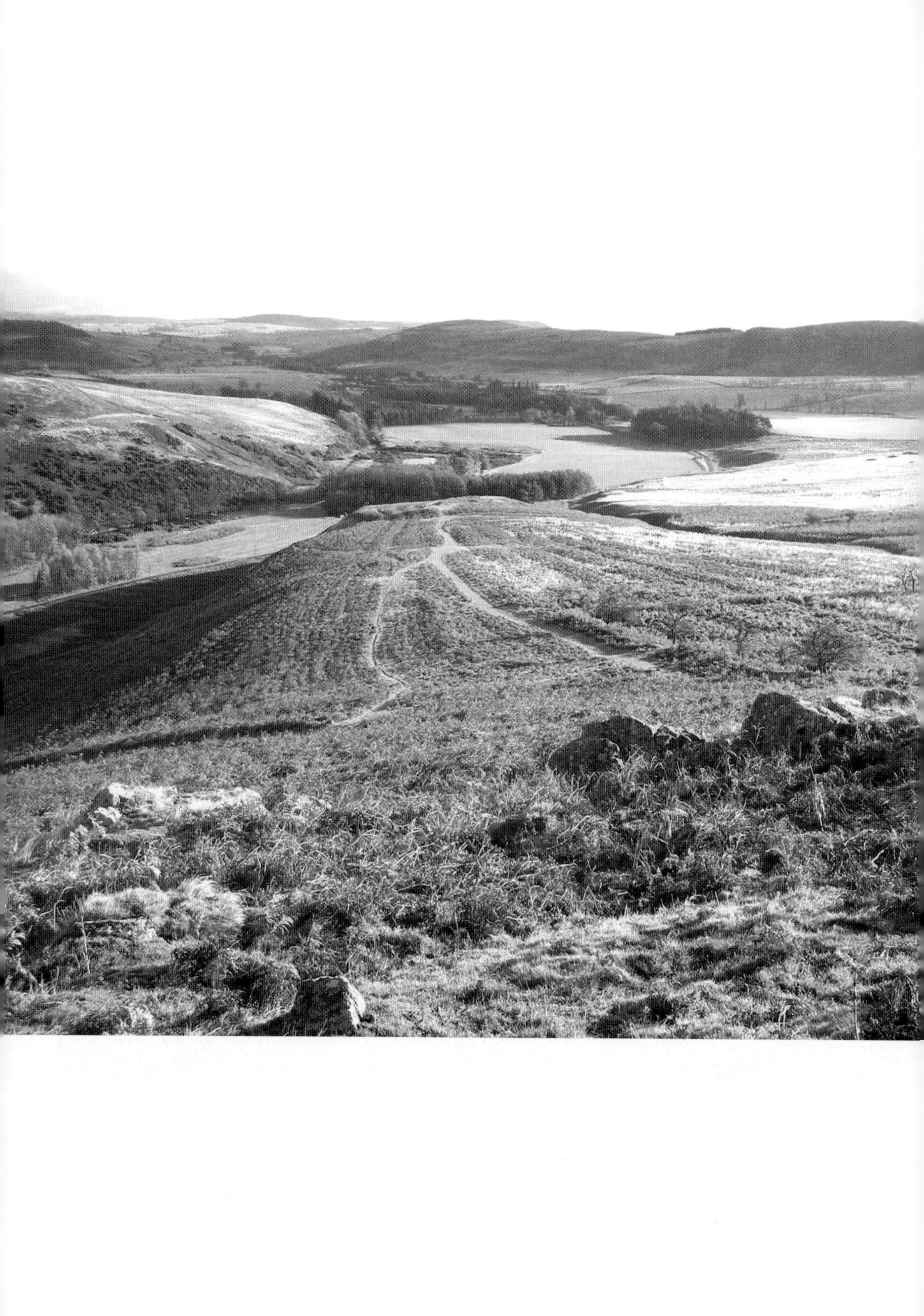

4

HILLS AND SCARPLANDS

HILLS

Visible from the coast are the Cheviot Hills and some of the prominent scarps.

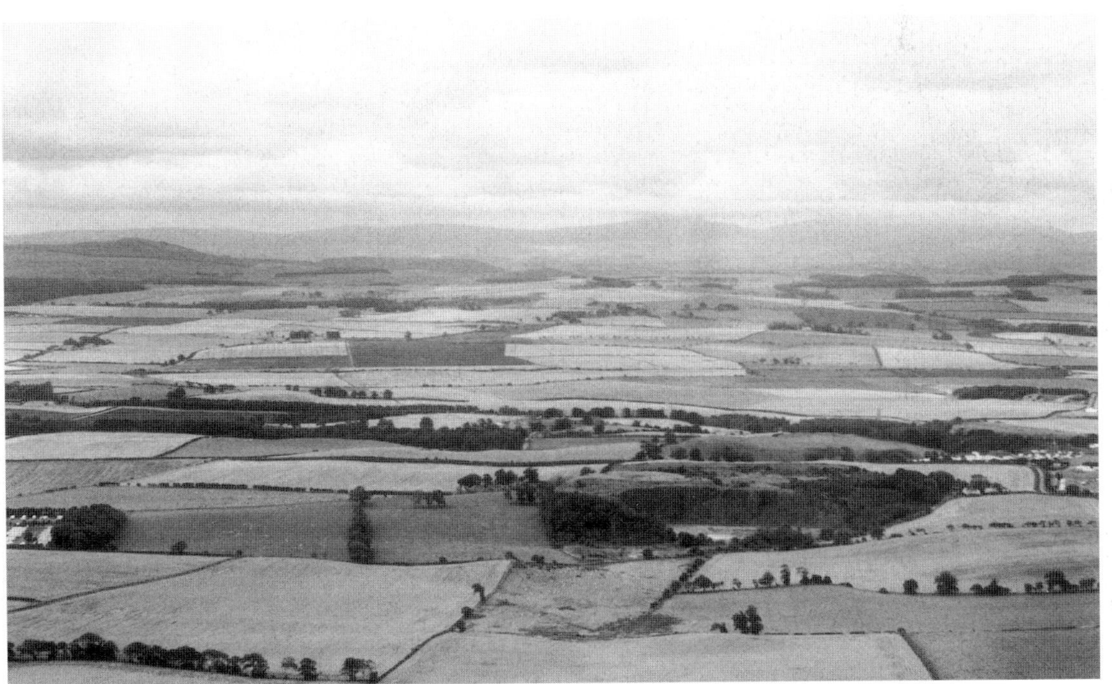

40 From coast to hills (Gordon Tinsley).

The fertile coastal plain has always been of importance for cereal growing. The regular field patterns are recent enclosures. There is a whinstone quarry in the foreground. Between fields and the Cheviot Hills is the relatively dark line of the Fell Sandstone scarp.

The Cheviot Hills are volcanic in origin, forming the north-west corner of the county, running into Scotland. They are characterised by rounded, ice-scoured profiles that are cut into by rivers and streams. The highest hill is The Cheviot itself; the meaning of this name is not known. It is clear that they have been cultivated for grain-growing, as the terraces, lynchets and rig and furrow systems show, although today they are mainly used for pasture. Not only do the field systems survive by being left under grass, but so also do many settlements from prehistoric times onwards, making them one of the most important ancient landscapes in Britain. In places, such as the quarries at Biddlestone, and in scars, the bright red and pink volcanic rock is visible.

The scarplands are made of Fell Sandstone, a sedimentary rock formed under the sea millions of years ago, part of a sequence that includes limestone, shale and coal. The scarps were fundamental to the movement of prehistoric people across the landscape and to the building of defences or enclosures with extensive views.

The 'dip slope' is gentler, and the major scarp running from north to south leads to the North Sea, whereas the scarp edge overlooks major river valleys. Towards Alnwick the main scarp veers south-west towards Rothbury and the Simonside Hills, then on to Elsdon and south-west Northumberland. One meeting place of volcanic rock and sandstone is near Alwinton.

This section gives examples of what is to be seen in the hills and from the scarps.

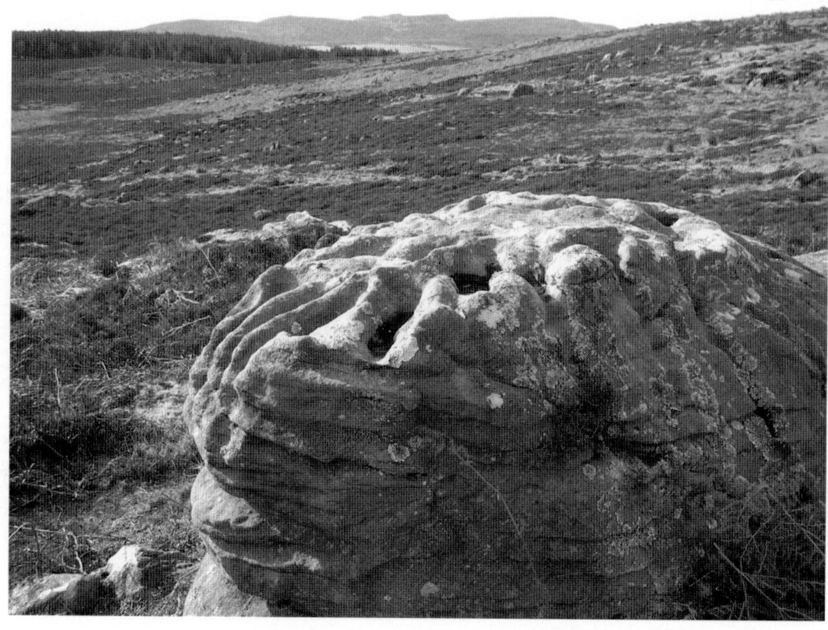

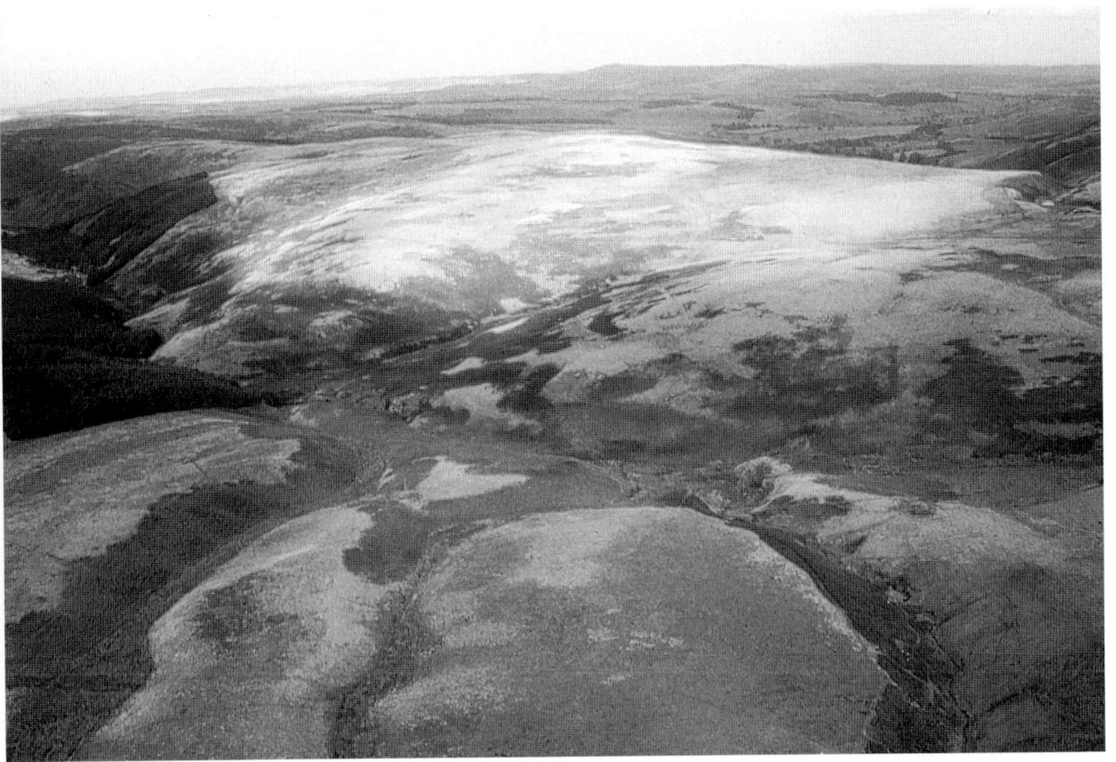

41 Cheviot Hills: landscape from Brough Law north-west.

Rounded outlines, deep valleys, thin soils and grass are characteristics of much of the hills. We are looking at a volcanic episode that began about 400 million years ago and at the result of ice sheets. At the centre is a granite core and around the edges are other volcanic rocks such as andesite. There is a great variety of rocks caused by the different rates of their cooling and crystallisation, but these differences are not immediately obvious from the air. The angularity of the scarp profiles contrasts with the general roundedness of the hills. Another difference is the general absence of heather.

The hills are intersected by many valleys, as we see in this picture, where trees grow. Today there has been a spread of planted forest throughout the hills and valleys.

The hills form the north-west border with Scotland, shared by both countries, distinctive, still with a special lifestyle and sharing a legacy of outstanding prehistoric landscapes and remains.

A major border industry is livestock, as it has always been.

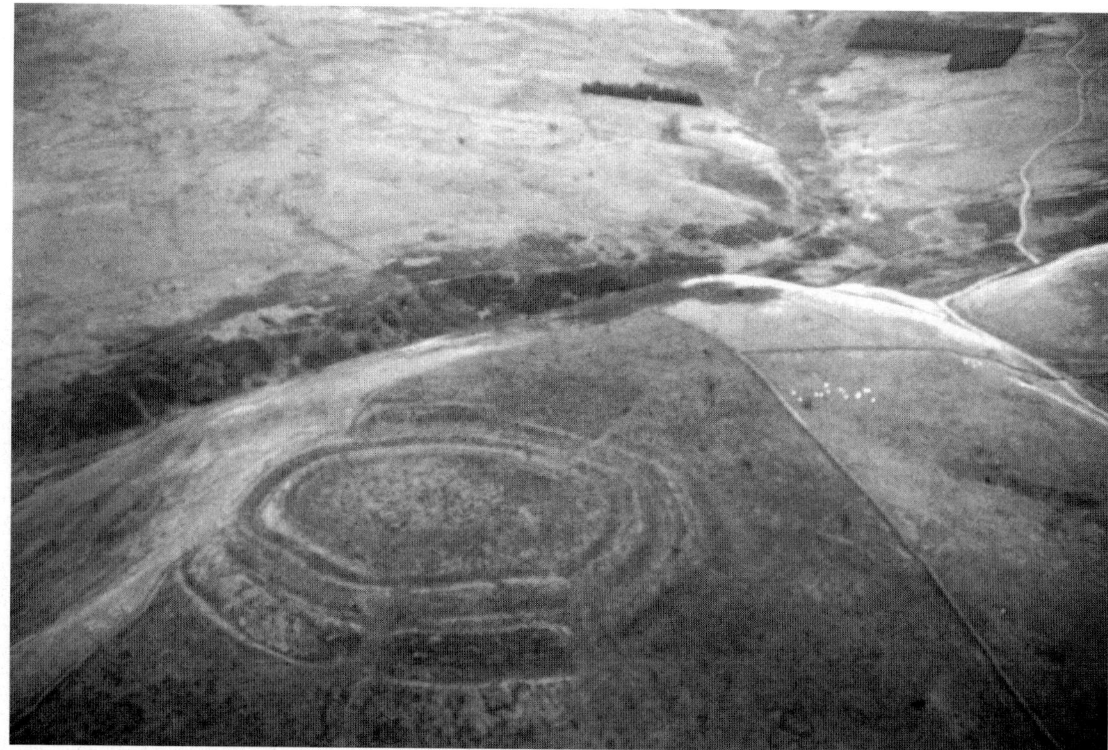

42 Alnham.

Lying on the southern edge of the Cheviots, Alnham is not only a village with a castle site, defensive tower, a church readapted to a shrinking congregation and a 'Salter's Road', but also a dramatically-placed hill settlement that continued to be used from the Iron Age through Roman times.

The settlement in the lower half of the picture is formed by a series of ditches built in linear sections, from which the upcast has been used to build the inner walls. These banks and ditches end at a slope to the left. It is not always possible to establish where the original entrances were, as farm vehicles have sometimes made new ones, but the likely entrances are at the bottom. It may have begun in the early Bronze Age, flourishing in the Iron Age, and extended during the Roman period, where it lies far north of Hadrian's Wall.

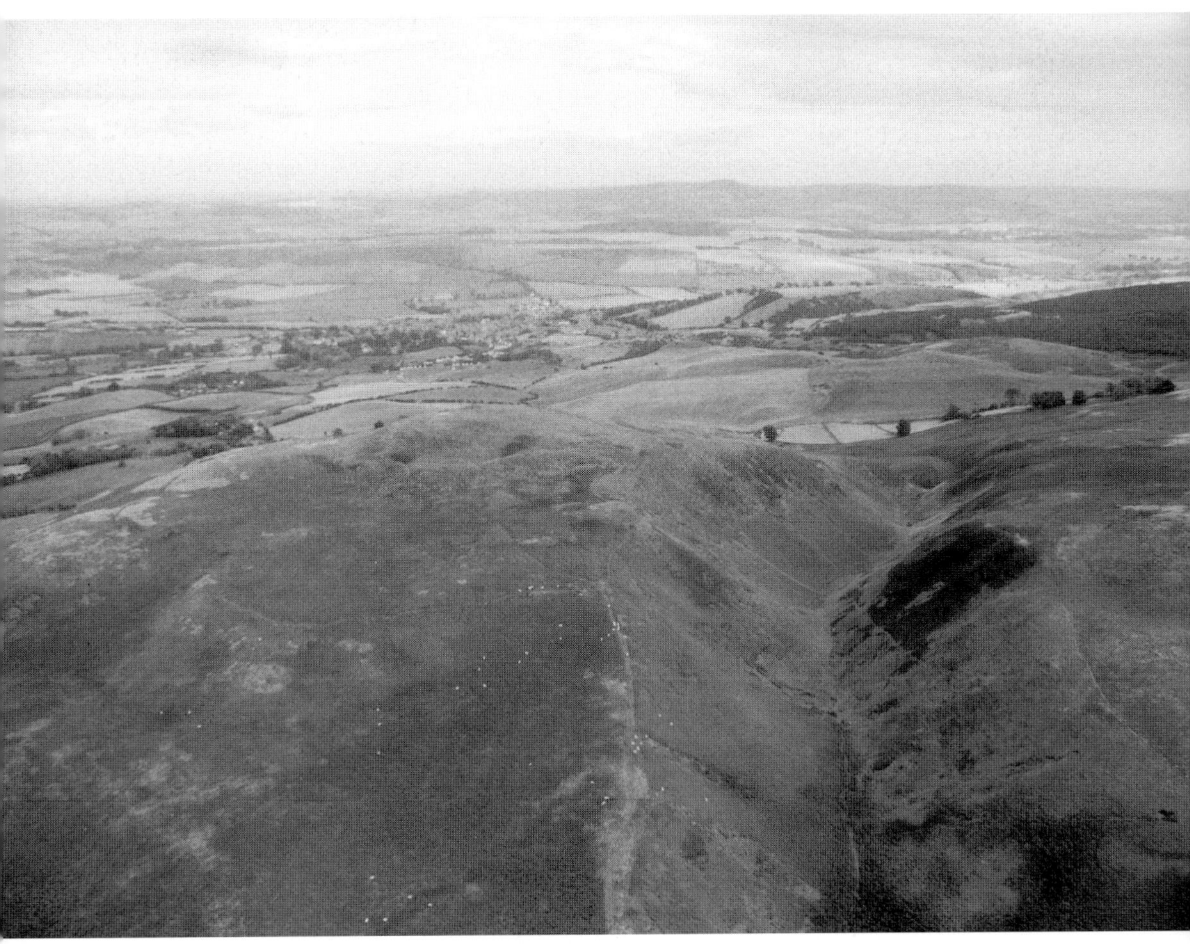

43 Humbleton Hill to Wooler.

Humbleton means 'bare-headed', or devoid of vegetation, and here the volcanic hill overlooking the Milfield Plain towards the scarplands and the North Sea provided a spectacular setting for a prehistoric burial mound on its summit and a later enclosure that developed to cover the summit. There are few signs here of anything more modern.

The ravine that lies on the right in this picture offers one reason for the choice of site, making access difficult for an attacker on that side.

Wooler lies in the top part of the picture, on the fringe of the hills, where the Wooler Water divides them from the next rise of sandstone scarpland.

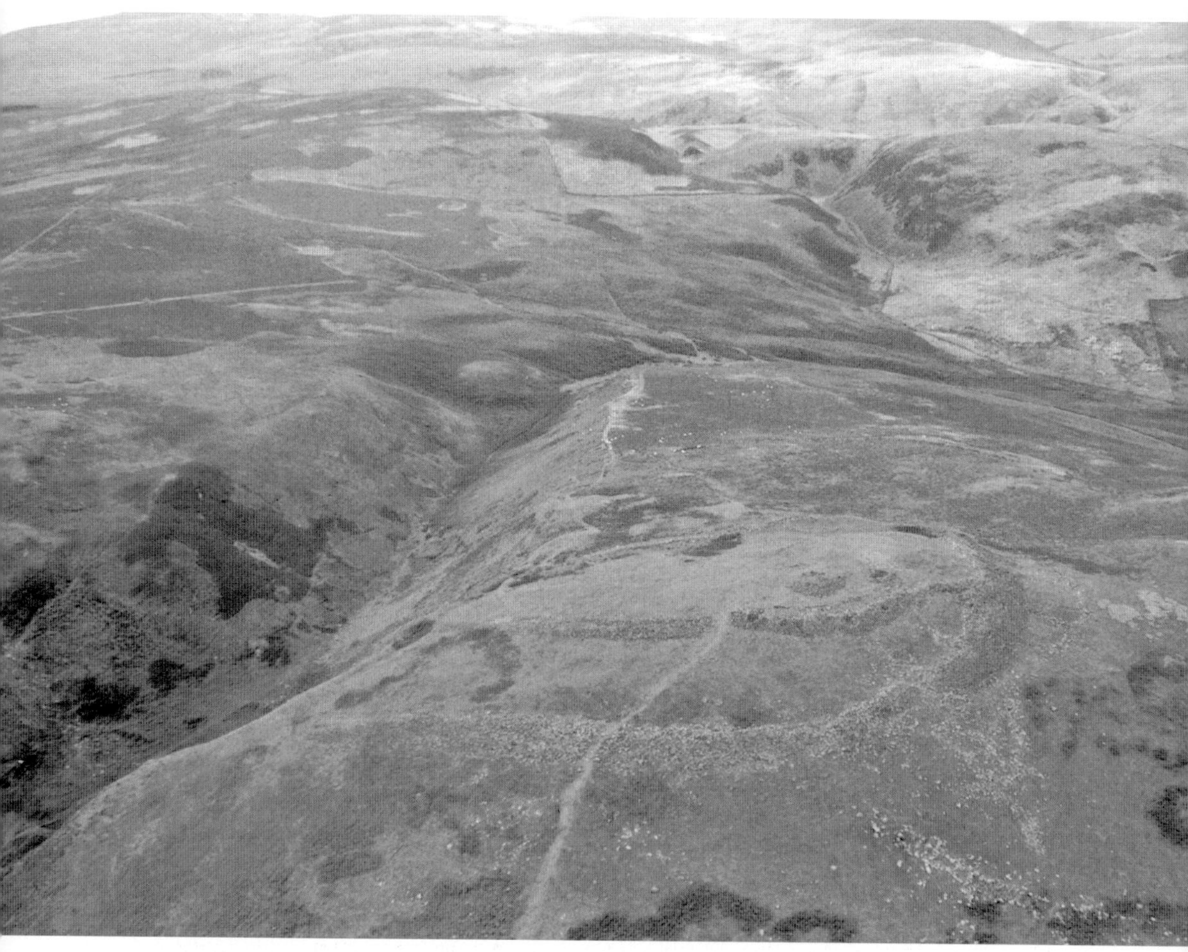

44 Humbleton to Monday Cleugh.

At the head of a small valley is a shelf of land (a 'cleugh' being a cliff or ravine) which is occupied by Monday Cleugh, a pre-Roman enclosure of curved walls and ditches, with some hut circles inside.

The sites of Humbleton Hill and Monday Cleugh settlements take advantage of steep slopes of the valley formed by the action of ice and running water. Humbleton, in the foreground of the picture, has walling that indicates development in its plan, forming several enclosures.

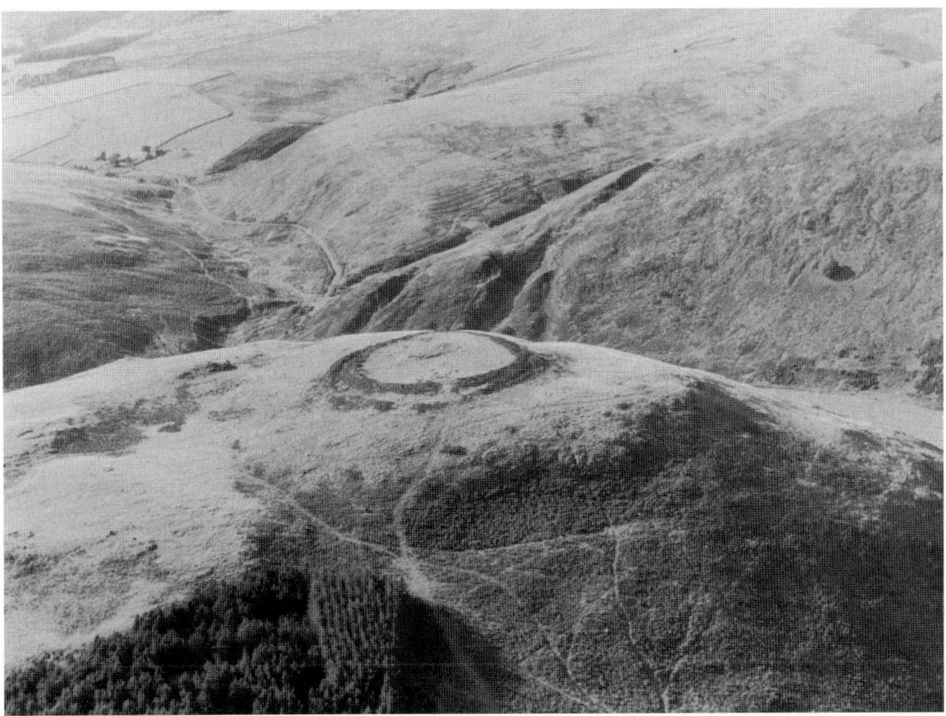

45 The Ingram Valley.

Ingram, taken from the Old English *angr-ham*, means a settlement covered with grass, and indeed the prehistoric field systems and farms are just that. The River Breamish ('to roar'), later the Till, cuts its way through the volcanic andesite rocks to give access into the core of the Cheviot Hills. The landscape has been intensively studied and excavated in projects involving the skills of many different professional and voluntary groups, so that much is known about what lies below the surface. Aerial photography has contributed enormously to an understanding of the landscape by revealing sites that were once invisible.

Officially-commissioned photographs cover much of the area, and show the relationship between settlements, farming systems and defences of many periods. It appears from the large number of sites that there were many people living here, but this is deceptive, as the evidence comes from a period of hundreds of years.

The above are but a few examples of what the Cheviot Hills contain. The saturation of the land with settlements, field systems and trackways continues throughout the hills, especially in the Alwinton area.

SCARPLANDS

We have already seen how important the scarplands are to people living in and moving through these areas. Other examples follow.

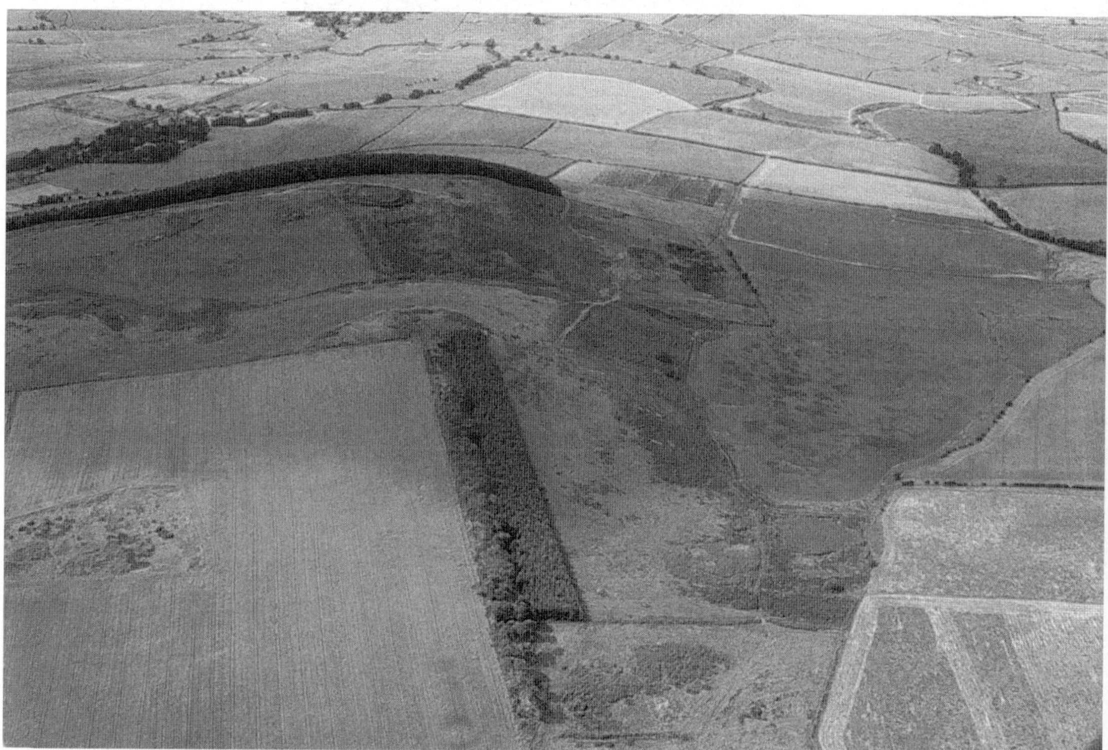

46 Chatton Park Hill.

Now famous for its prehistoric rock-art sites on outcrop sandstone and on the floor of a rock overhang, the picture shows that much of the scarp has been cultivated, with a fringe of trees along the scarp edge (top). To the right is a valley leading to large rolling cultivated fields. The uncultivated parts on the scarp are used for grazing. The name Chatton comes from the Old English *ceatta*, which could literally mean a wild cat or was perhaps a nickname for someone who behaved like one.

Just below the thin fringe of the plantation running from left to right is a small enclosure of walls and ditches, pre-Roman, which encloses an outcrop of rock pecked with prehistoric motifs at least 4000 years ago. Such motifs extend across the area above the field boundary that runs parallel to the wood.

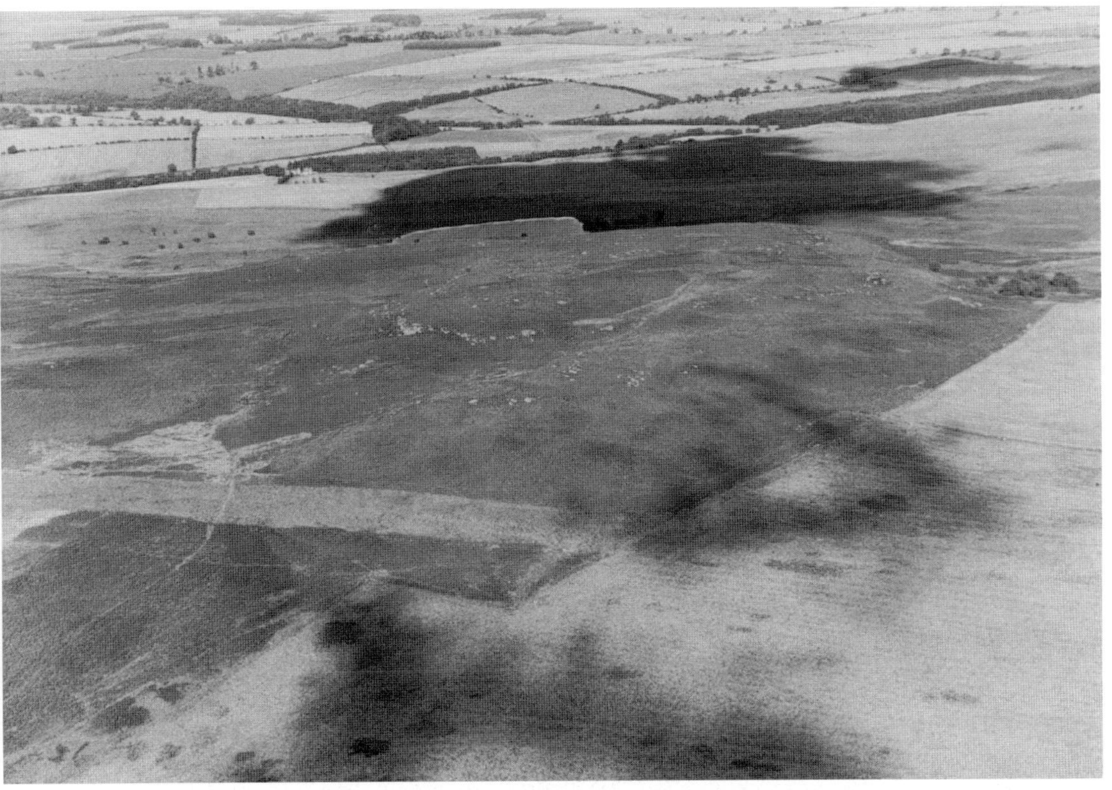

47 Hunterheugh.

A varied landscape; the central point is heather and bracken moorland on a low sandstone crag that is part of Beanley Moor. Leading into the cultivated field, right, is the line of a major gas pipe. Above the moor is Kimmer Loch, then cultivated fields running towards the North Sea. Significant prehistoric sites have been discovered here, and some have been excavated.

Little was known about this area until quite recently; it was the digging of the gas pipe trench which led to the discovery of complex prehistoric rock-art, although a Later Iron Age complex of enclosures was already recorded. The author recorded extensive rock-art in detail, leading to an excavation. The moorland, which contrasts with the cleared and cultivated fields to the upper right, extends well beyond the left side, known as Beanley Moor (see over the page).

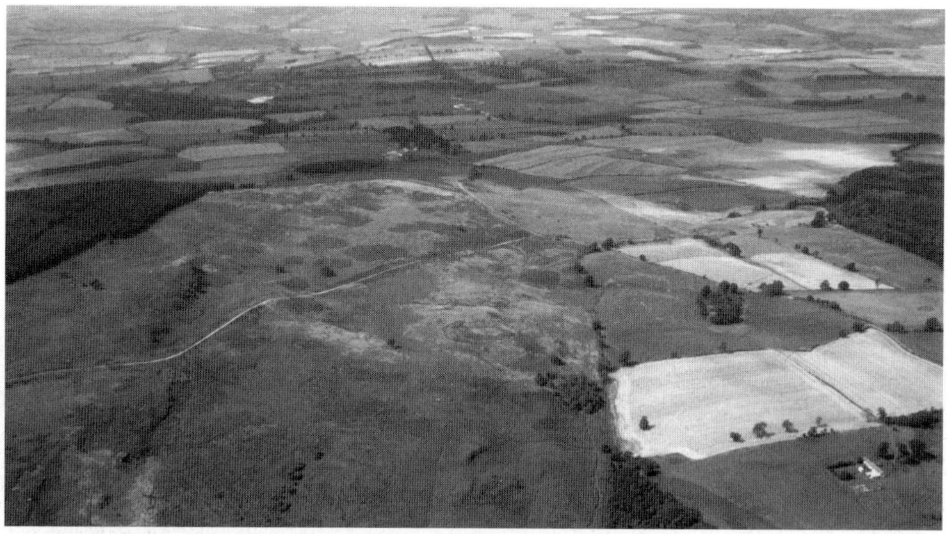

48 Beanley Moor.

A wide view of Beanley Moor shows the moorland vegetation, with the Ringses hillfort at the centre. The name means that beans were grown there.

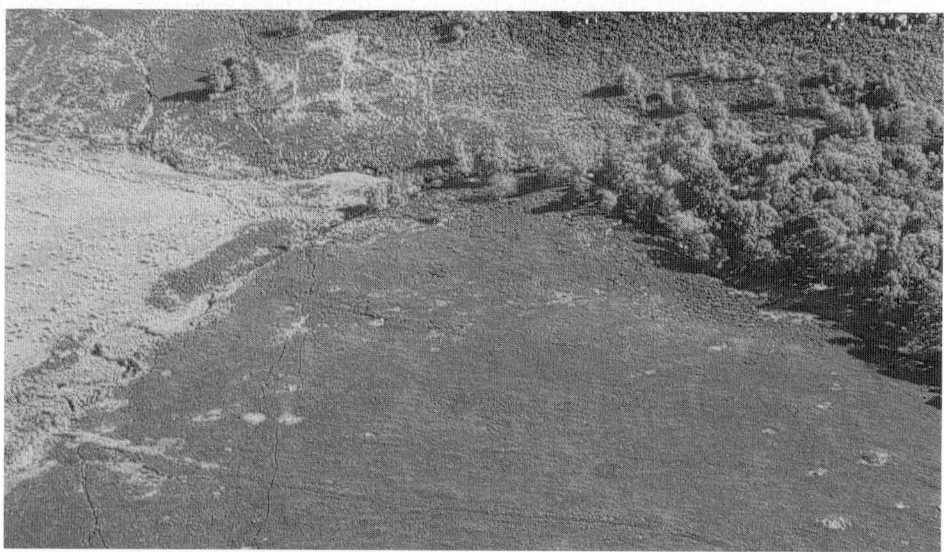

49 Debdon Whitefield.

Part of a large area of moorland adjoining the Cragside estate, this has thin soil covered with grass and heather. Some mounds here are burial cairns, while others are the upcast collar of bell-pit mining. 'Whitefield' suggests that grass which turned white grew there. There is a small prehistoric village of round-houses in the triangle formed by the junction of the two streams (upper centre).

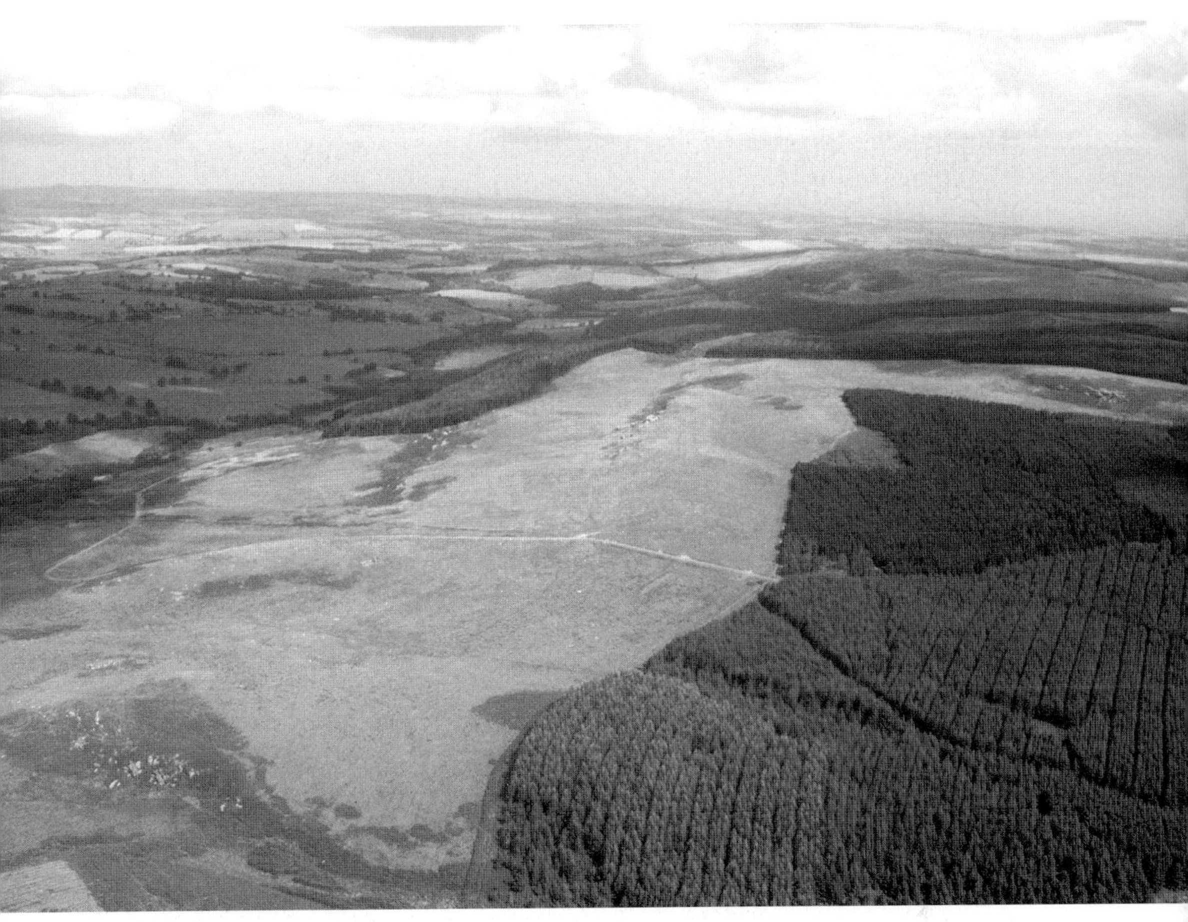

50 Caller Crag.

Caller Crag, named after calves, is part of the scarp running from Rothbury to Alnwick. The crag outcrops occur like steps and the top one has some extraordinarily beautiful shapes caused by erosion. A flat area beneath the crags would have made an ideal platform for gathering together herds of cattle. Below, the scarp has been planted and now cleared of coniferous trees; in parts it is extensively quarried for stone.

To the right, the forest has been planted in the last 50 years. Timber has become a major industry in Northumberland; more of it is now processed as hardboard at the Egger factory in Hexham.

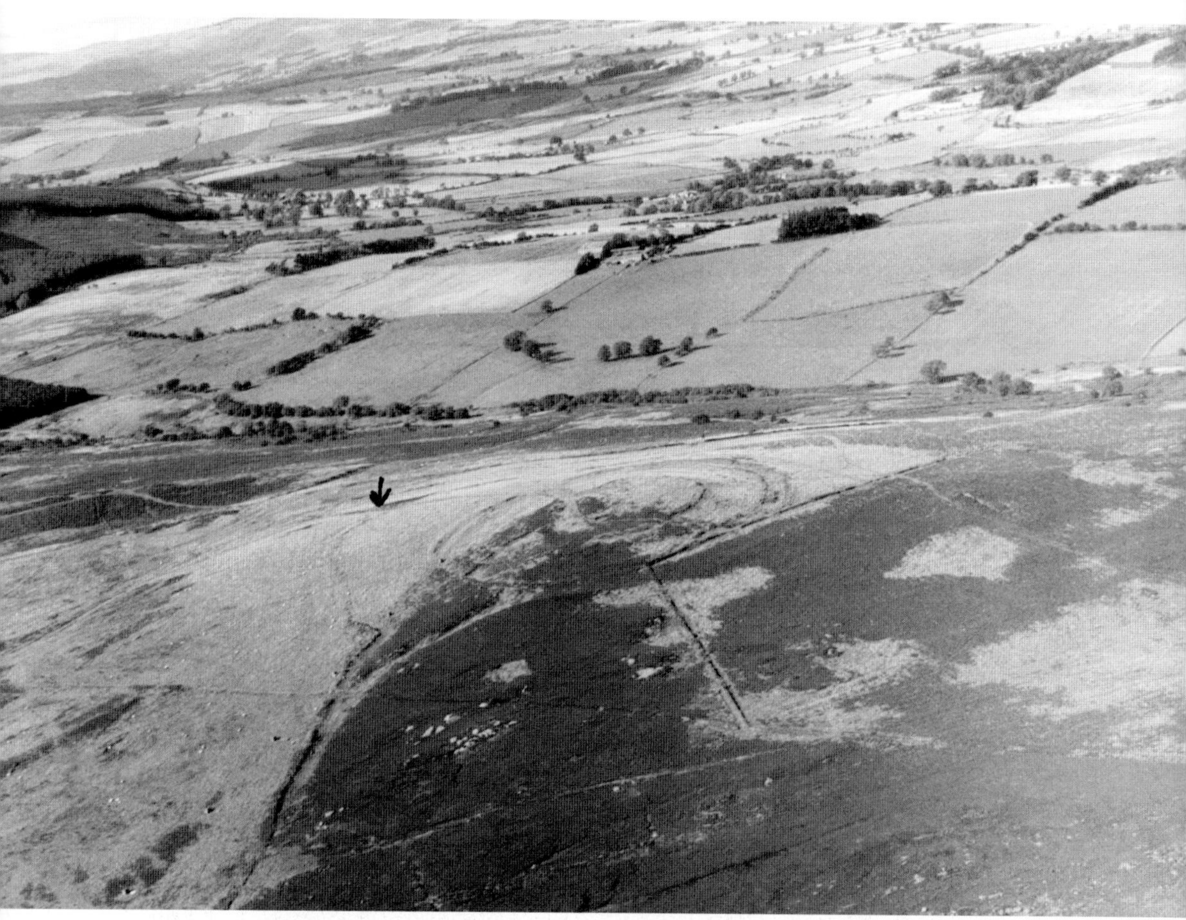

51 Lordenshaw.

The Simonside Hills are visible from many places in Northumberland and must have been a good reference point for travellers. The tops have prehistoric burial cairns. The hills overlook Lordenshaw, a lower part of the scarplands whose name may mean that it is a ridge difficult to cultivate. Here we have a view to the Coquet valley over the hillfort. An arrow marks the position of a large outcrop marked with prehistoric motifs, one of many in this moorland area.

The moorland bears evidence of use over thousands of years, from prehistoric burials and settlements, followed by a deer park, quarrying, narrow rig and furrow ploughing for arable cultivation, and grouse butts. It is now an important part of the Northumberland National Park.

5

TOWNS

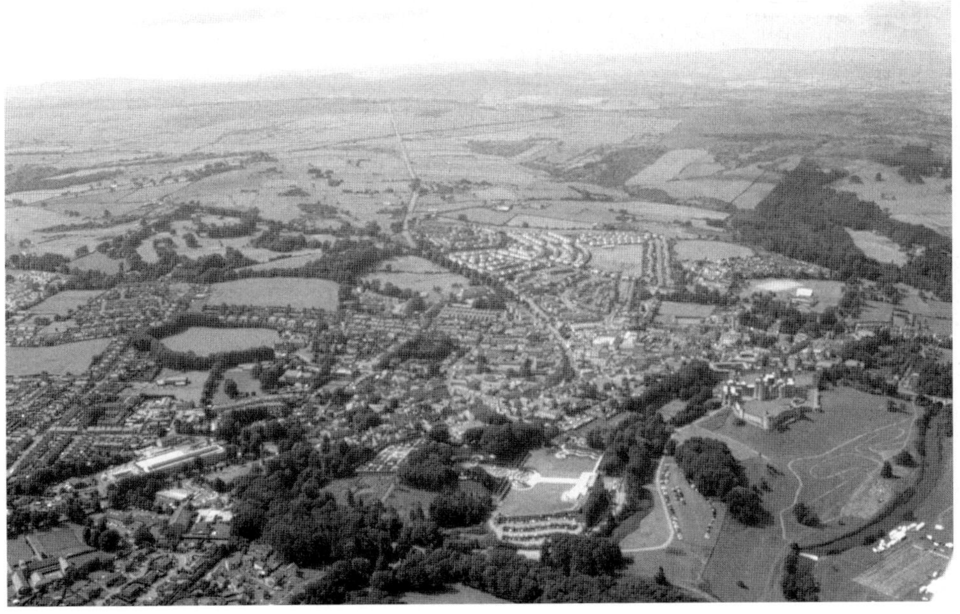

52 Alnwick.

Like Berwick, Alnwick's strategic importance is buried in the past. Here we see the survival and development of its castle above the main crossing place of the River Aln, and the way in which the old town has kept close to the protection of its walls. Outside its once-walled perimeter, estates, industries and shops have spread.

The pattern of main streets forms a triangle, in which the Market Place lies. Radiating from the streets are thin strips of land that were the 'burgages' owned by townspeople where their houses were built and their gardens stretched out at the back.

The castle grounds have been developed with the addition of gardens, a water garden and a tree house, increasing visitor numbers (and congestion) in the town.

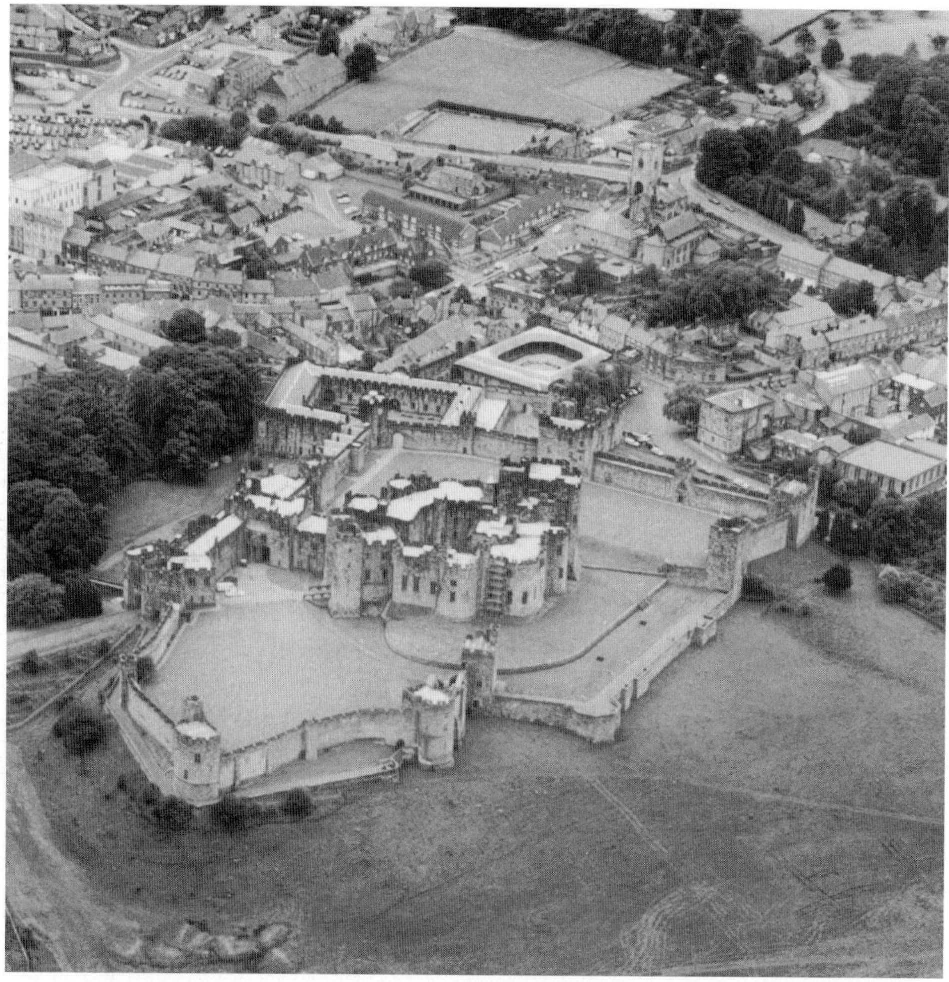

Opposite 53 Alnwick Castle (Gordon Tinsley, 1998).

The castle is one of the most important strongholds in Britain, the power-base of the Earls/Dukes of Northumberland. It overlooks the River Aln at its crossing-point. Here we see the keep and arrangement of mainly round towers linked by walls that form a small courtyard. Although there has been much development and alteration to meet the demands of a quality residence, the basic plan of a keep at the centre of two baileys or wards is dominant. To the right is an added gun-platform. At the top is a barbican entrance, like a small castle. The Guest Hall is top left, part of a modern rectangular courtyard. Outside the castle, right, is Bailiffgate, with buildings that have been used as a College of Education and school, the furthest right being a purpose-built library.

The town centre is off-left. The site of one of the town gateways (Pottergate) on the line of the town wall is seen protruding like a church tower (top). Top left is the beginning of a council housing estate.

MORPETH

Morpeth became the county's administrative centre when Tyne and Wear was formed. It is odd that the River Wansbeck separates the castle and church from the rest of the town, which lies across the bridge on the north bank. One of the main streets crosses this bridge; the others run to and from the Market Place.

Its name either means 'the path across the moor' or 'murder path'.

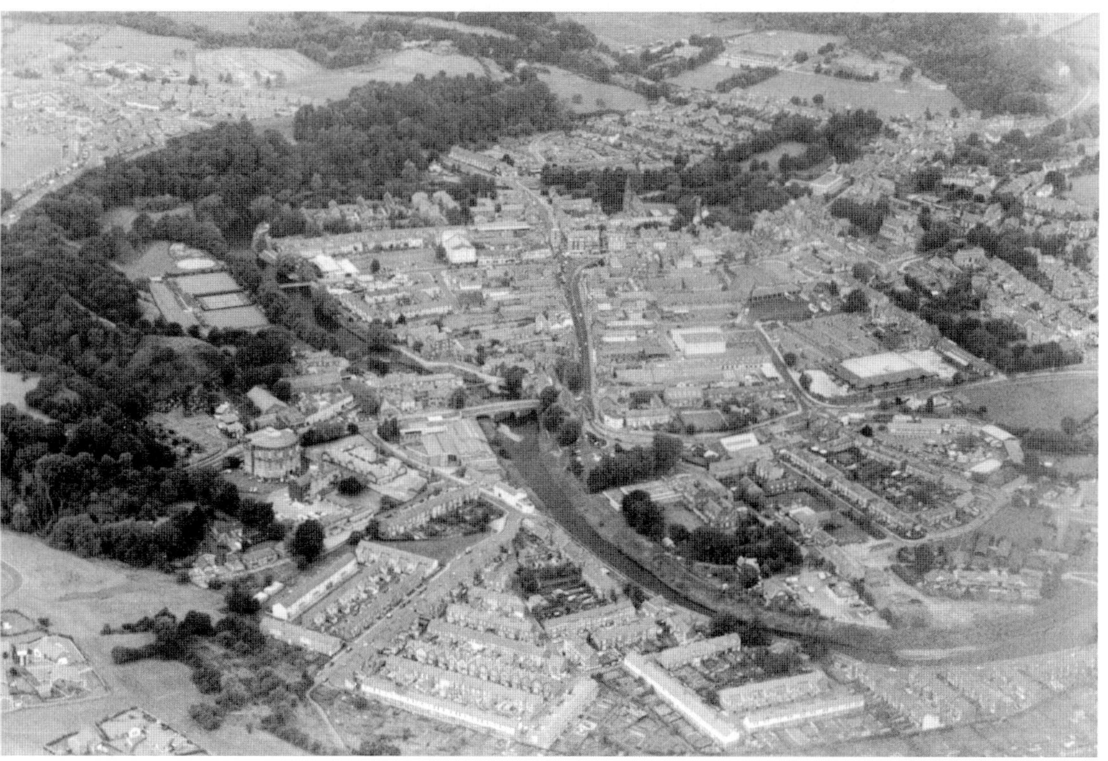

54 In the photograph the bend in the river is clearly seen, with the modern bridge replacing a partly-preserved old one, now a footbridge. The bridge carries the road from the south that passes the green site of a castle opposite a substantial-looking gaol. The straight road that runs through the town is the main one, with a bell tower near the junction where the road turns north to join the modern A1. Park land is retained to the south of the river, where another footbridge leads over it to a car park and leisure centre. Although open grassland and woodland are preserved, especially for use as a golf course, much of the periphery is taken up with estate housing.

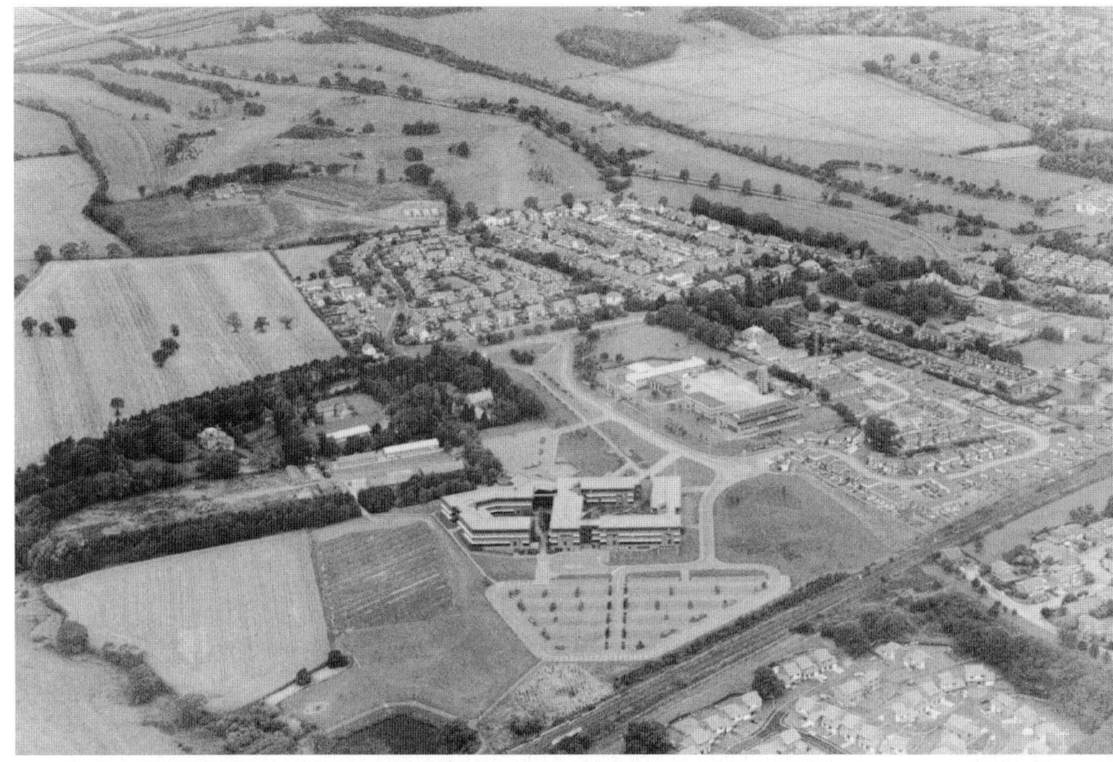

55 Morpeth.

The far south of the town figures County Hall and its large car park, and other public buildings. The railway line in its coastal route to Berwick is seen as a straight track at the bottom of the picture. Beyond County Hall, on the west side of the main road with its housing estates, is the golf course, where medieval rig and furrow ploughing has been well preserved. The new bypass is visible in the top left-hand corner.

The scale of the building of County Hall and its continuing position at the centre of a new unitary authority emphasises the growing importance of Morpeth since Northumberland became administratively separate from Newcastle. However, Alnwick continues to vie with Morpeth for the title of 'county town'.

HEXHAM

Hexham (the settlement of a young Anglian son of a man of some substance who could not inherit from his father but had to find land for himself) owes its foundation to St Wilfrid, who established a monastery there in the mid-seventh century which in its day was regarded as one of the finest buildings north of the Alps. It is now called Hexham Abbey.

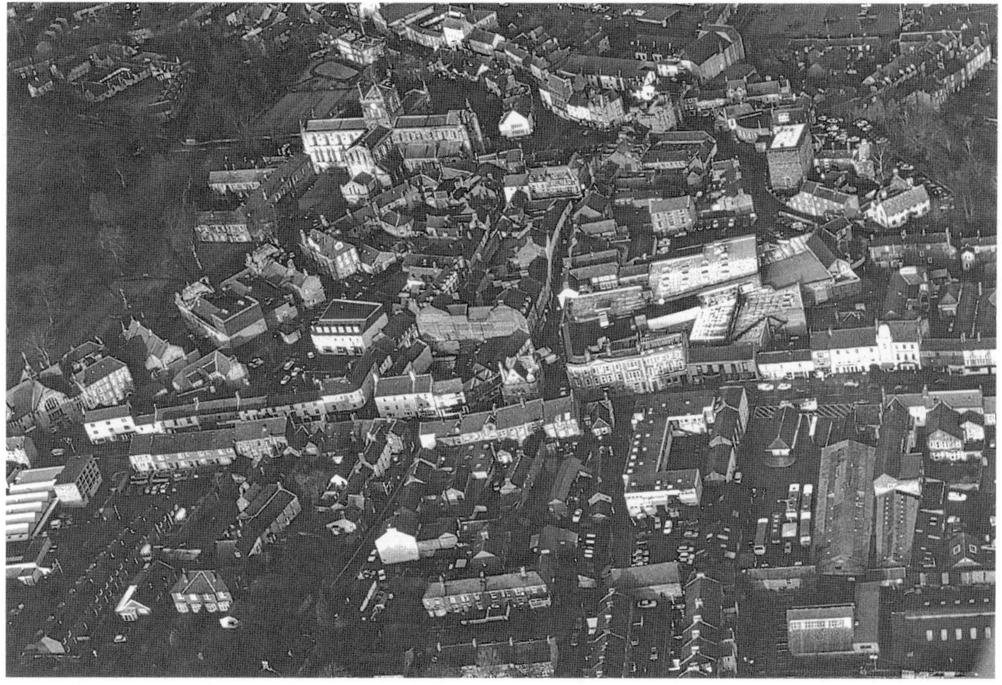

56 Here the view is from the south-east, with the Abbey top left. The street called Battle Hill and Priestpopple (meaning a hill with a building on it, and small plots of land owned by the priests) runs from left to right.

The street pattern to and from the Abbey and market place reflects the importance people placed in living close to the market, priory and civil administration, closely packed. Buildings have developed on the sites of much older ones and around them, but the historic centre has managed to retain much of its integrity. Historically, the parkland to the left of the Abbey (west) has been defended from further encroachment by its owners.

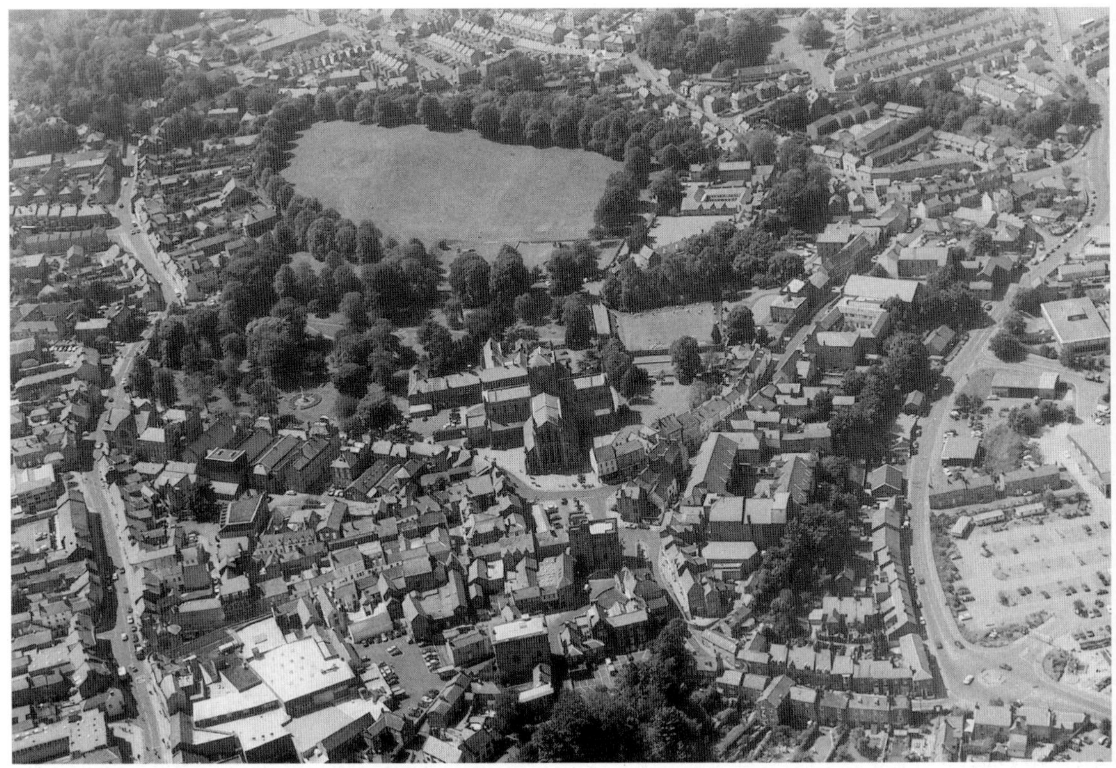

57 Hexham.

The site is a glacial platform, flanked by the River Tyne to the north and by streams to the west and east. The town grew up around the market place, with the Priory on the west and the fortified administrative centre on the east. The heart of the town has been little disturbed, with today's streets focused on it.

After the Dissolution of the Monasteries, the Priory became the town church and most of its enclosing wall decayed. Part of the Priory became a home for Lords of the Manor. The grounds were mercifully preserved by the owners, so that you may see extensive parkland there today. A new road was built from the market place through priory grounds to join the main Haydon Bridge-Corbridge road that runs from east to west at the south of the town.

Despite changes in use and style, buildings are tightly-packed in the historic centre, following the old pattern of long narrow burgage strips (as they do at Alnwick, for example). All new development took place outside that centre from the eighteenth century onwards and the town continues to expand into every available space. Old industries like tanning died out and new ones arose, with Egger chipboard factory, the most recent, dominating the eastern approach.

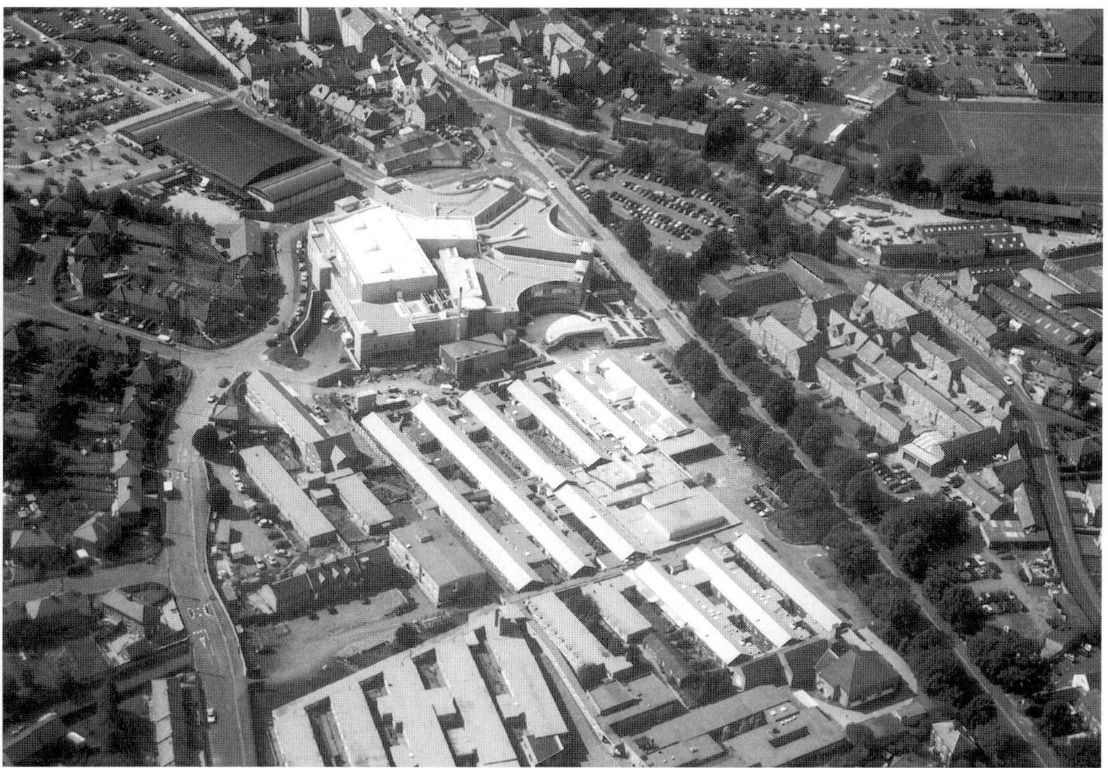

58 Hexham east (Matthew Hutchinson).

This photograph, although recent, is already part of the historical record, as it shows the old hospital's rectangular huts being replaced by the new Hexham Hospital. The well laid-out housing on the left is the response to slum clearance in the 1930s. The Corbridge road runs to the right, with the old Workhouse building further right. In the top left-hand corner is the Co-op and its car park, about to change ownership to Marks and Spencer in June 2008.

This opening up of Hexham to large retailers is an obvious recent trend, designed to take some trade away from the Metro Centre in Gateshead. It also threatens some smaller businesses and adds to traffic congestion. However, as yet nothing detracts from the beauty of the town centre.

PRUDHOE

As the name suggests, the settlement lies on a ridge (like Cambo or Ingoe) high above the River Tyne. The castle, with a keep, baileys and gatehouse, was established in Norman times by the Umfraville family, and lies closer to the river than the modern town. The photograph shows the spread of industry on the lower ground towards the castle, but it has not been allowed to encroach on the strip of green that divides it from the castle. The castle itself has a deep valley to the east and is on the ridge that has had a ditch cut around it except on the north-west side. The picture shows the keep standing proud within the walls of the inner bailey, the outer having a barbican entrance. The medieval bridge to the castle lies over the dene to the east. There does not appear to be any trace of the village settlement, because so much of the area is covered with recent developments.

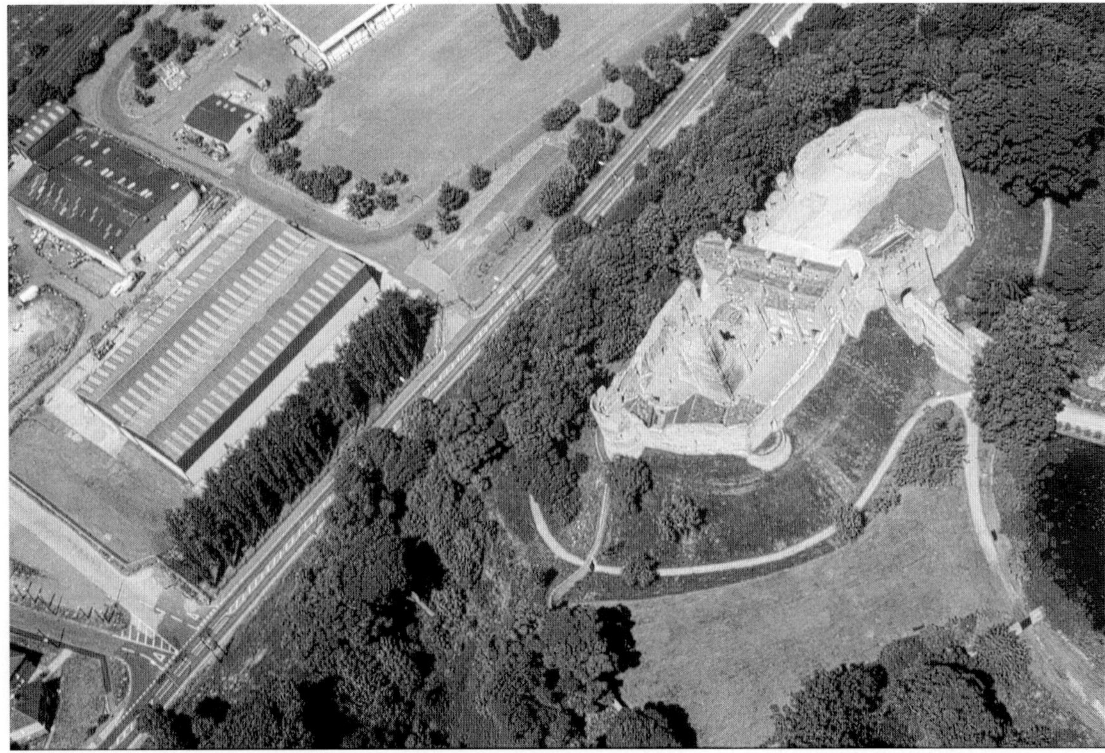

59 The castle in its setting.

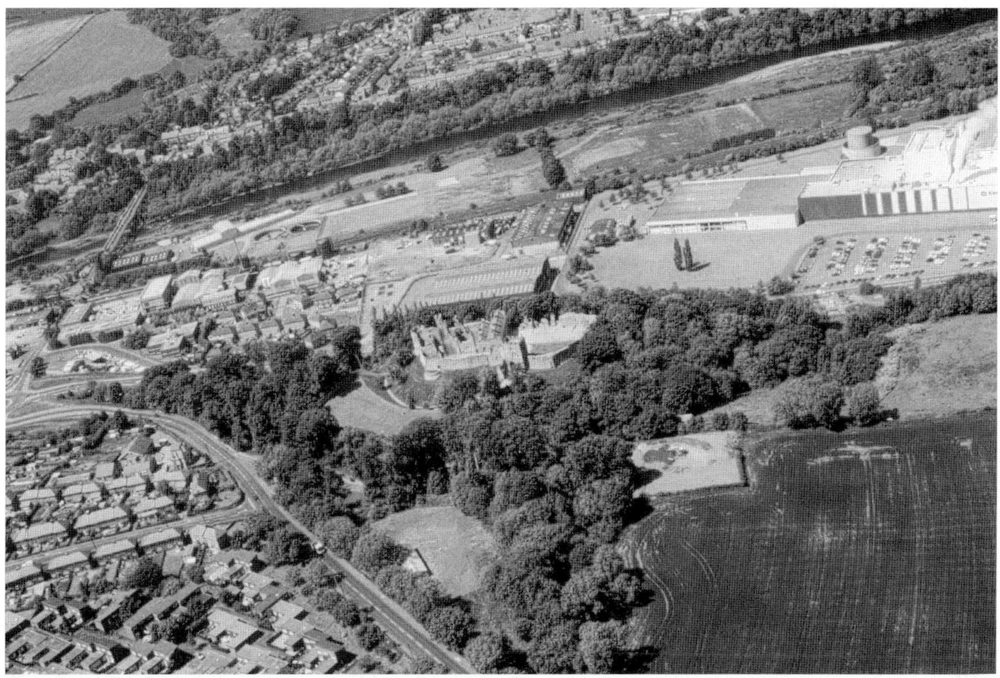

60 Prudhoe.

The castle, fringe of the town and industry.

BEDLINGTON

Even before the first coal mine was sunk in 1840, Bedlington had a long history. Its name dates back to 1050 and means a settlement named after Bedla or Betla. It was the centre of Bedlingtonshire, part of the County Palatine of Durham. However, only a few old houses and wide main street survive amid the newer architecture of the pit village. It had a famous and important ironworks and was renowned for the manufacture of locomotives and malleable iron rails.

When heavy industries pass the days of their effectiveness, there always seems to be great haste to get rid of everything, good and bad. It is often too late to realise that much of what has been destroyed would have been of enormous interest to future generations. These south-east Northumberland towns have had to re-invent themselves particularly since the coal mines closed, but with the end of the traditional industries has gone a way of life that offered an established purpose and stability to people living there.

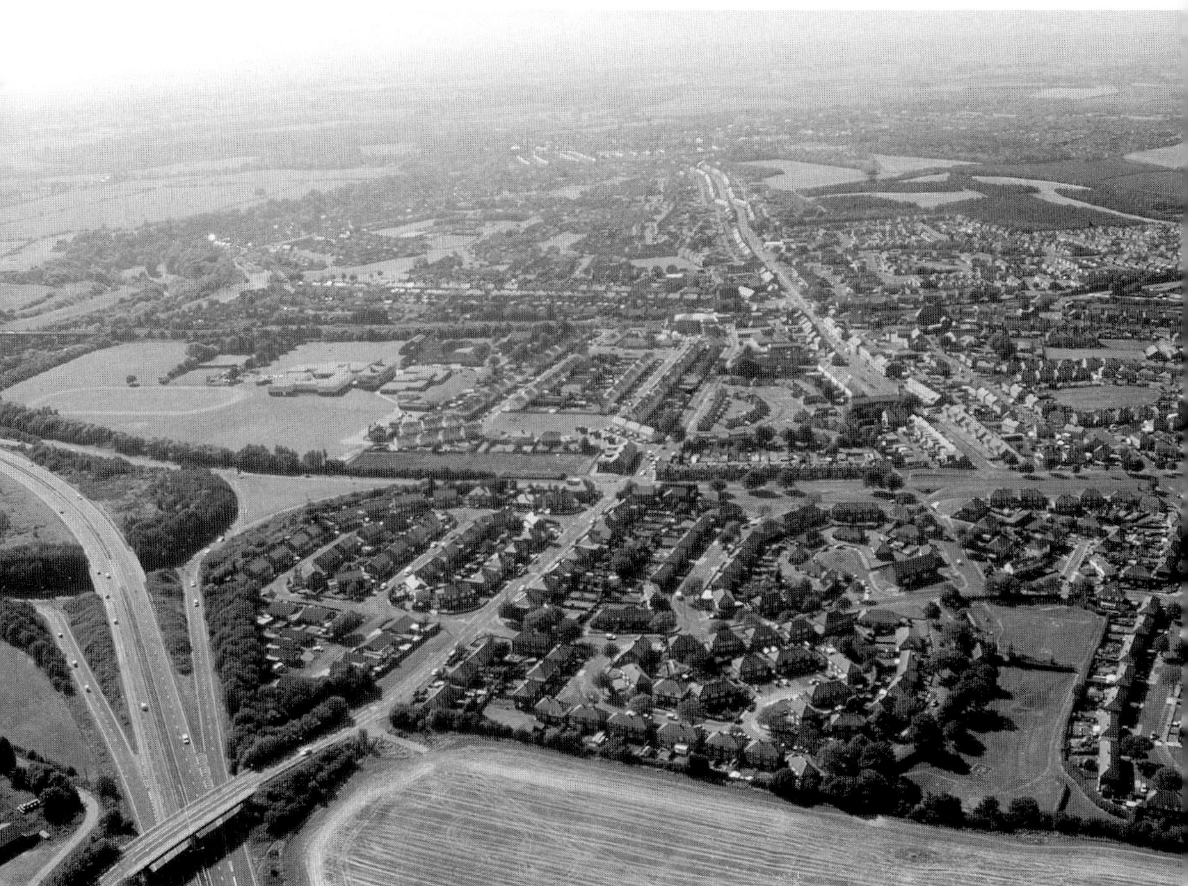

61 Bedlington.

Bottom left to centre is a main road intersection, to the right of which, above fields, is a housing estate. Above the sports field, marked by a running track, a railway line runs central from left to right. The straight road which crosses it, towards the top of the picture, is flanked on the right by houses arranged in a crescent, then by another estate and woodland. To the left of this road is the river valley, with houses and schools in between.

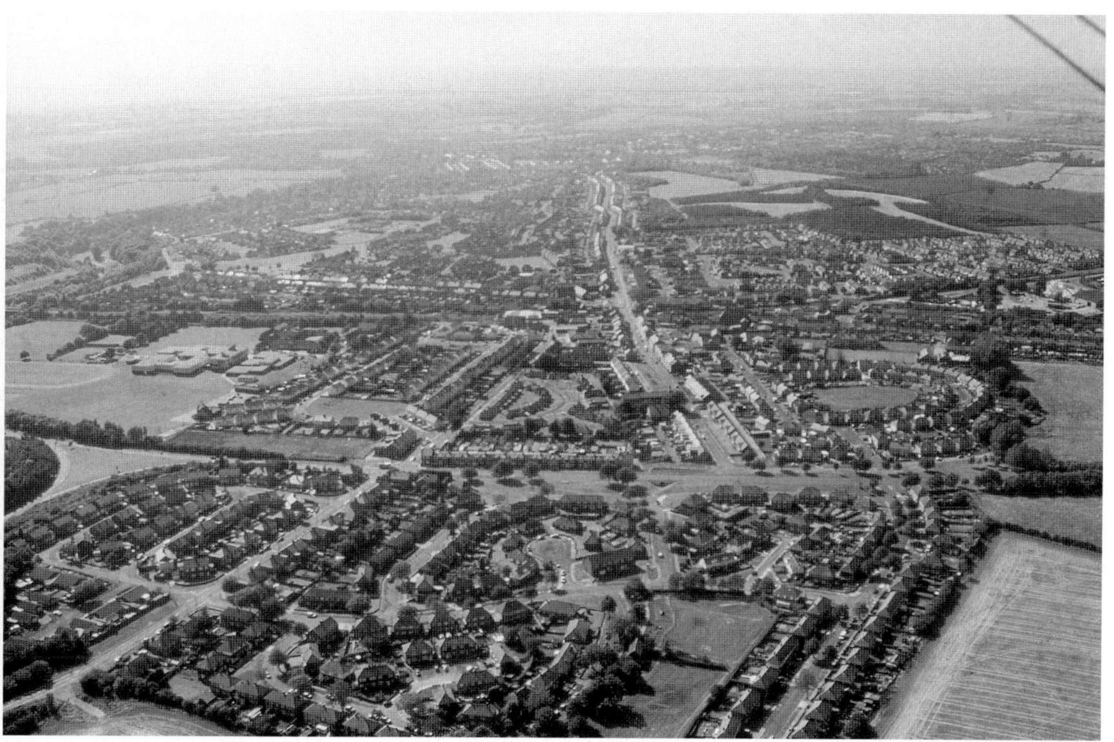

62 Bedlington.

We see more detail, with the road running through the town clearly defined in a north-east to south-west direction. What stands out is the number of green spaces within the urban area, running into farmland.

Great care is being taken to retain some 'rural' or parkland character within some of these industrial towns. Much derelict industrial land has been landscaped to provide pleasant places for local families to visit. The industrial past has not been forgotten, and some local schools are investigating with archaeologists some of the sites of iron manufacture.

ASHINGTON

Originating surprisingly as 'the valley where the ash trees grew', the town is entirely the creation of industry, although the single farm from which it takes its name still survives on the fringes of the modern town. The reason for the town's existence is the abundance of coal, which fuelled the Industrial Revolution, and its easy access to the sea for export of the coal.

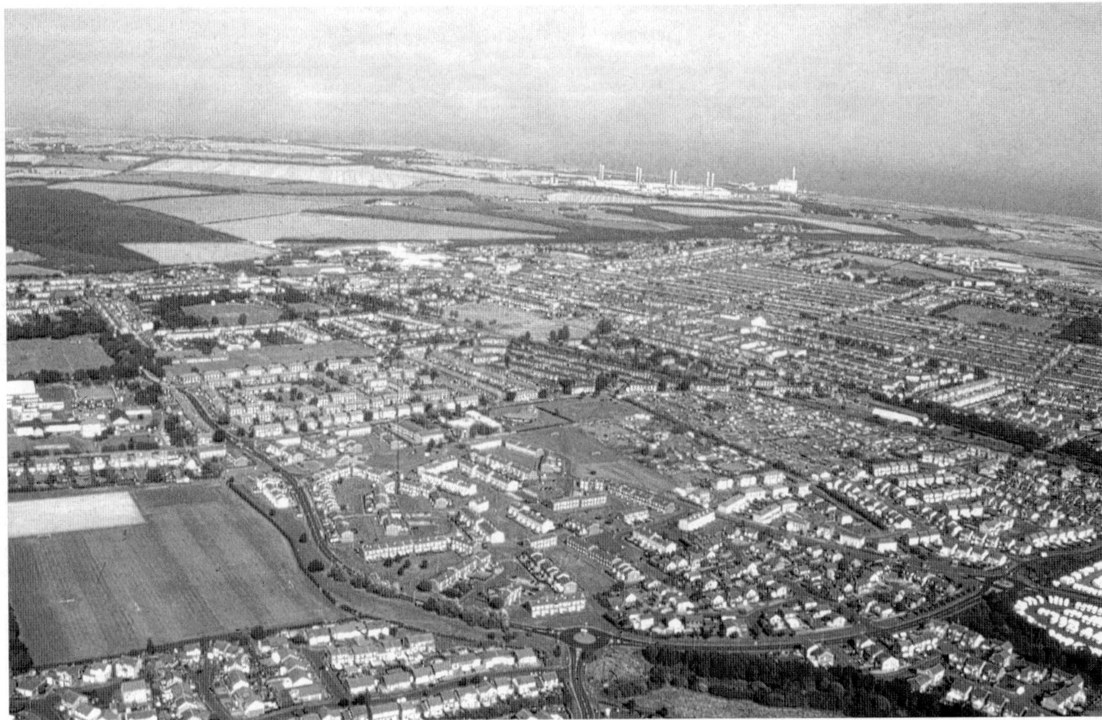

63 The Ashington Coal Company built the first houses from 1855-78, all based on terraced rows, a pattern that continued as the town developed. At the top of the picture is the Alcan aluminium smelting plant at Lynemouth, on the North Sea coast.

There is a clear division between the geometrical arrangement of terraced housing of the Hirst area (centre-right) and later estates, although these are not the oldest terraces. Much of the left-hand site is occupied by houses, schools and open spaces, but towards the town centre the building becomes more crowded. Appearing in the bottom right-hand corner is the edge of the main industrial estate.

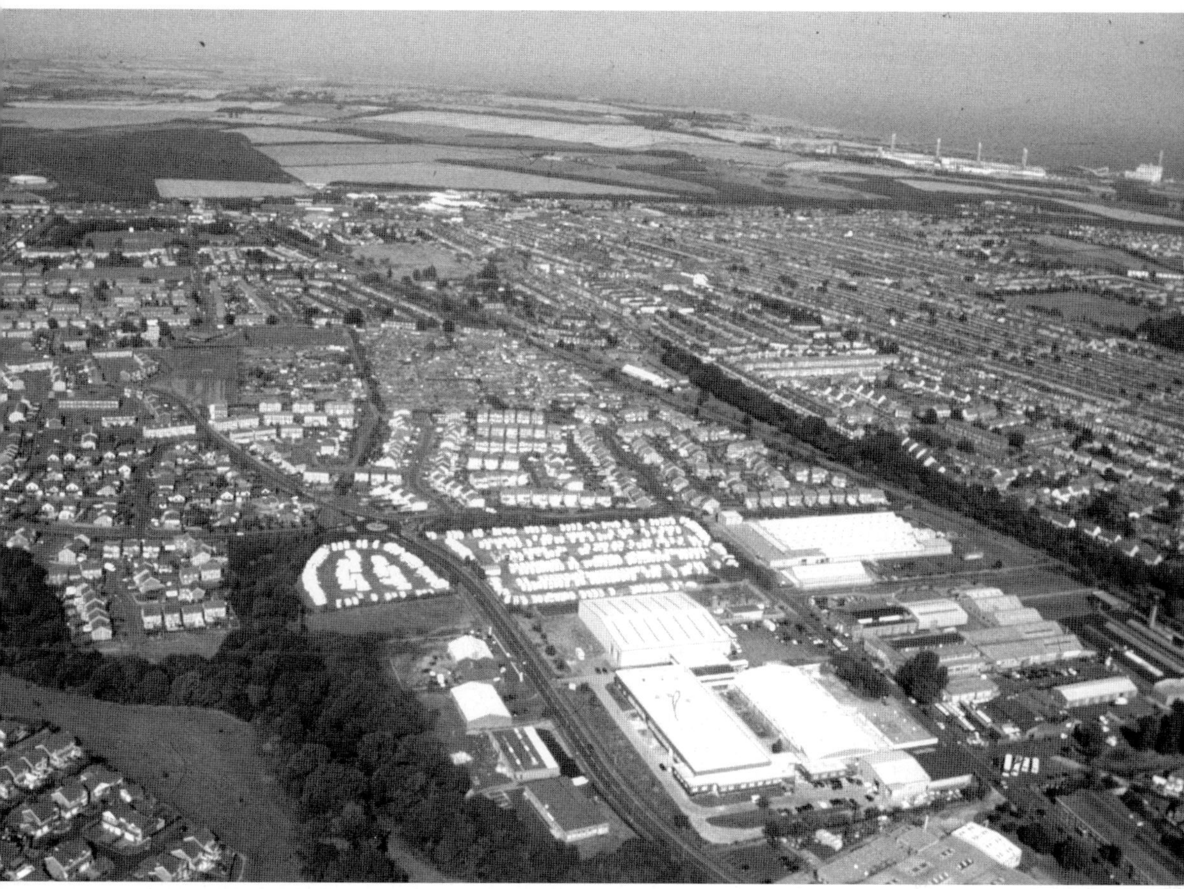

64 Ashington.

Taken in the same direction, we see the railway and A196 (dividing the Hirst area, Wansbeck Hospital and North Seaton from the rest) running from north to south, with the east end having the earliest housing and industries. Ashington College campus is in the south-east and schools are identified by their playing fields. The industrial estate is close to the River Wansbeck just west of the main road, seen here at the bottom of the picture.

Queen Elizabeth Country Park is seen to the top right, marked by its small lake.

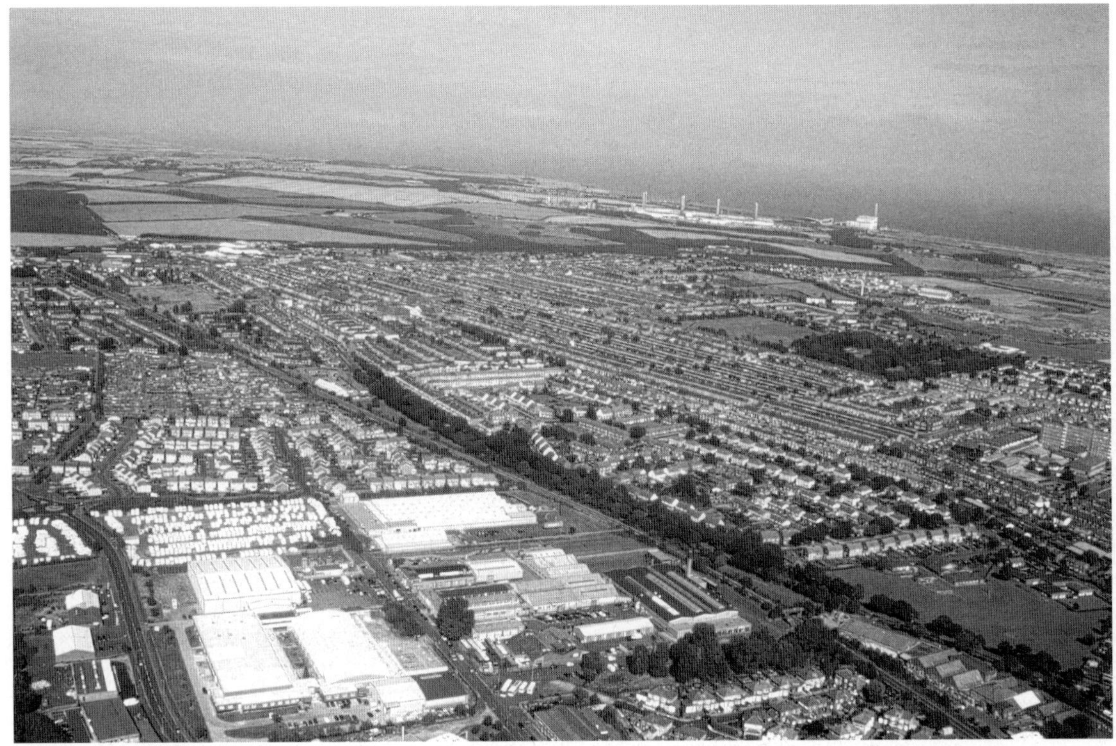

65 Ashington.

This shows most clearly the division between the east and west part of the town, with more detail too of the 1870 terraces. Ashington College campus is in the lower right-hand edge of the picture. The wind generator and Wansbeck Hospital are at the top right-hand corner of the town.

The town owes its origins to coal and other industries shattered in the Thatcher era, but there is an awarenes that if new methods of using coal cleanly and for storing carbon dioxide can be developed, the North-East still has about a quarter of its reserves waiting in a time of energy crisis, when dependence on overseas sources of energy could cripple us. Offshore coastal windfarms have also been developed at places like Blyth, but this is not enough.

PEGSWOOD

Pegswood is a modern offshoot of the larger towns nearby, but in 1242 it was recorded as 'Peggiswrth', meaning Pegg's enclosure.

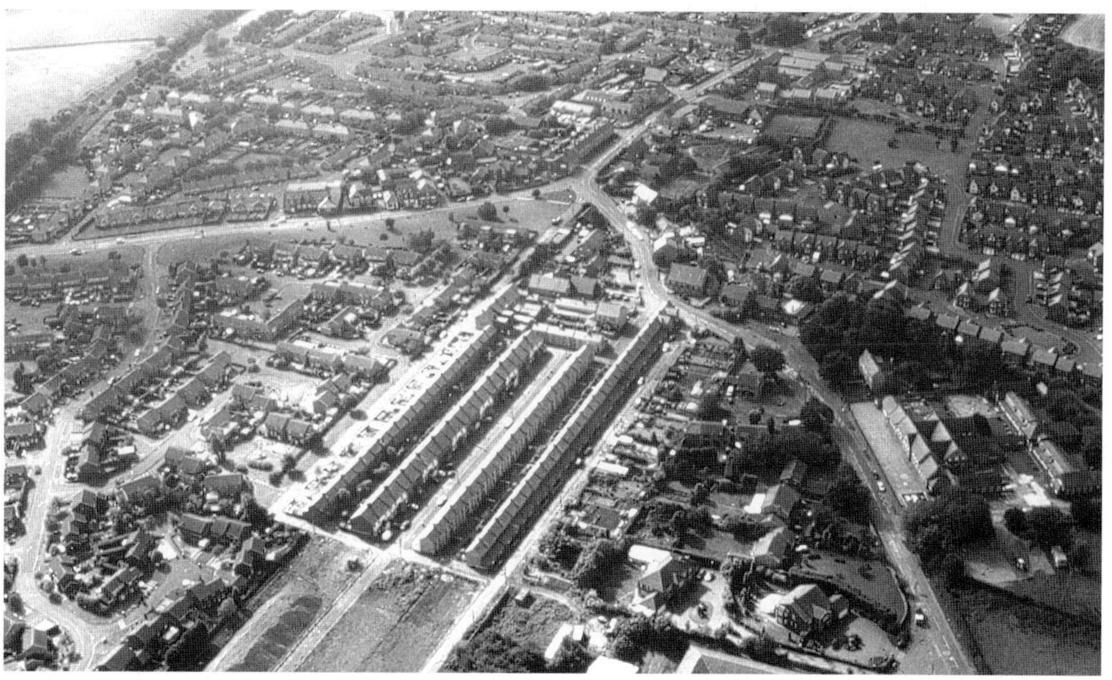

66 Viewed from the east, there is a prominent rectangular arrangement of terraced houses at the bottom centre of the picture. The railway runs to the left and is crossed by the A197, which meets Butcher's Lane running to the bottom right-hand corner. Other housing estates are more varied in their layout than the strict terraced plan. At the far top left is the River Wansbeck, en route from Morpeth, with cultivated fields between it and the settlement.

The picture illustrates two different approaches to life, based on economics. The coalfield demanded quickly-built, regulated, compact back-to-back housing; modern living favours spaced-out housing with individual gardens.

WOOLER

In many ways Wooler can be considered a village rather than a town, but its position in the north-west of the county, the presence of a ruined castle and its status as a market could qualify it as a small town. Its position gives it its name, which means 'a promontory by a spring'; it is on the margins of the Wooler Water – a high place that commands extensive views across the Milfield Plain.

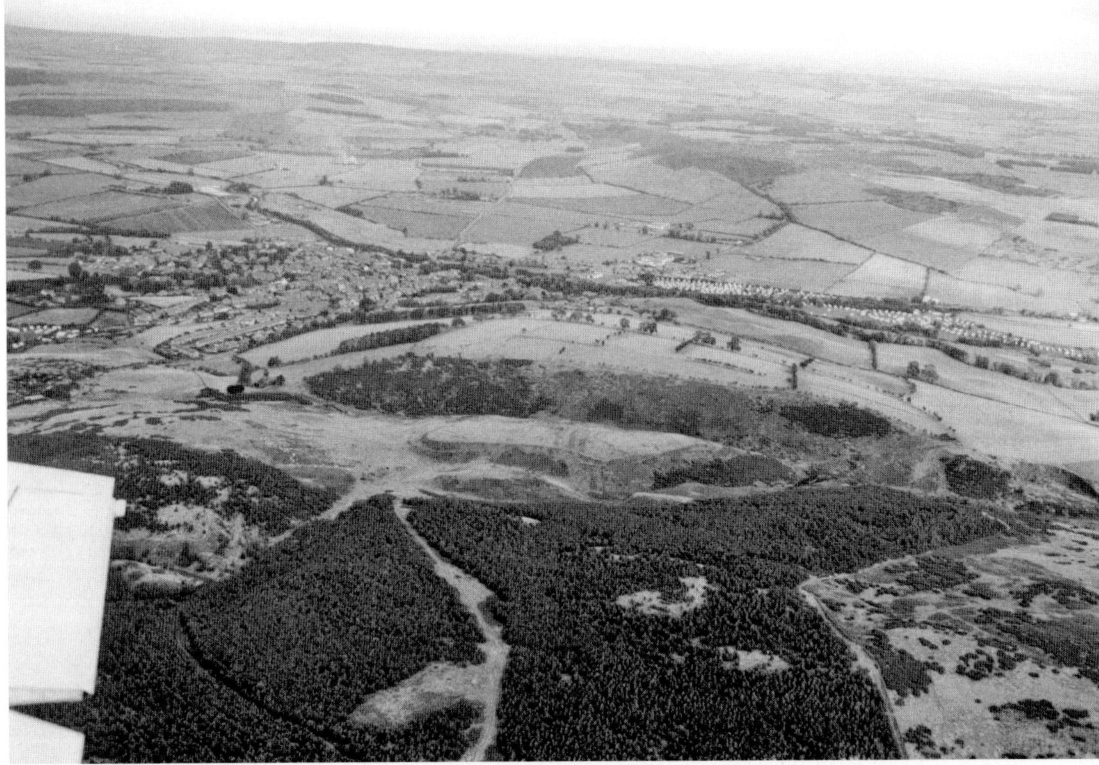

67 In the photograph, Wooler is centre-left; to the right is a caravan site that in 1503 was where the English army camped before moving to the Ford area to fight the Battle of Flodden. It lies on the margin of the volcanic outcrops overlooking the Milfield Plain. Above the caravans, Weetwood and Fowberry Moors, which are outlying scarps of Fell Sandstone, overlook the Plain and lead on to the North Sea. Above the woodland at the bottom of the picture is an elongated prehistoric enclosure in a strong position. The A697 runs through the caravan sites, appearing as a dark line, onwards towards Coldstream (see also picture 43).

6

VILLAGES

Much of the interest of Northumberland is enshrined in its villages, with a considerable variety of locations and building materials, and much evidence of long histories.

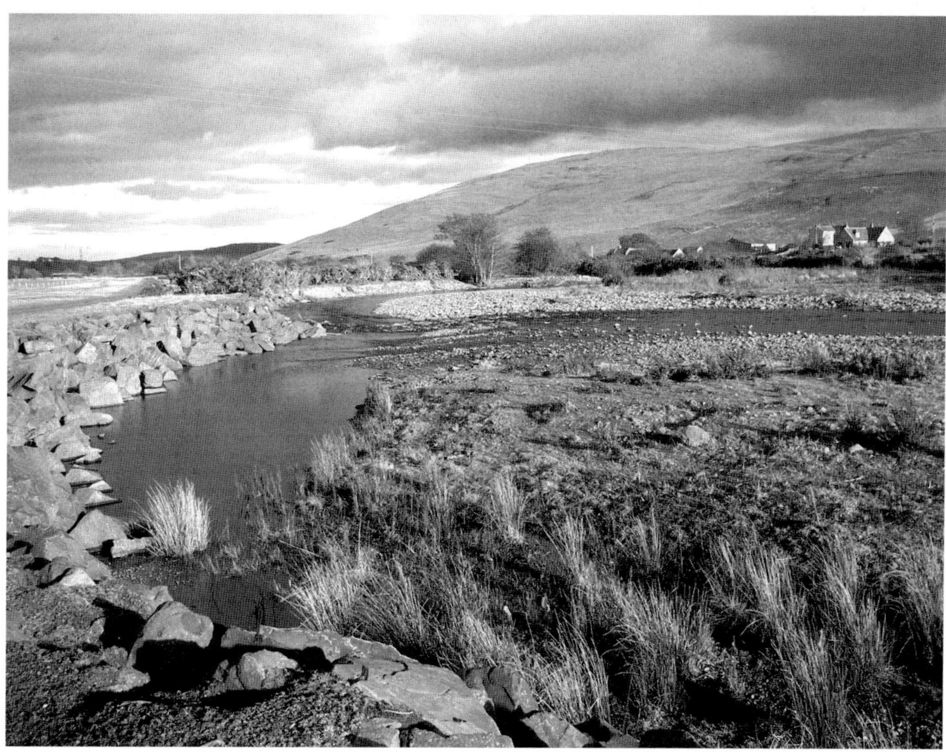

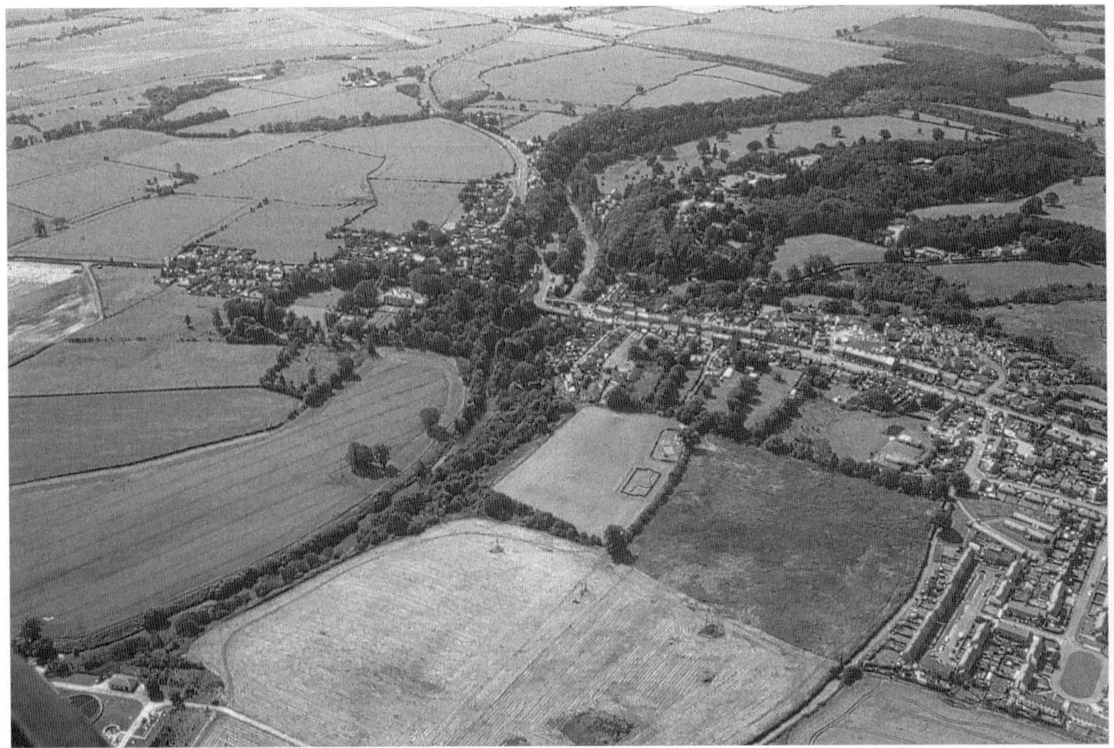

68 Felton.

Now by-passed, Felton once lay on the A1, the Great North Road, at an important crossing-place over the River Coquet. 'Feltona' in 1166, it was a farm in large cleared fields. The old bridge, like that at Warkworth, has been preserved with a modern bridge in tandem. The village is spread on either side of the road in a ribbon and the number of inns, a gasworks, brewery, bank, chapel and reading room indicate its importance to travellers.

The east (bottom) has the village's recreational fields, to the north of which (right) are council houses, a village hall and a graveyard. Recently there has been some up-market housing development. The wooded river valley, stretching from corner to corner of the picture, has Felton Park at the top right, where the old architecturally-enigmatic parish church and a modern Roman Catholic church stand away from the village. There are well-preserved remains of a watermill. To the south (left) is level farmland, which includes a Second World War airfield, now used by microlights and other small planes (see 116, 117).

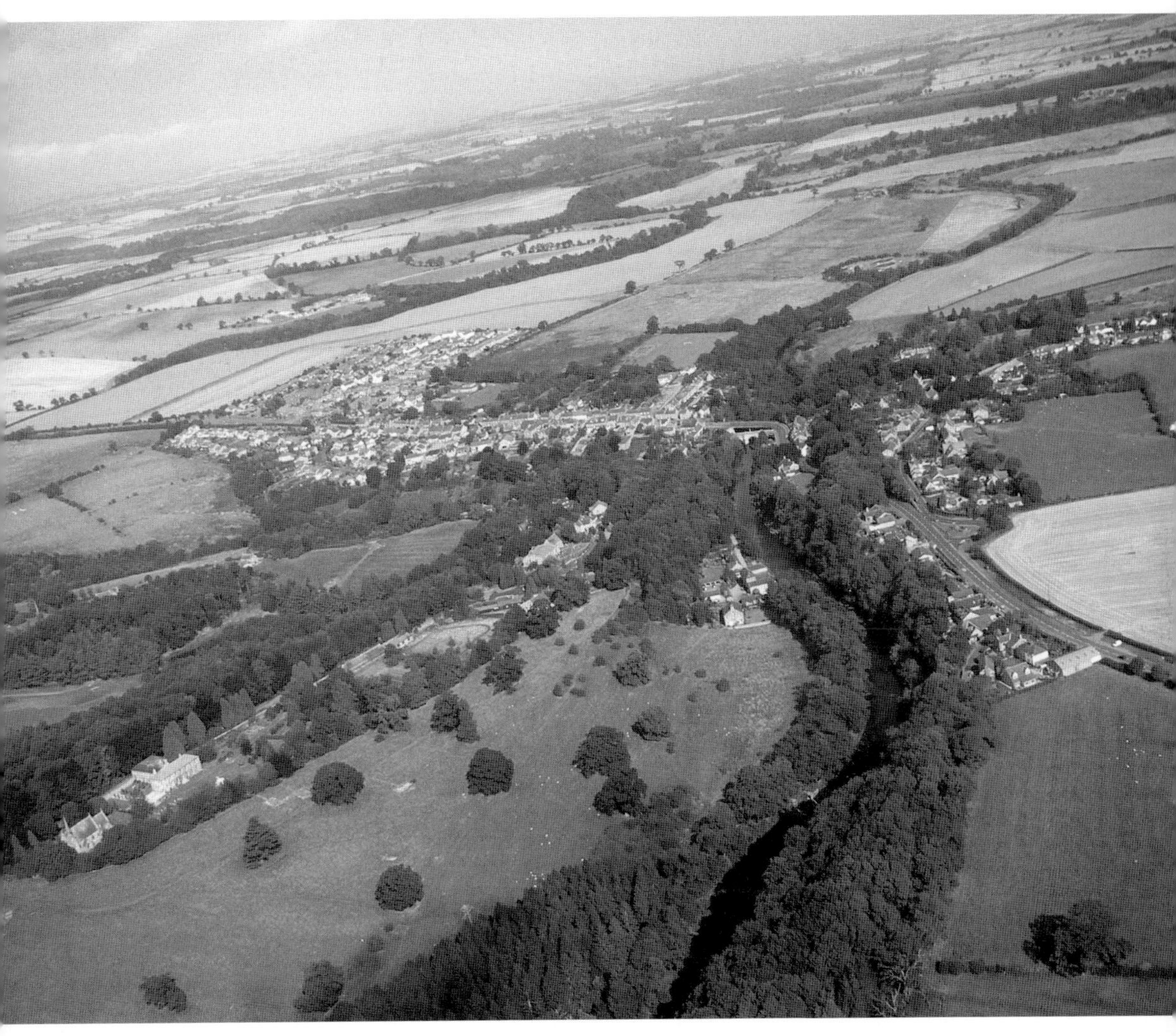

69 Felton from the west.

The River Coquet is flowing from the bottom, with its banks tree-covered. To the left is Felton Park, with the remains of the old house and its 'Riding Field', meaning a clearing. We reach the village from here via the church. To the right of Felton, over the bridge, is Thirston. The river winds its way to the sea via Acklington and Warkworth.

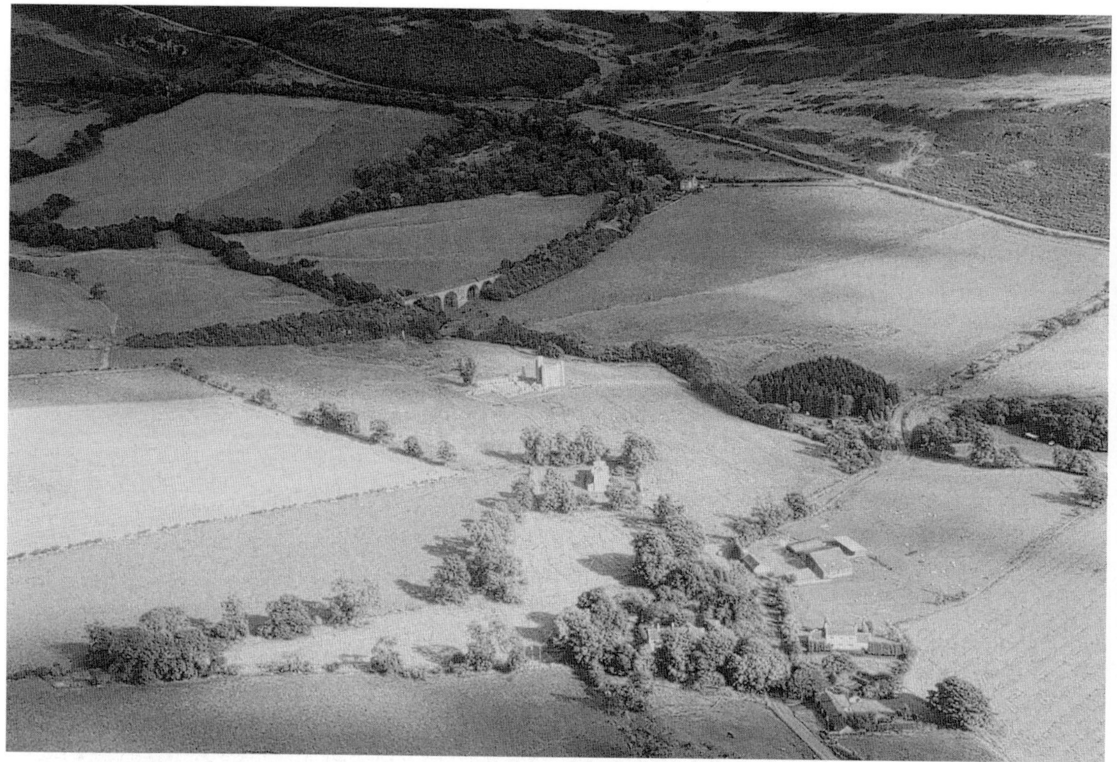

70 Edlingham.

Edlingham is one of several village names that can cause confusion: Eglingham, Ellingham, Ellington, Elrington and Eltringham. Those ending in -ingham, which means that they belong to the descendants of a named Anglian, are pronounced *injum*. The suffixes depend on which person or feature they take their name from: Egwulf, Ella, a place of elder trees, or Elfhere. Edlingham is named after Eadwulf.

The view of a railway viaduct, castle and church, all below the scarp along the line of which runs the old turnpike road from Alnwick to Rothbury, and extensive grassed rig and furrow ploughing, all point to a long history in an important place.

The castle was built in a valley rather than on a hill and its building has evolved. Its structure has been revealed and reinstated by modern archaeology (see also picture 96). The scarp that shelters the land on one side has extensive quarries and timber plantations, bell pits for small-scale coal working, and prehistoric sites, along with some dramatic small cliffs. On the other side is good farmland.

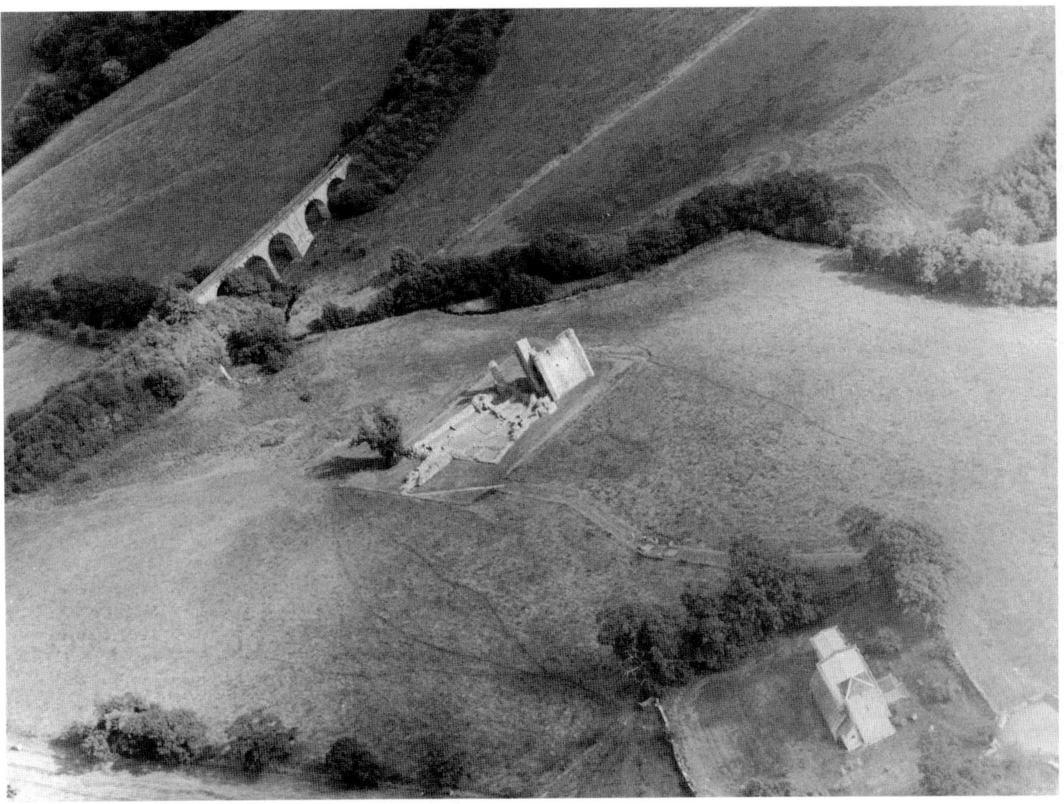

71 Edlingham.

This picture focuses on three of the principal buildings that define the history of the area. At the bottom right is the church of St John the Baptist within its large walled graveyard, its nave dating to at least early Norman times. The tower, squat, with thick walls, seems out of keeping with a church, but its position in the Border lands explains why it was built like a fortification. These were turbulent times.

The castle, centre, is seen more closely in picture 96. It stands close to the burn in what is now a cleared area; in one field a large medieval grave-slab, now in the church, was unearthed during ploughing.

The railway viaduct was built north-east of the castle around 1885, perhaps incorporating some castle stone, and carried the now-defunct railway from Alnwick to Cornhill.

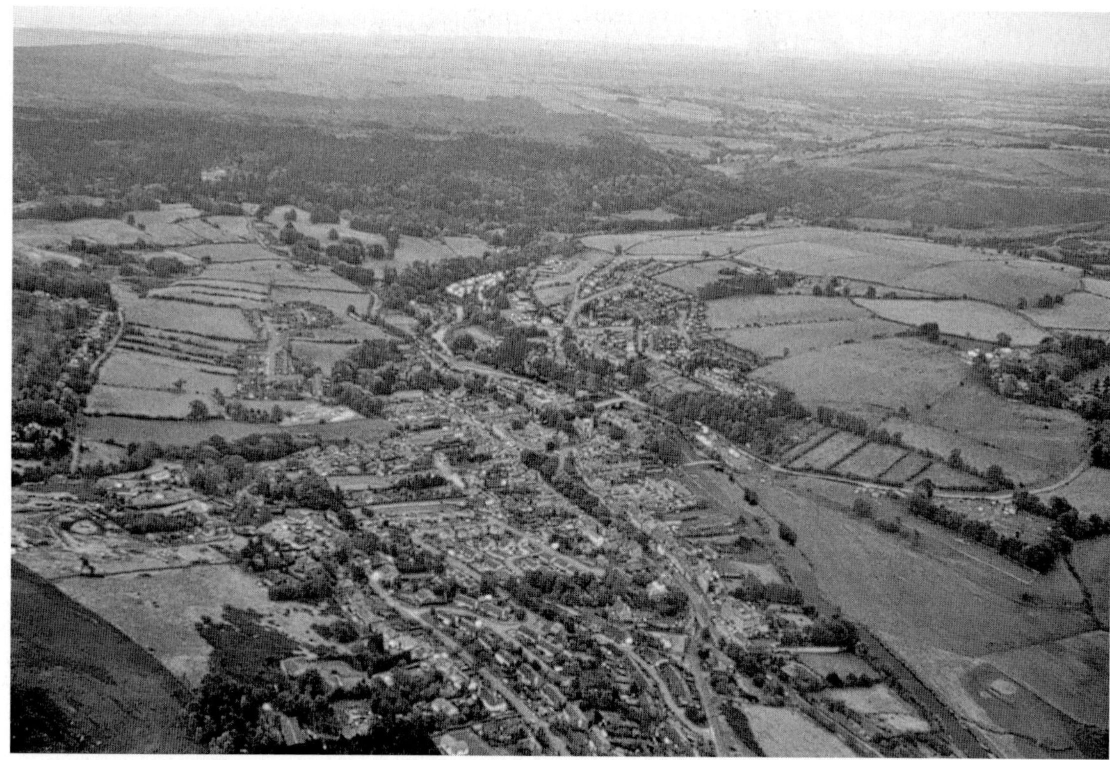

72 Rothbury.

Rothbury is the principal village of the Upper Coquet valley before the river winds its way eastward to Warkworth. The old bridge has been widened at this important river crossing. The name suggests it may have been a burgh and thus may have been fortified early in its history. It has parts of an early foundation in its church, and the outstanding remains of an Anglian stone cross, part of which is in the church and the rest in the Museum of Antiquities, Newcastle. Most of the village is, however, geared to the needs of a market centre, to the people who work in the area, to commuters and to tourism.

The view shows that the main road follows the river, with housing development on the valley slopes on either side. Strips of land once belonging to individual cottages are clear, and on early maps these carry the owners' names. Roads run east to Brinkburn and Alnwick, and south to Hexham.

To the left is the beginning of Cartington Moor, with new housing nibbling at its edges. Top left is the extensive plantation of Cragside with a variety of trees to enhance the importance of Cragside House.

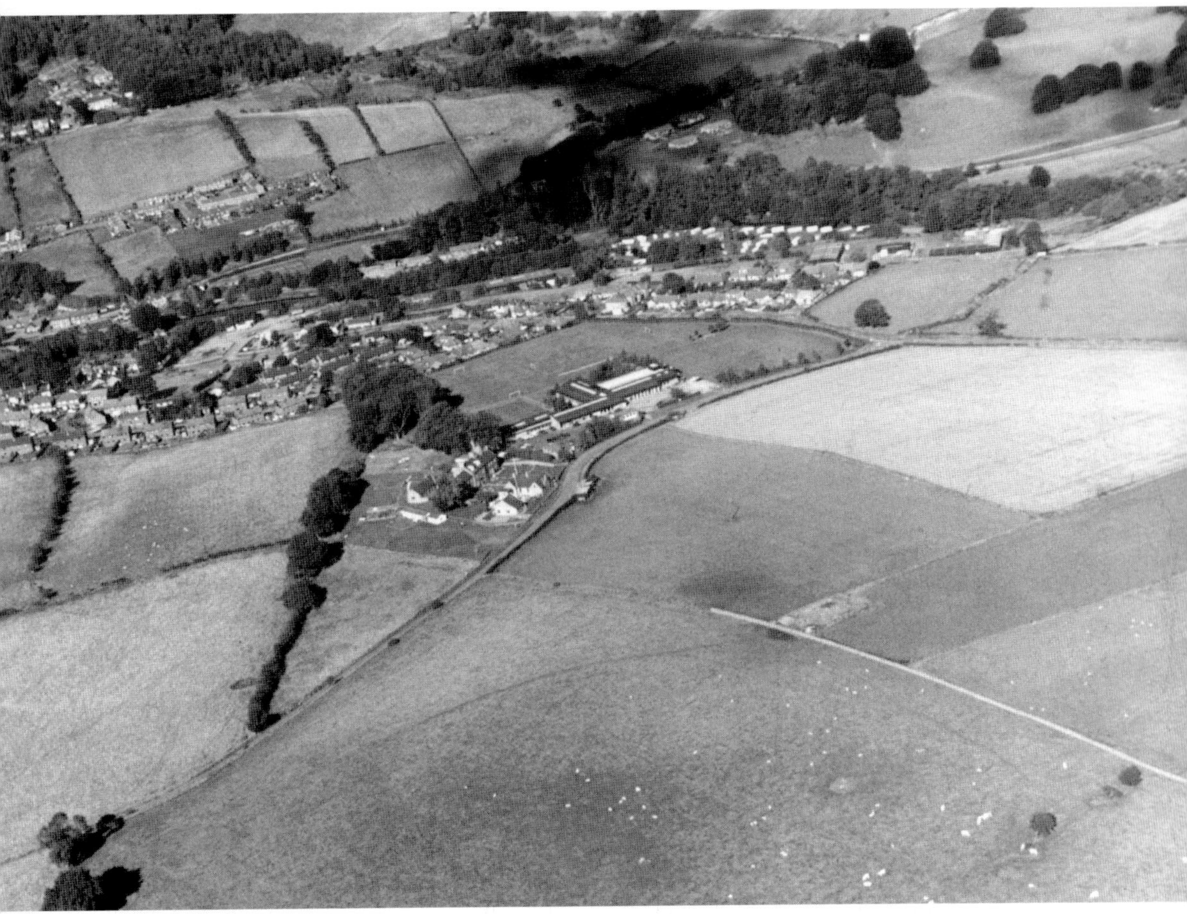

73 Rothbury.

Overlooking the village from the south is the Middle School with its boarding wing and swimming pool. Originally built as a secondary school, it serves one of the largest and most thinly-populated areas in the county, the swimming pool originally having been built largely as a local effort, but now run by the County Council. This must have one of the finest outlooks of any school in Britain. Housing development has slowly crept up the hill to reach the school. On the opposite side of the valley are the strips of land to which I have already referred.

The field at the top end of the lane which passes the school has now been filled with houses. At the bottom of the picture is the beginning of what used to be Rothbury's golf course, now relocated.

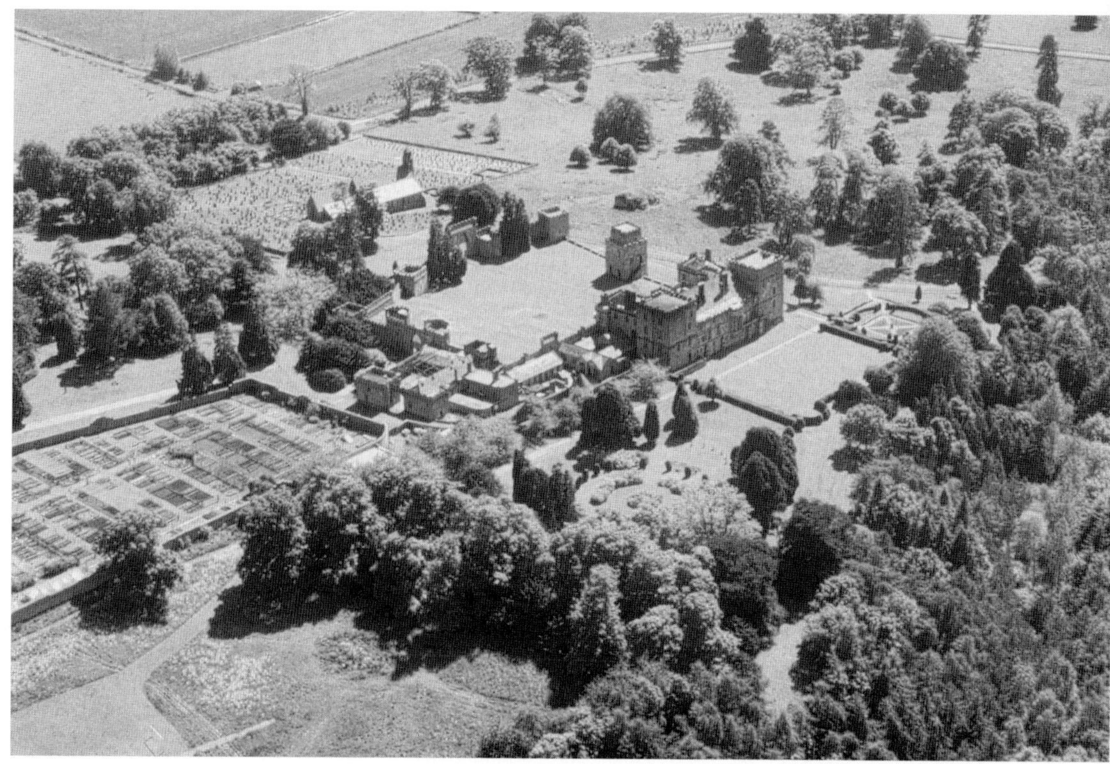

74 Ford.

Castles and fortifications have played a large part in the history of the Border. At Ford, as the name suggests, the castle was built to overlook a crossing place of the River Till. We see an artificially-created landscape of buildings and parkland. The original fourteenth-century castle was built on a courtyard plan with four towers at the corners, but has been extended. The church is earlier, but heavily restored, and lies outside the castle wall along with the village, which occupied the field at the top of the picture, with a small vaulted defensive tower thought to be for the parson. The village was rebuilt to the east by the Marchioness of Waterford, who was responsible for much of the landscape that we see today. The castle, rented from Lord Joicey by Northumberland County Council, has for years been a remarkable residential education centre for hundreds of children and adults. This has ensured its preservation as well as providing a unique opportunity for study.

The large walled garden to the left is now a commercial nursery. There is strict control by the Joicey Estates over any developments within the landscape which might spoil it.

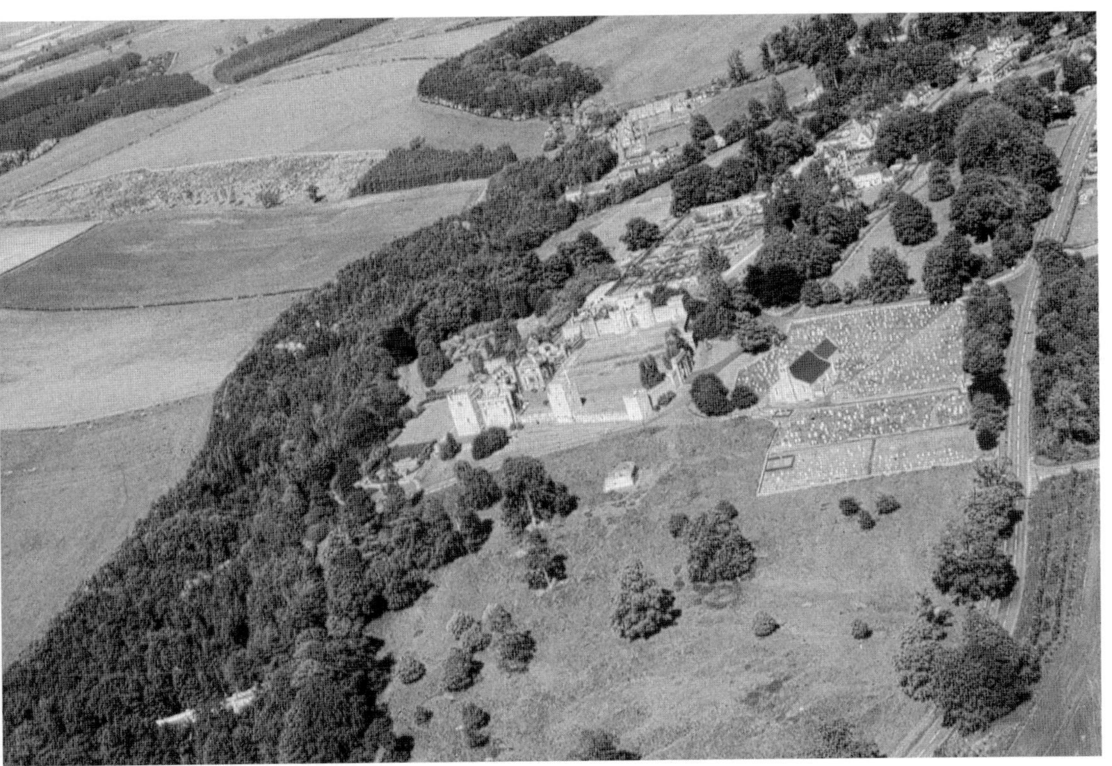

75 Ford Castle.

The castle and church from the west, over the site of the old village and remains of the 'parson's tower'.

overleaf 76 & 77 Etal.

The River Till flows north from Ford via Heatherslaw Mill to reach another castle and village at Etal. The river is seen at the bottom of picture 77, where there is a weir and watermill site. The castle lies centre-right, with two freestanding towers and another absorbed into a farm adjoining the Heritage centre. It is today reached by a miniature railway. The village is largely modern on either side of the road leading to the gatehouse. Etal Hall and the church lie on the other side of the Ford-Duddo road. Like Ford, this is very much a landscape created as an estate, centred on a defensive site. The name means that it was Eata's grazing land.

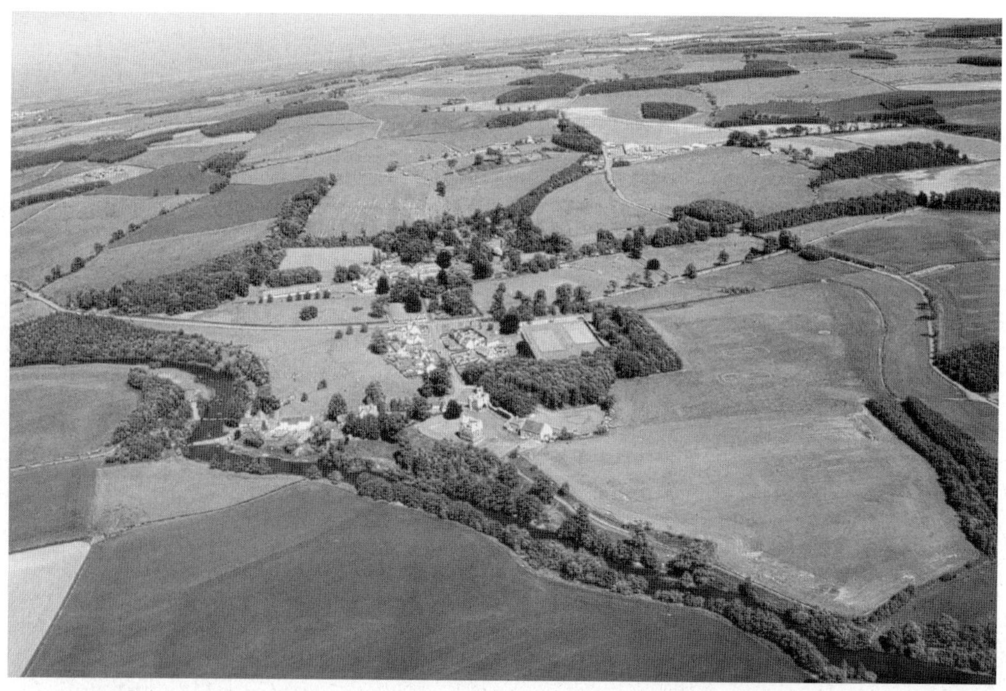

76 (above) & 77 (below) Etal.

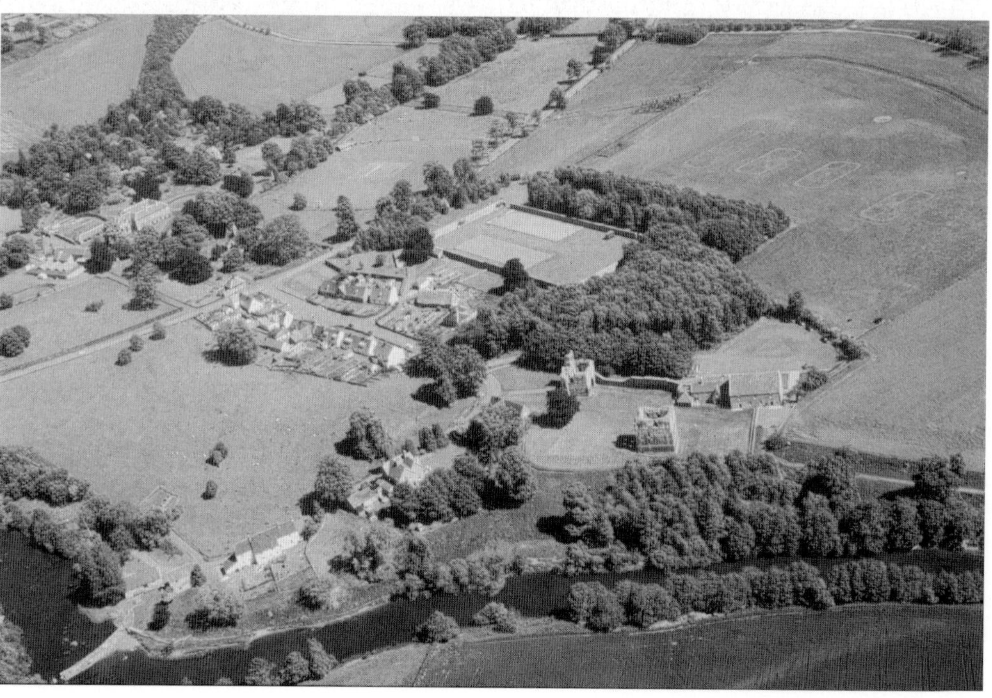

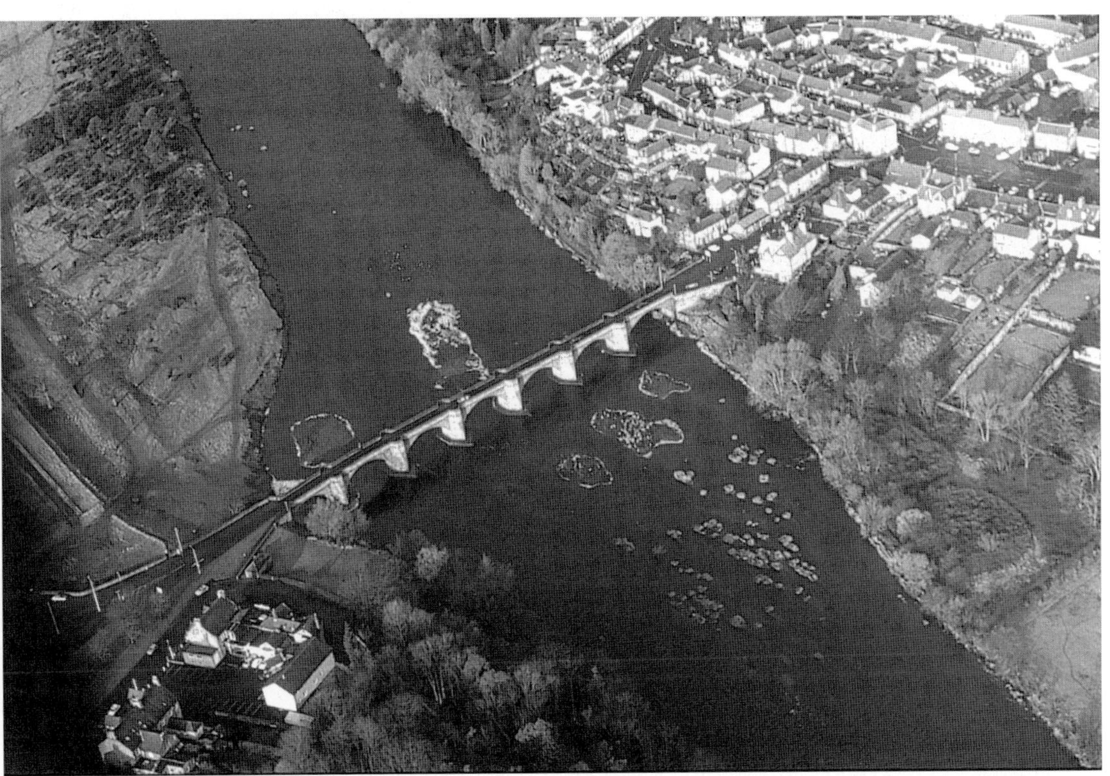

78 Corbridge.

The bridge that crosses to Corbridge across the River Tyne on the north side with seven spans dates to 1674, and was the only Tyne Bridge to survive floods in 1771. There has, however, been extensive flooding recently on the south bank. The Romans built a fine bridge downstream that has recently been excavated on the south side, with a ramp made of very large sandstones taking the road over the bridge to Coria, one of the largest Roman settlements in the north. This emphasises the importance of fording places and bridges to the development of settlements, as Roman and medieval Corbridge are military and market centres. Roman stone was to provide masons with ready-made material for such buildings as Hexham Abbey crypt and the western tower of St Andrew's church, Corbridge.

A car park has now been built on the south bank (bottom left) by the bridge end to offset some of the congestion in the popular village centre; it also gives access to a walk along the south bank to the reconstructed ramp of the Roman road where it led to a bridge over the Tyne to Coria.

Flooding in this area has recently been a major problem.

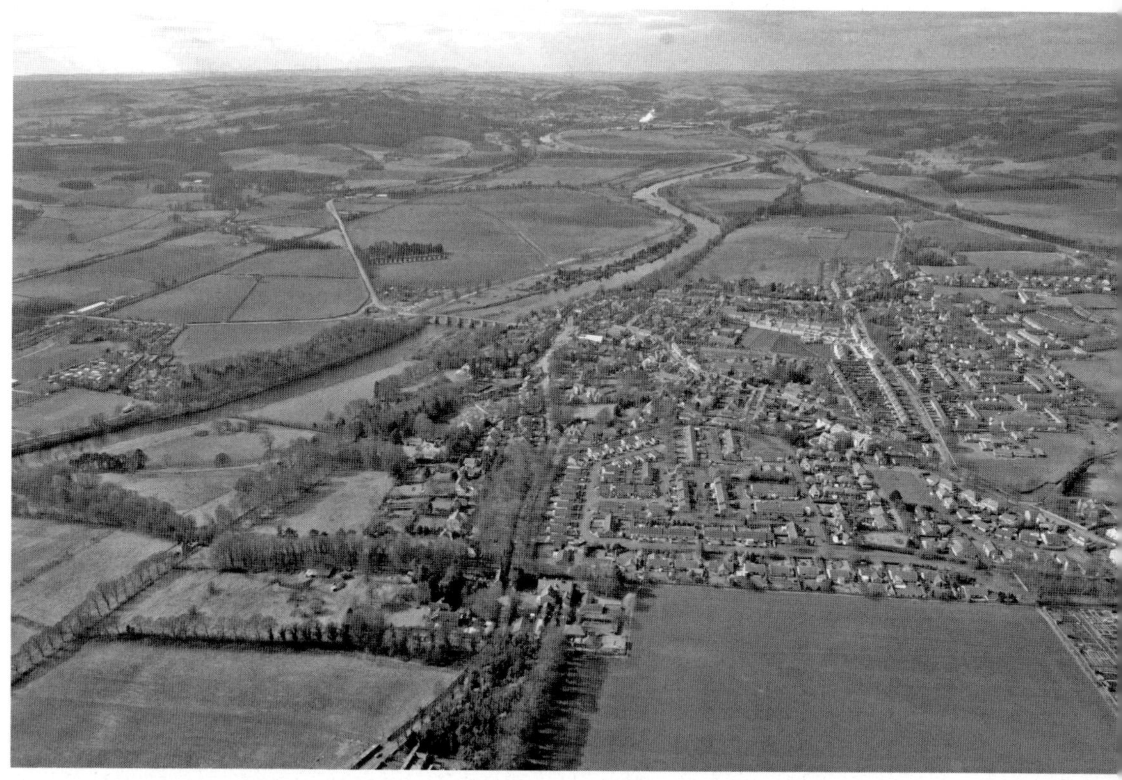

79 Corbridge (*The Hexham Courant*).

Once one of the most important settlements in the county, it is now a large village. The attraction for settlement was the River Tyne, with its fertile haughs on either side providing flat fields overlooked by the valley slopes, and fording places which were then bridged. From the left end of the bridge a straight road is crossed by the Carlisle-Newcastle railway via Hexham, marked by the steam emitted from the Egger factory (top). Both the Roman settlement of Coria and the modern village lie on the north bank. The excavated part of the Roman site is seen as a small square within a field; there is the museum and some of the building foundations. Originally this was a key fort on the early Antonine frontier, and the building of Hadrian's Wall increased its importance as a supply base to the south of that wall.

The medieval settlement, which made good use of some Roman building material, covers the rest of the area up to the ploughed field at the bottom, where we see a spread of housing estates. What remains of the old town is largely around the church, market place, and Vicar's 'pele'; it still retains its plan of parallel streets running from east to west (bottom to top). An oblique road (B6321) runs from the bridge north-east past Aydon to reach Hadrian's Wall and the military road.

WARKWORTH VILLAGE

Warkworth, an important seat of the Earls of Northumberland, occupies land enclosed by a big loop in the River Coquet. Named after a Lady, Werce, the motte and bailey castle has a planned village leading up to it from the north. As we see in the pictures, the land holdings on either side of the road are arranged as burgage strips (here called 'scribes') each with a house and garden. At the north end is the Norman and later church, then a fourteenth-century bridge with a strong tower.

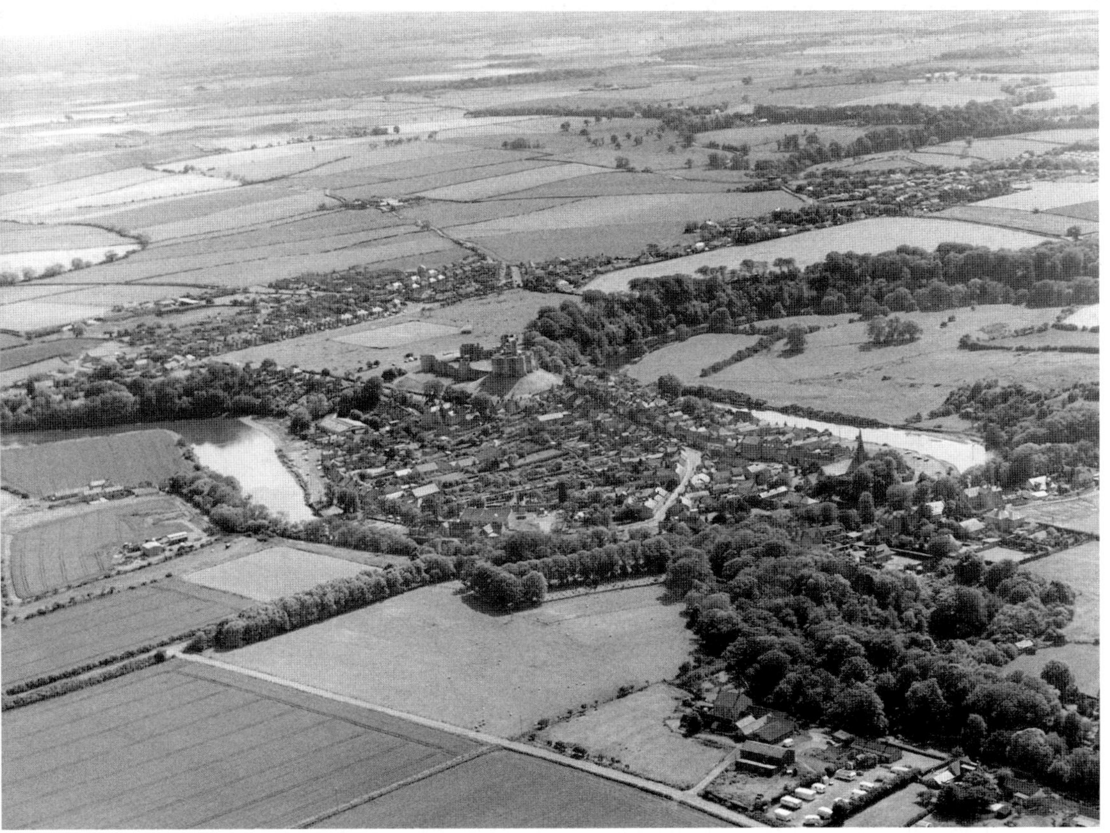

80 This view, from the north-east, includes the village, its surrounding fields and recent housing developments. The position of the castle and village within a bend in the River Coquet, gives it a ready-made strategic advantage. To the right, the river has flowed from Morwick, where there is a mill and some of the finest prehistoric carved spirals in Britain, on a sandstone cliff rising from the river.

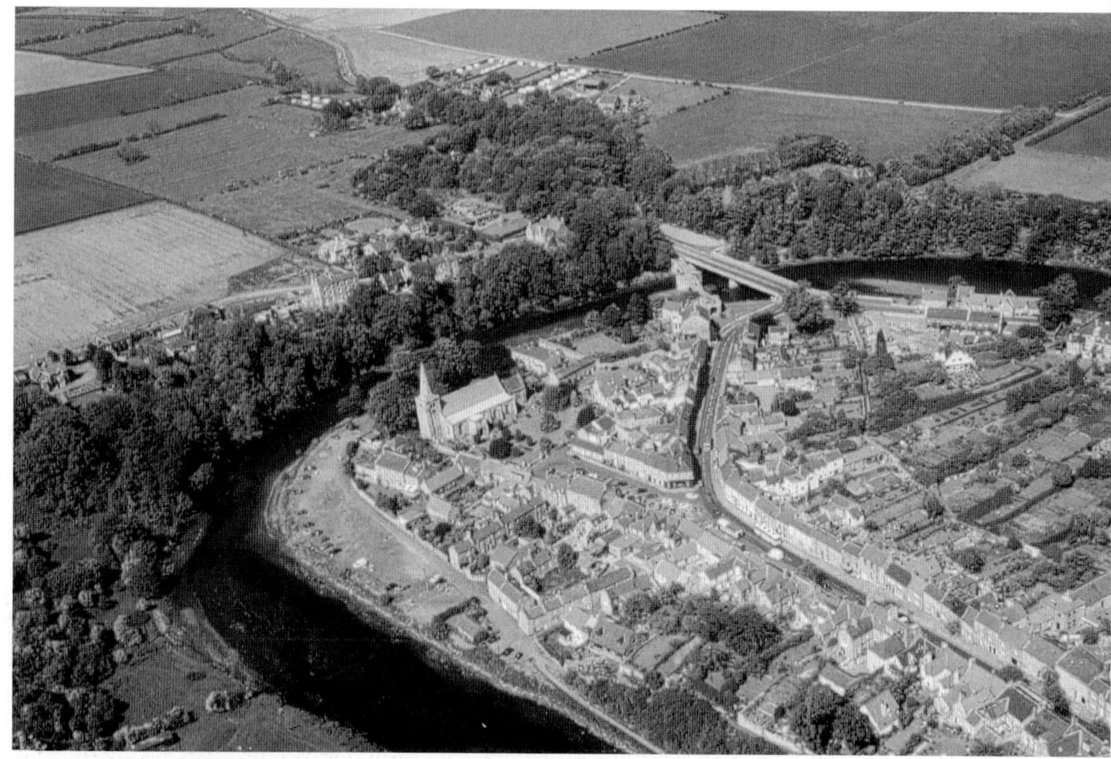

81 Warkworth.

The north part of the village is centred on the main road to the castle, with strips of land on either side. The church is at the top left and the bridges are clearly seen at the end of the road, which goes on to Alnmouth (see also under 'Castles').

The church of St Lawrence, largely Norman, with a tower and spire added later, faces the small market place and from here there is a small lane which gives access to a river walk (left). This marks the edge of the medieval settlement, to which strips of holdings run from the main street above.

Outside the village there has been a spread of caravan parks, a feature of many of these popular coastal areas, where proposals for new ones often meet with considerable opposition from people living there.

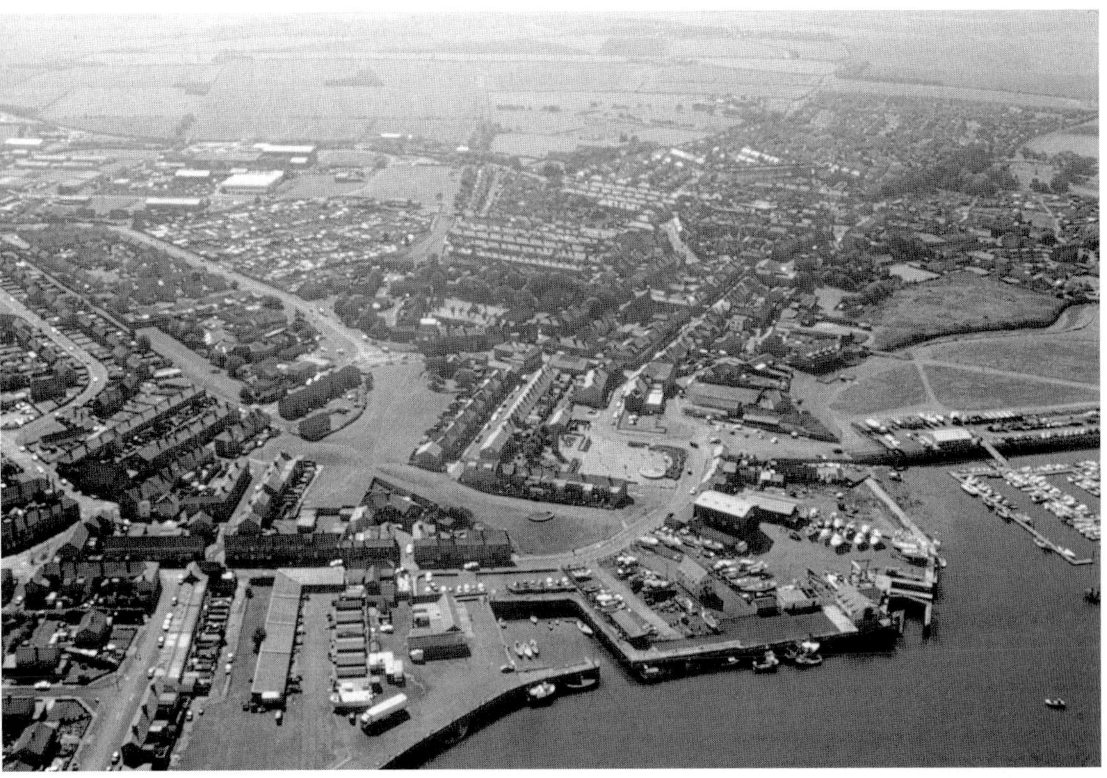

82 Amble.

The coastal village appears as 'Ambell' in 1204, meaning 'Anna's promontory', but the present settlement is anything but ancient. Originally its harbour was known as Warkworth Harbour, constructed in the early nineteenth century. Attached to it is the Queens Street planned town.

It is still a small working fishing port, with the addition of sea trips for tourists, and it has expanded its buildings and caravan parks. To the south are coastal country parks, many the result of reclamation from defunct mining.

In this picture we see the main harbour at the bottom and the marina to the right. The view is to the west.

This harbour attracts many different species of birds, especially when the fishing boats come in. Among the residents are black and white (male) eider ducks, known as 'Cuddy's ducks' after St Cuthbert; cormorants are often seen spreading their wings in the sun.

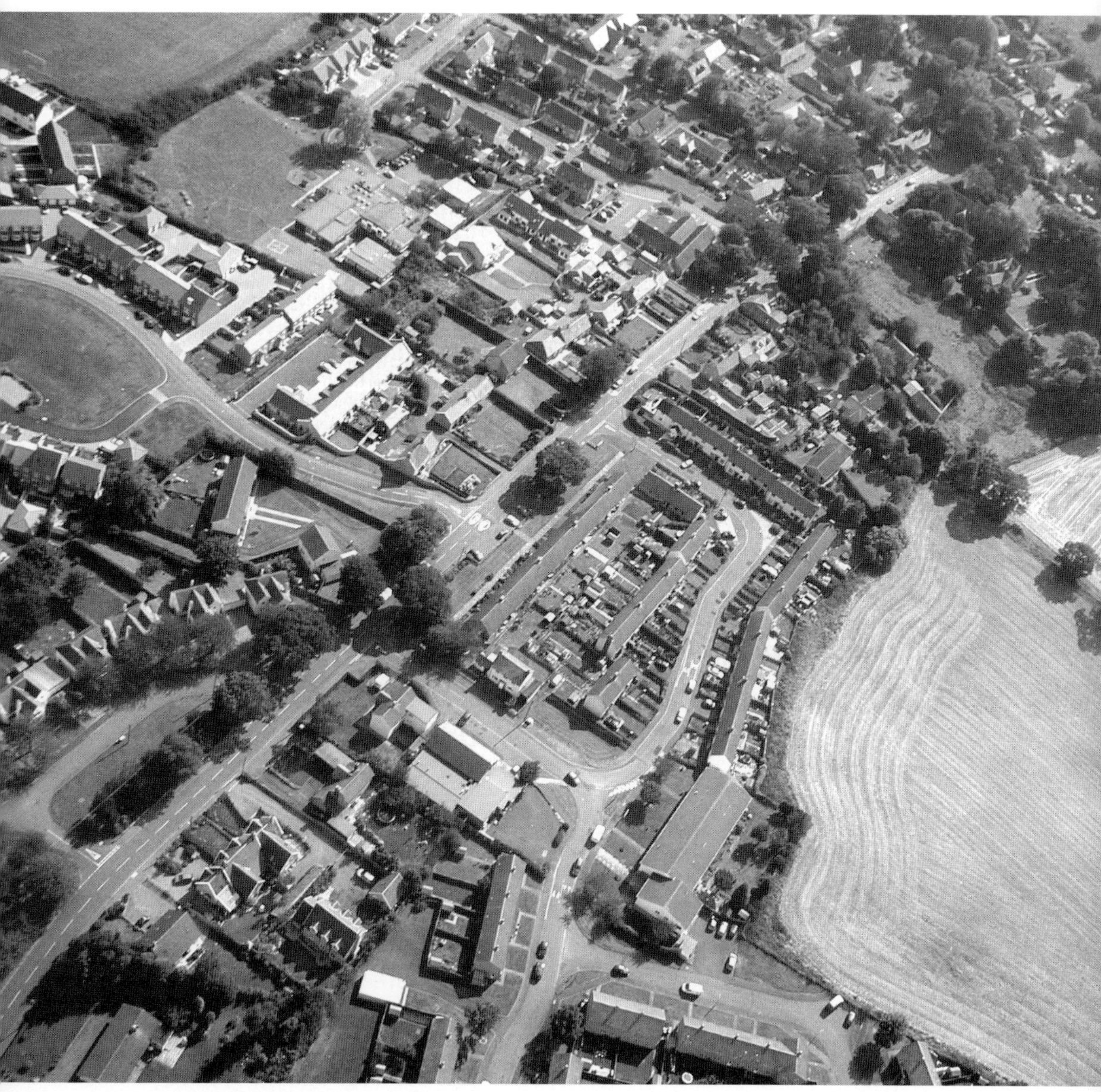

83 Longhoughton.

This is the north part of the village, an extension of its line, which includes houses built for armed service people and their families. One long-roofed structure is the NAFFI (Navy Army and Air Force Institute). It is a reminder that this area houses important radar systems. Its 1242 date and the spelling of the name show it to be a settlement on or by a spur.

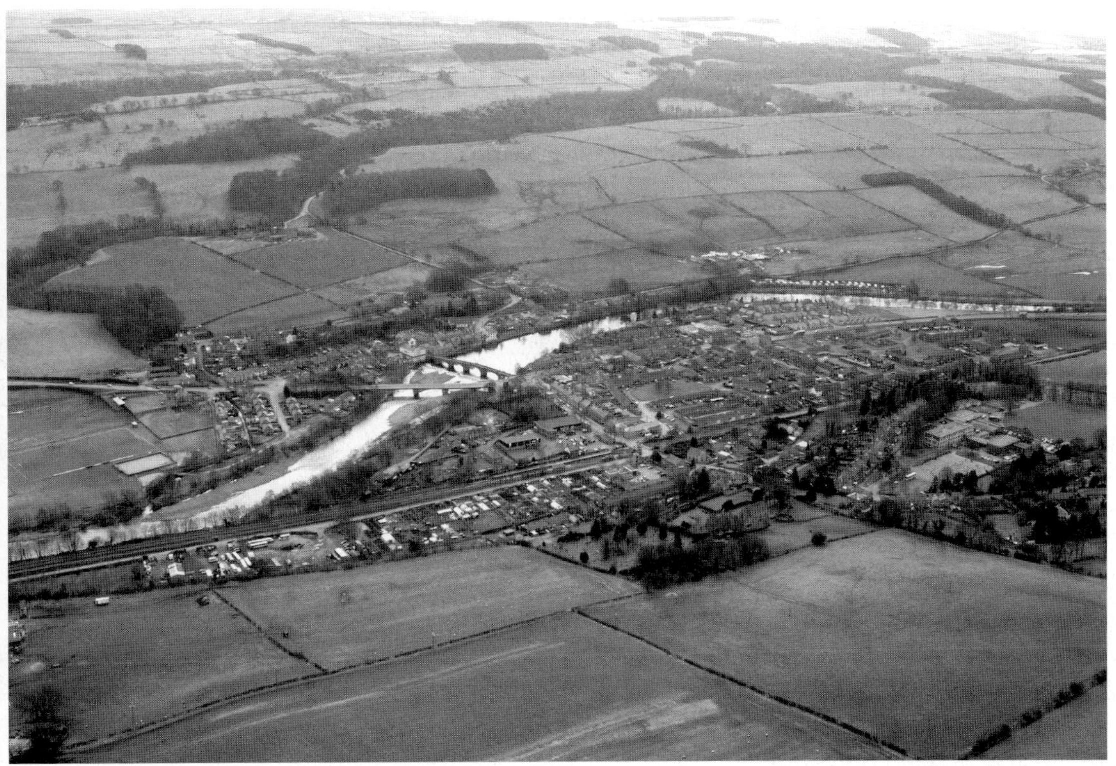

84 Haydon Bridge (*The Hexham Courant*).

Haydon Bridge ('Hayden' in 1236) is being transformed by the building of a bypass, for which residents have campaigned for many years, as the main road through the village on the north bank of the Tyne is almost impassible for residents and for modern traffic.

The village grew up as a crossing-place and, partly because it was administered by the Greenwich Hospital Commissioners, it has some fine buildings. However, the original village church lies half a mile to the north along with some old 'bastle houses' of the unruly Border past. There was an important lead mining and smelting industry, though short-lived. The Newcastle-Carlisle railway has a station here, crossing the north-bound minor road. Near this, lower right, is the school campus.

On the opposite bank of the river, spanned by modern and older bridges, is a large hotel built by the Commissioners. The fields at the top of the picture are being severed by the building of the bypass. To the left, the dark woodland runs along a tributary valley which includes the course of a disused railway and the A686 road on the way to Langley Castle and Carts Bog.

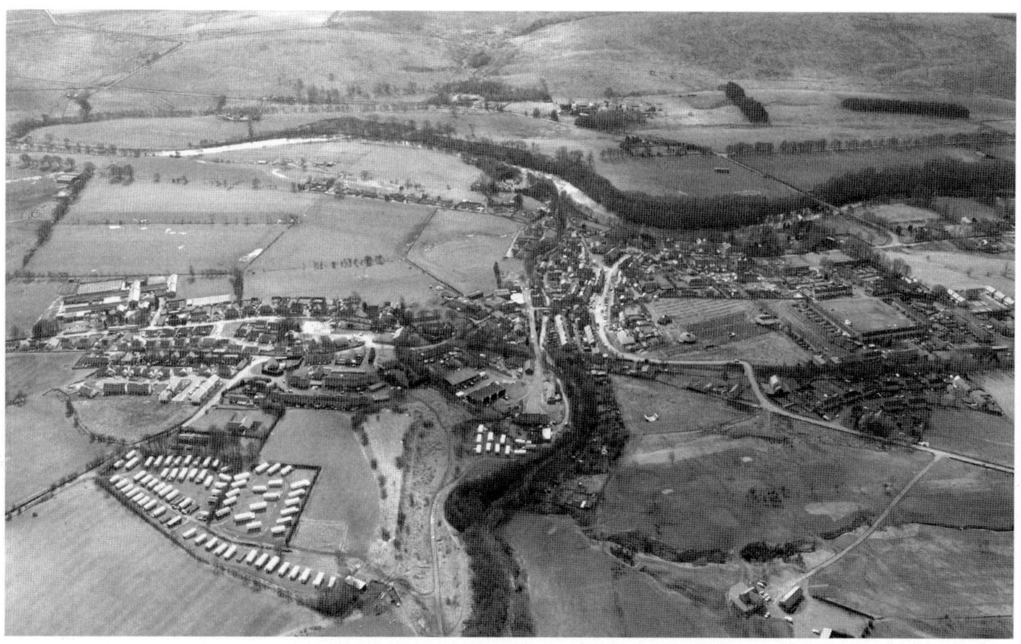

85 Bellingham (*The Hexham Courant*).

Bellingham may be regarded as a town for its important and rather lonely role in the life of the North Tyne valley. There is not much that is very old, although its name, 'Bainlingham' in 1050, means either a hill-dweller's farm or a farm belonging to the Bel family. Its ending is pronounced *injum*. The church is of exceptional interest.

The River North Tyne, with its fringe of trees, runs from top right to left. It is joined by the wooded valley of the Hareshaw Burn, which flows from the bottom centre of the picture. There is a large caravan park to the left, adjacent to fields which have rig and furrow ploughing visible. To the right of the burn (north) is a golf course and clubhouse in an open space, joined to the B6320 on its way to the main A68 road to Scotland. A small group of white-topped caravans and larger dark-topped buildings occupy the space left by a short-lived, but large, iron-smelting site which relied on the locality for its raw materials, employing hundreds of people. There is now a car park giving access to this beautiful and interesting valley and to Hareshaw Linn, a waterfall. Otherwise the oldest part of the town clusters around the main street, with its nineteenth-century shop fronts. It includes an eighteenth-century three-storey house and a Town Hall with a lead clock tower and spire.

Elsewhere are the remains of the terraced houses of the iron workers and more recent housing development. To the left of the burn (south) above the caravans lie the schools. A denuded mound in this area was the site of a small castle. Beyond the haughs on either side of the river is rising ground with pasture and moorland (top); the division between the two different kinds of land is marked by the road to Hexham, which crosses the river by an 1834 bridge.

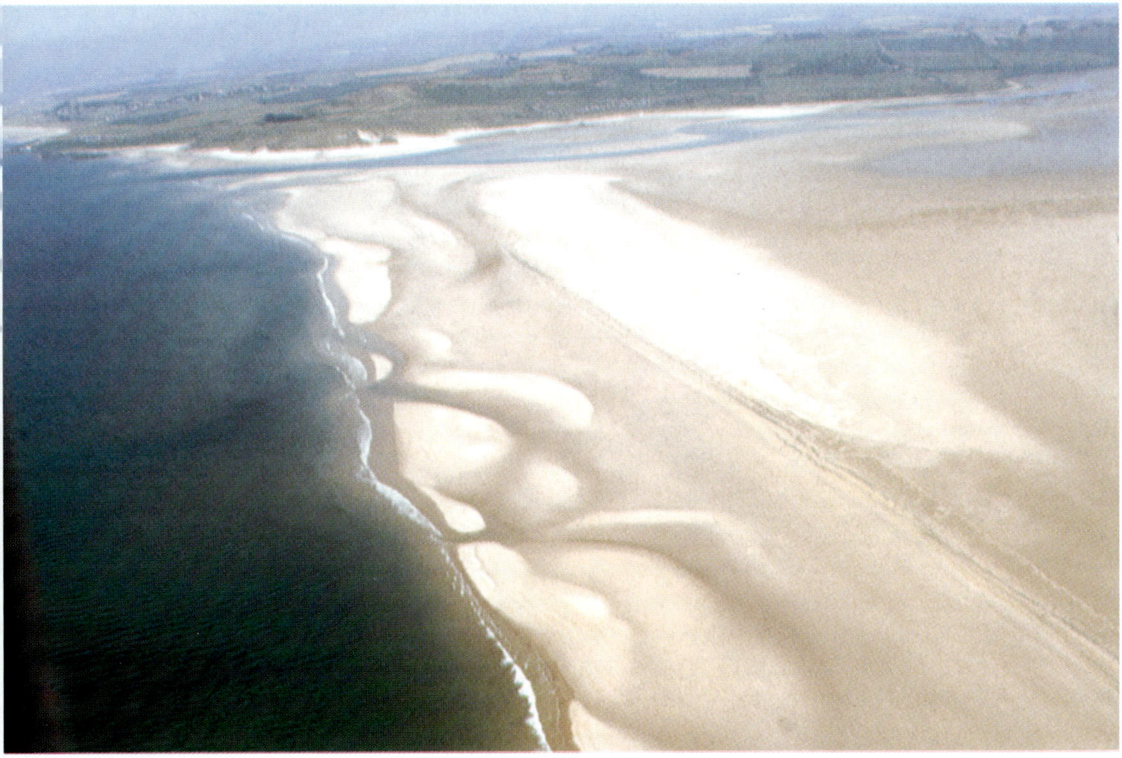

1 Ross Links

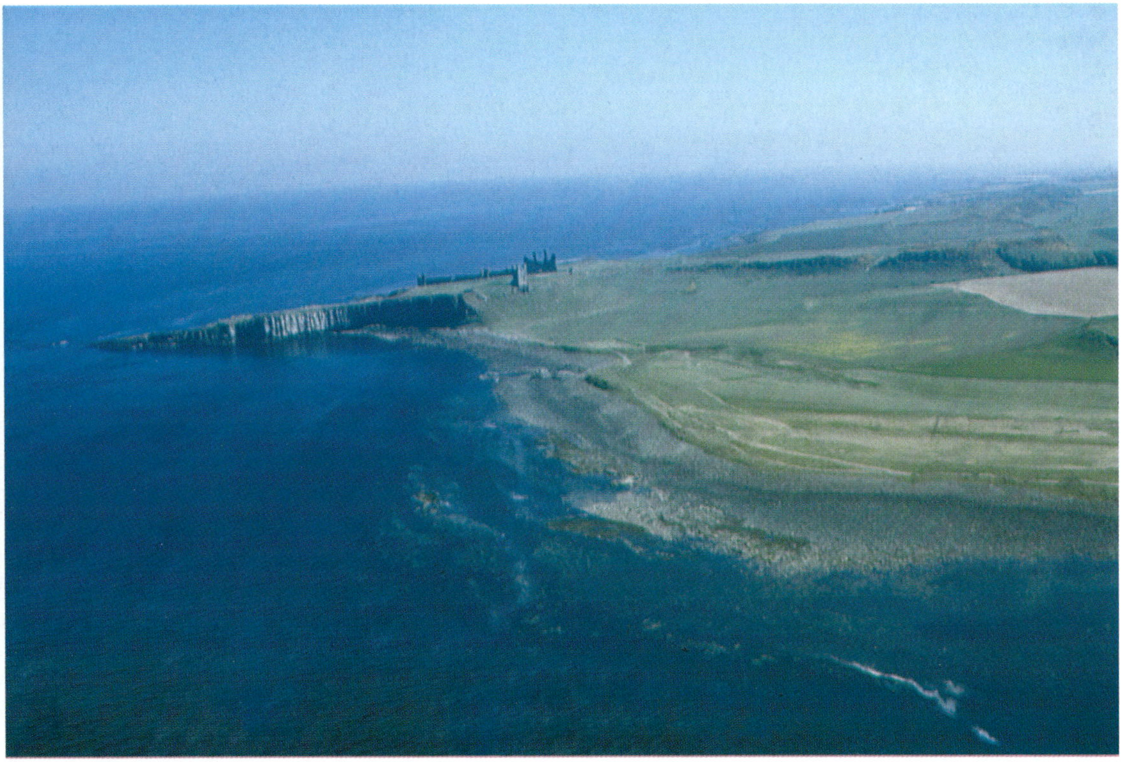

2 Dunstanburgh

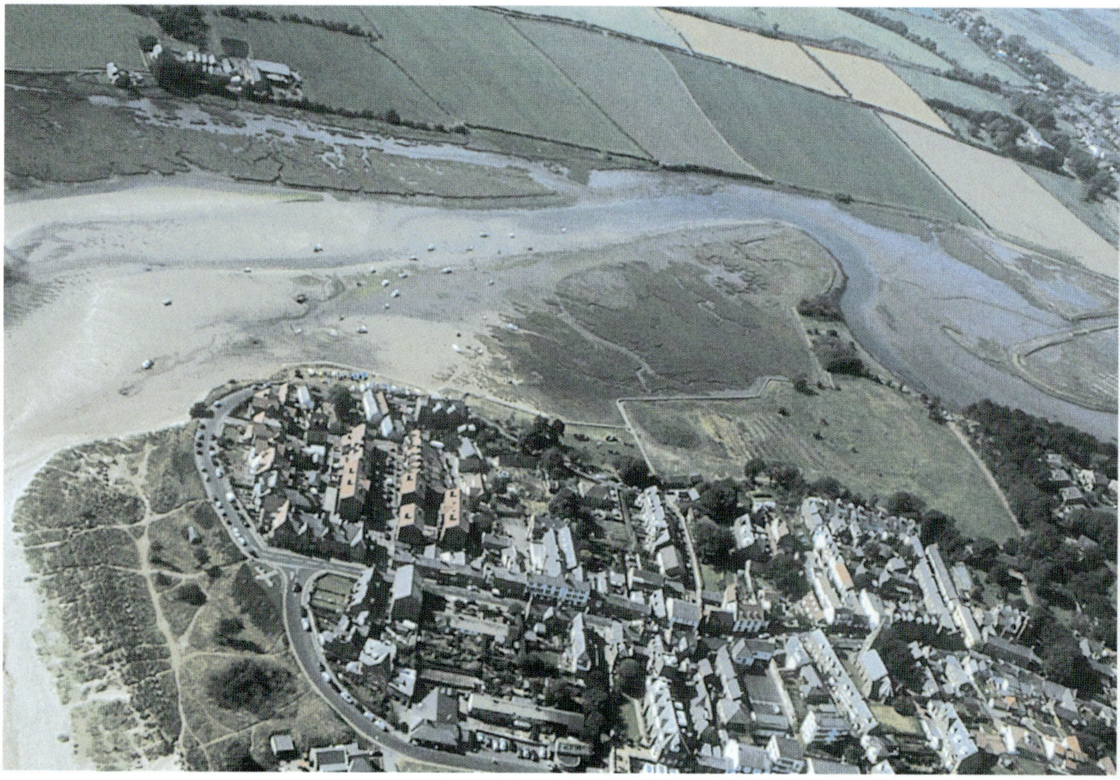

3 Alnmouth

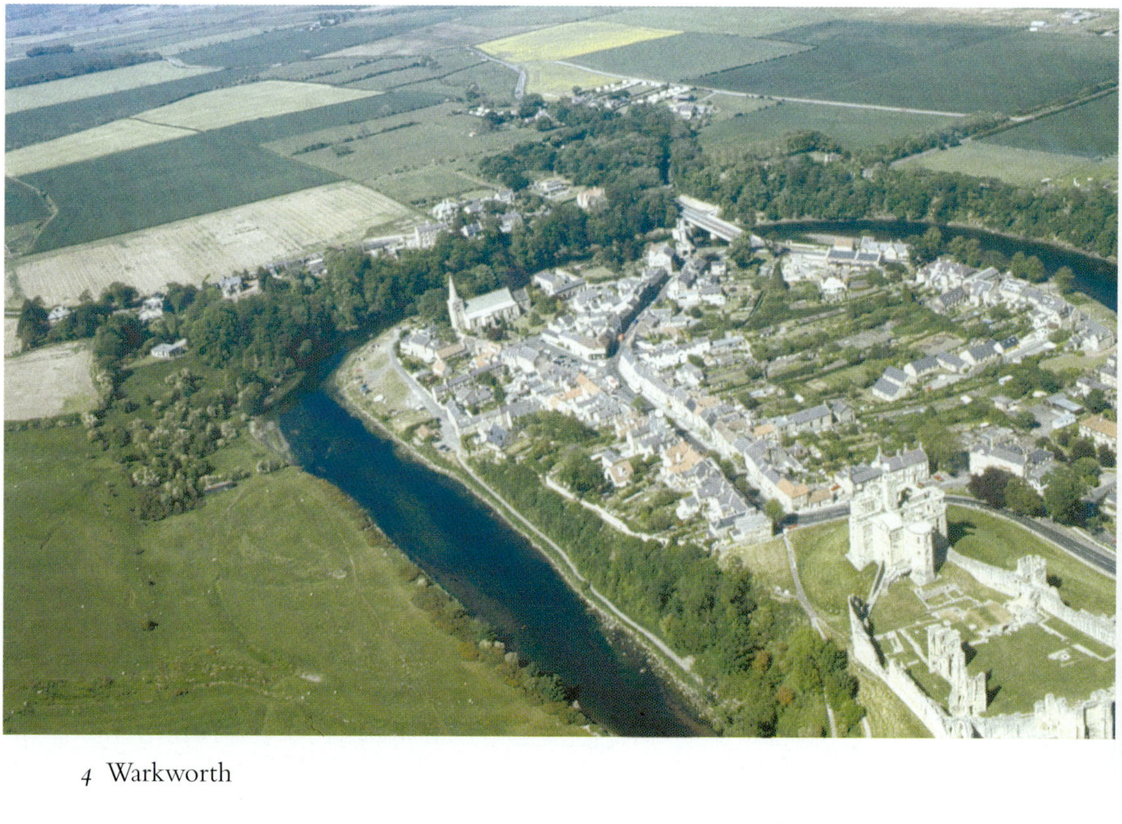

4 Warkworth

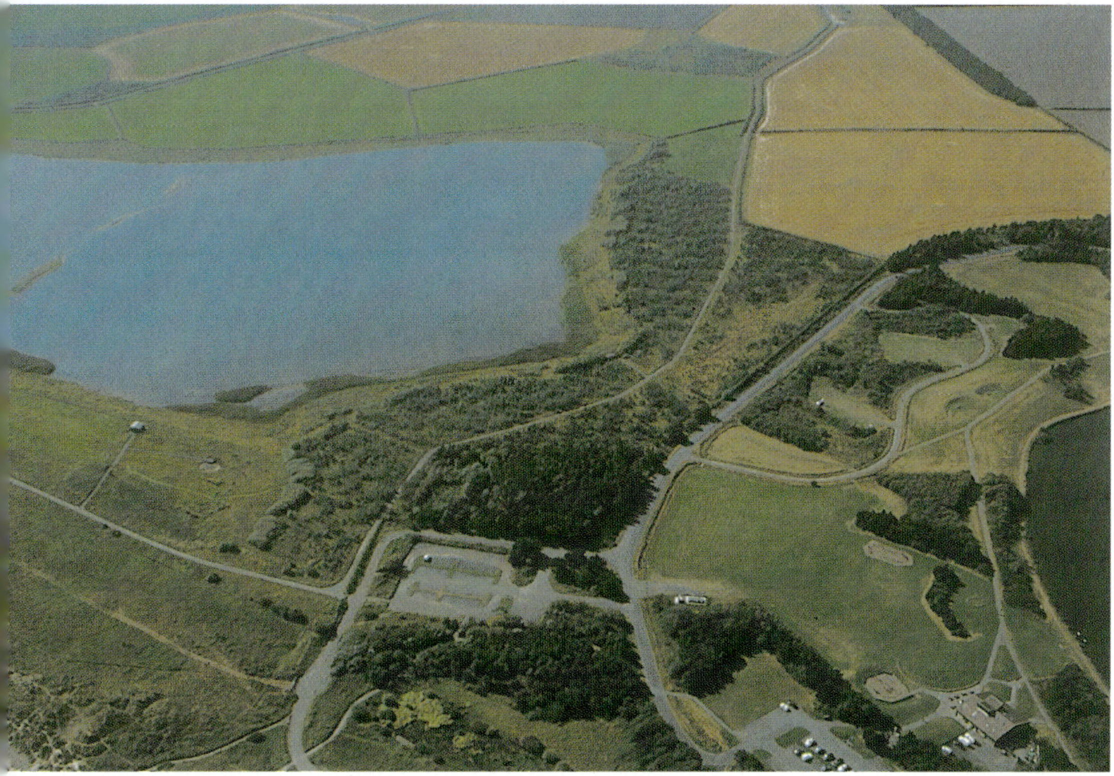

5 Landscaped industrial area on the east coast

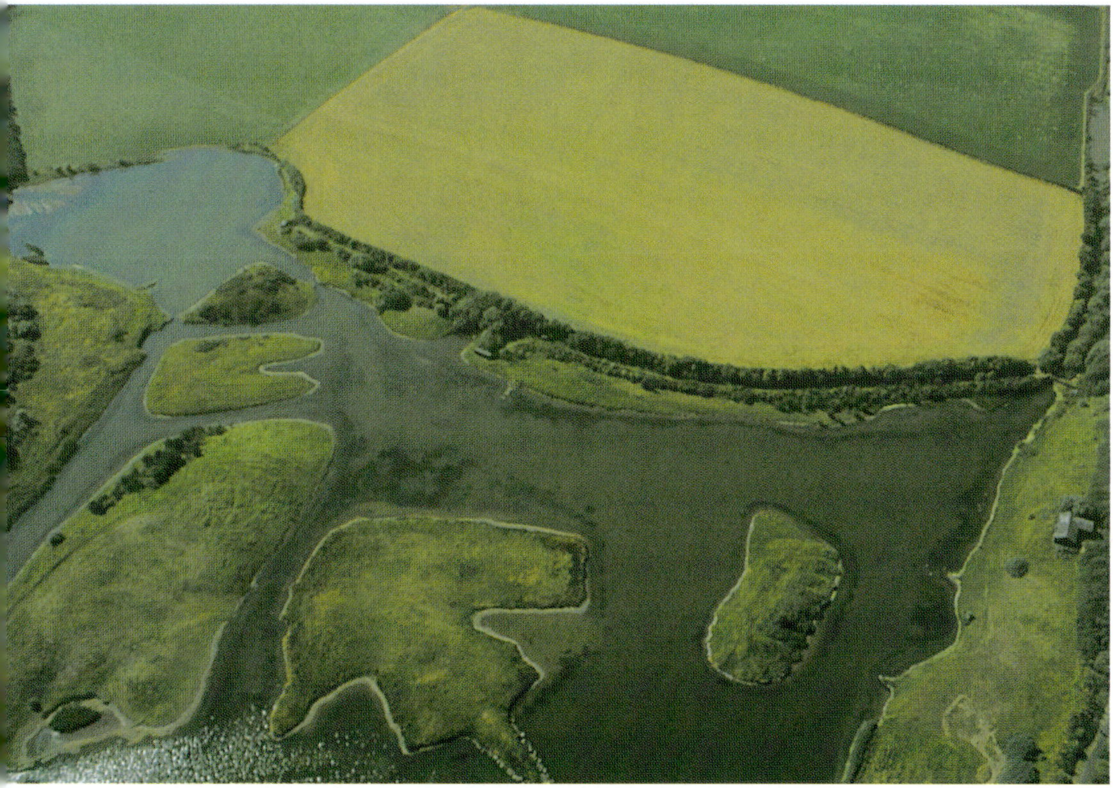

6 Landscaped industrial area on the east coast

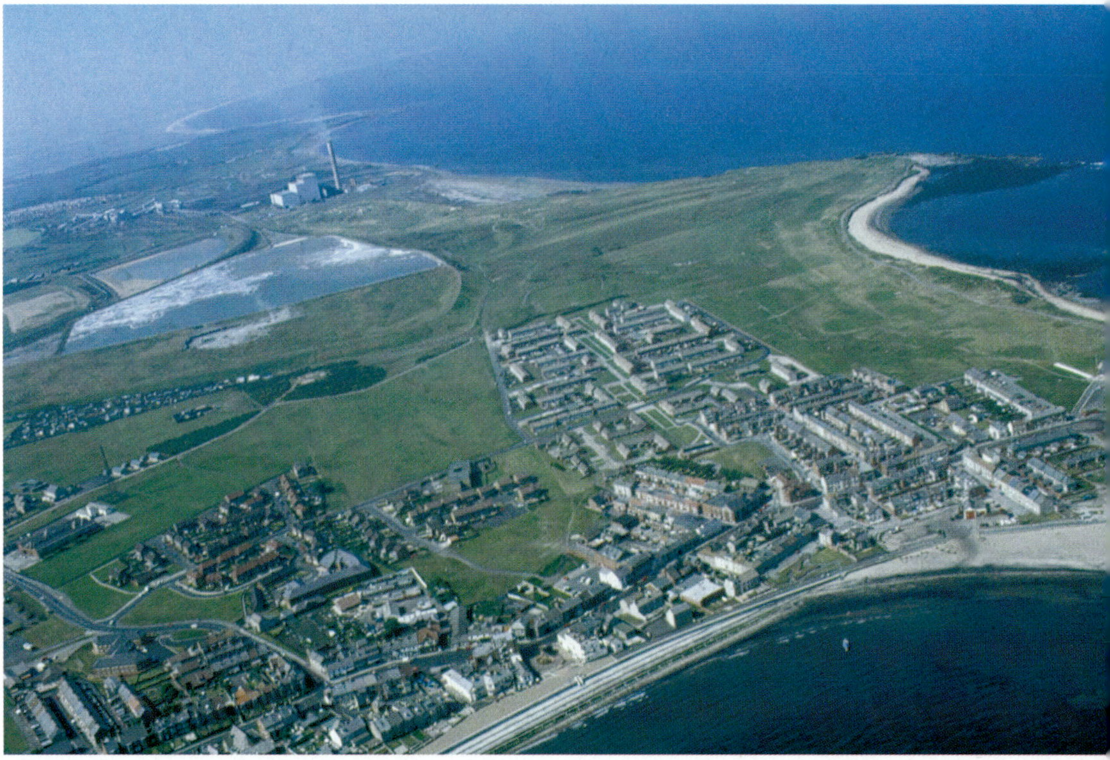

7 Newbiggin-by-the-Sea

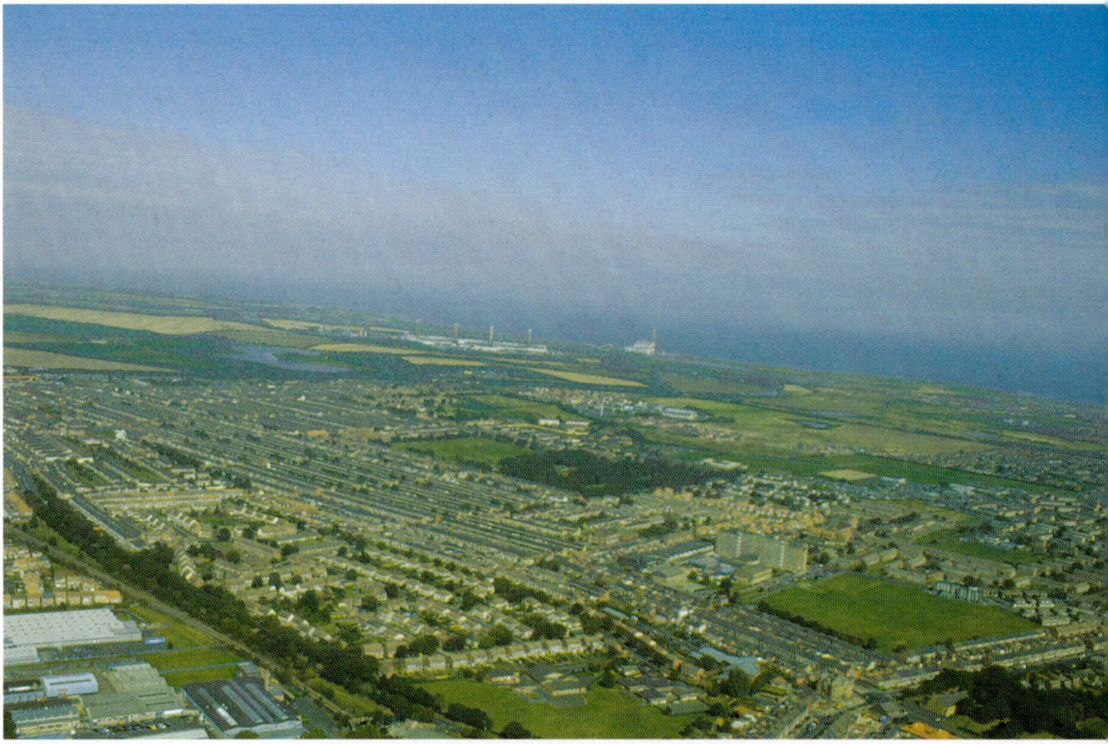

8 Ashington

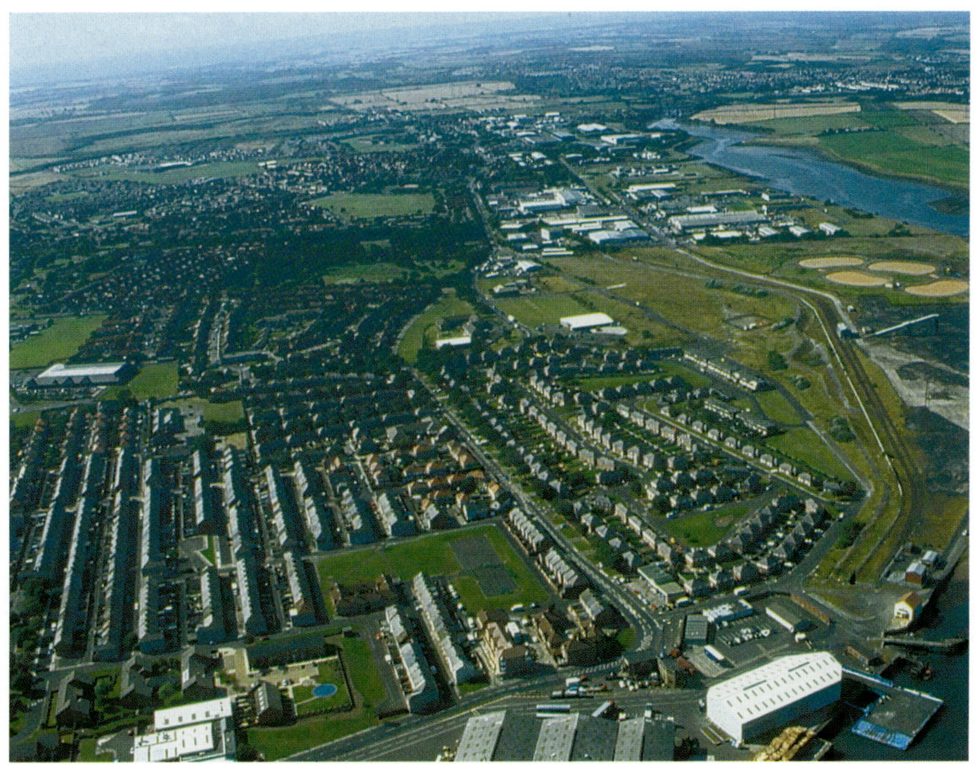

9 Blyth

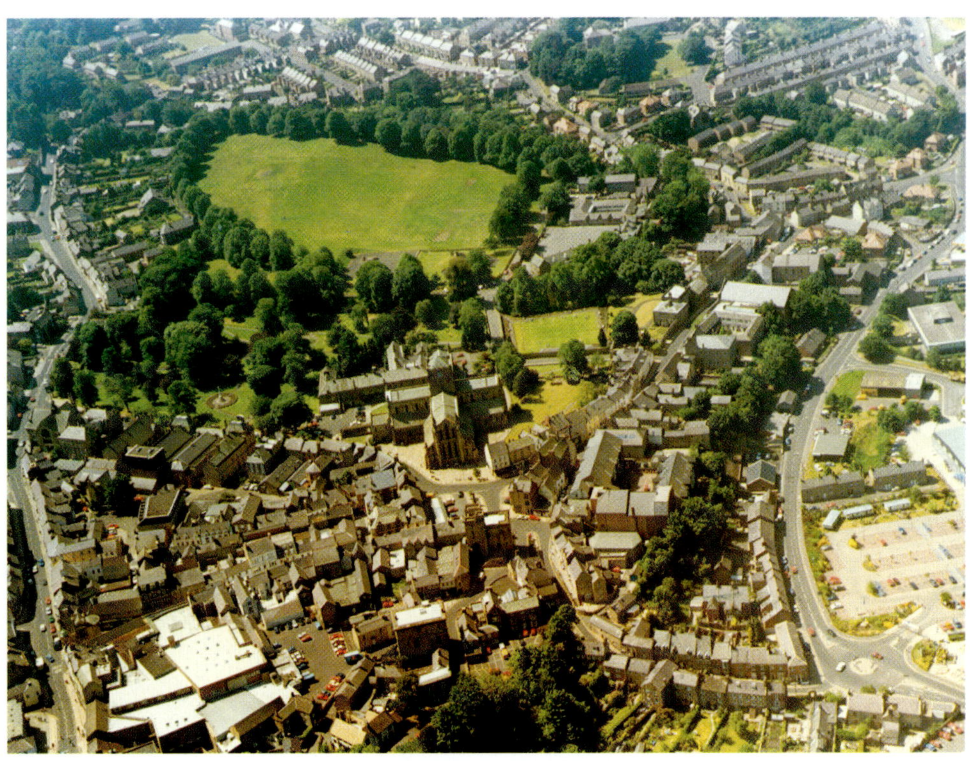

10 Hexham

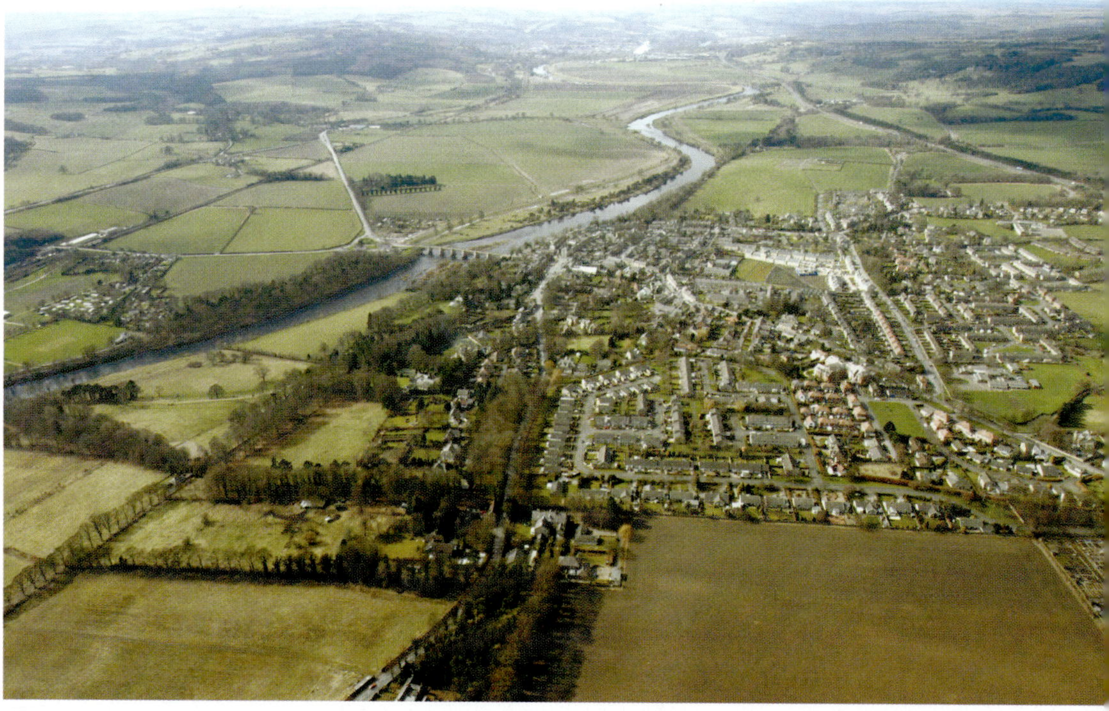

11 Corbridge (The Hexham Courant)

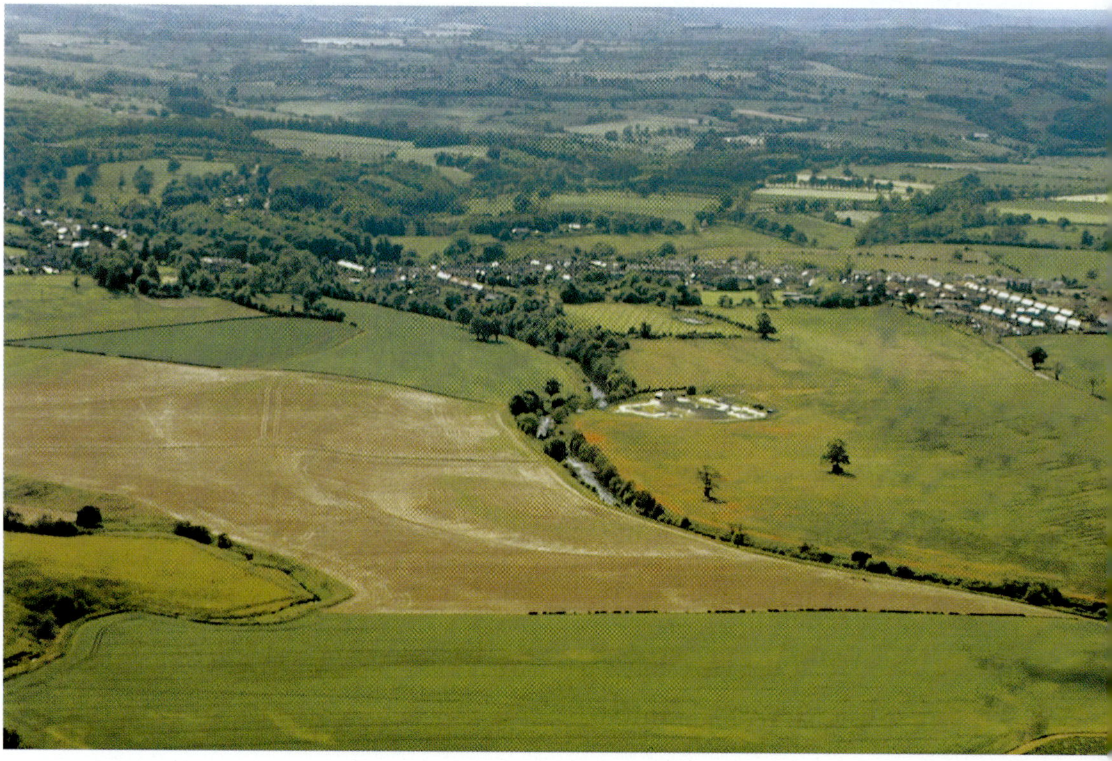

12 Felton

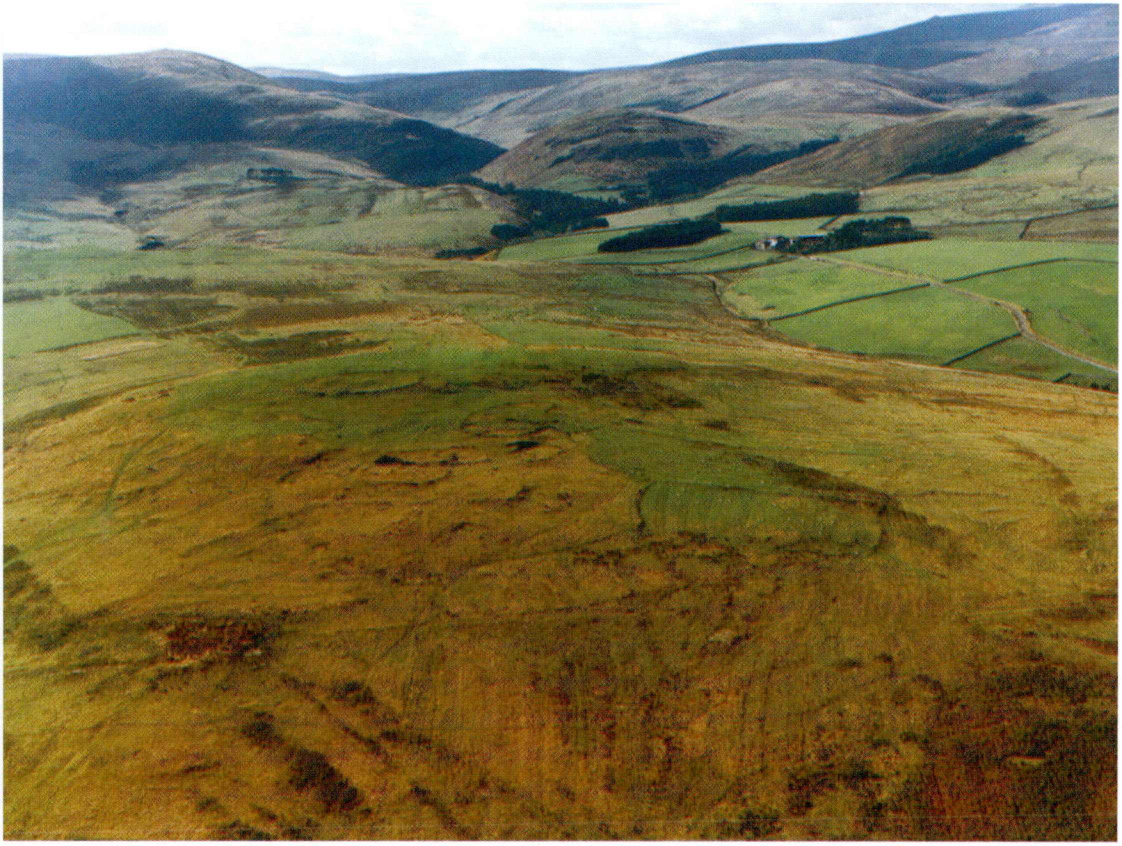

13 Hartside, Cheviot Hills

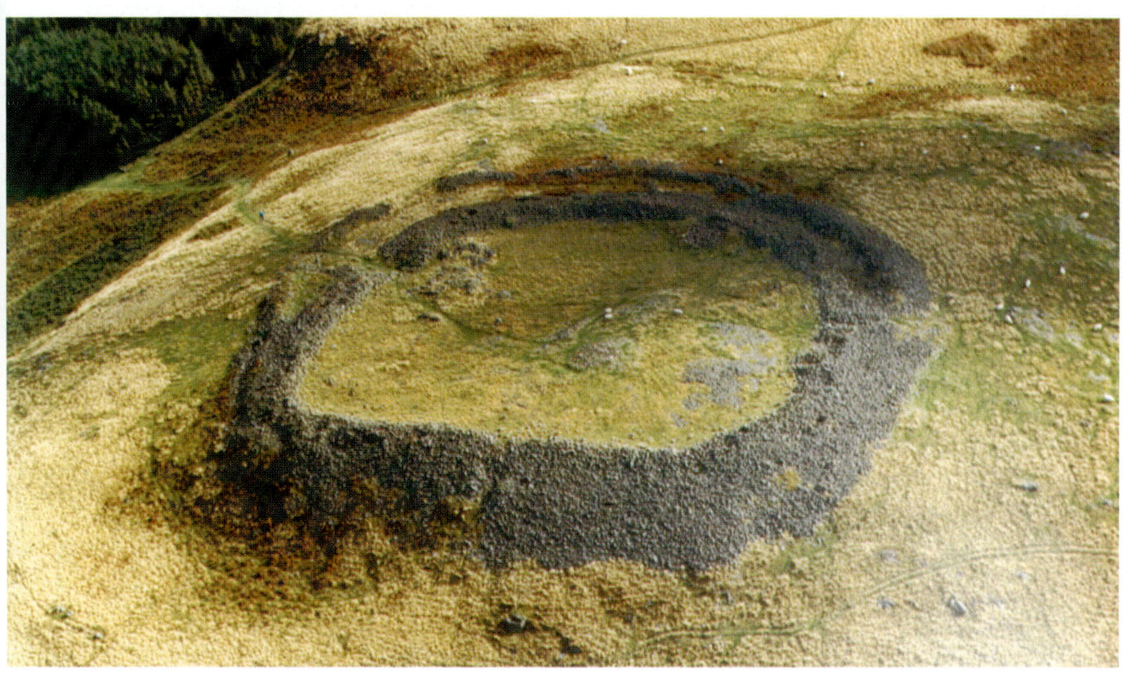

14 Brough Law, Ingram valley

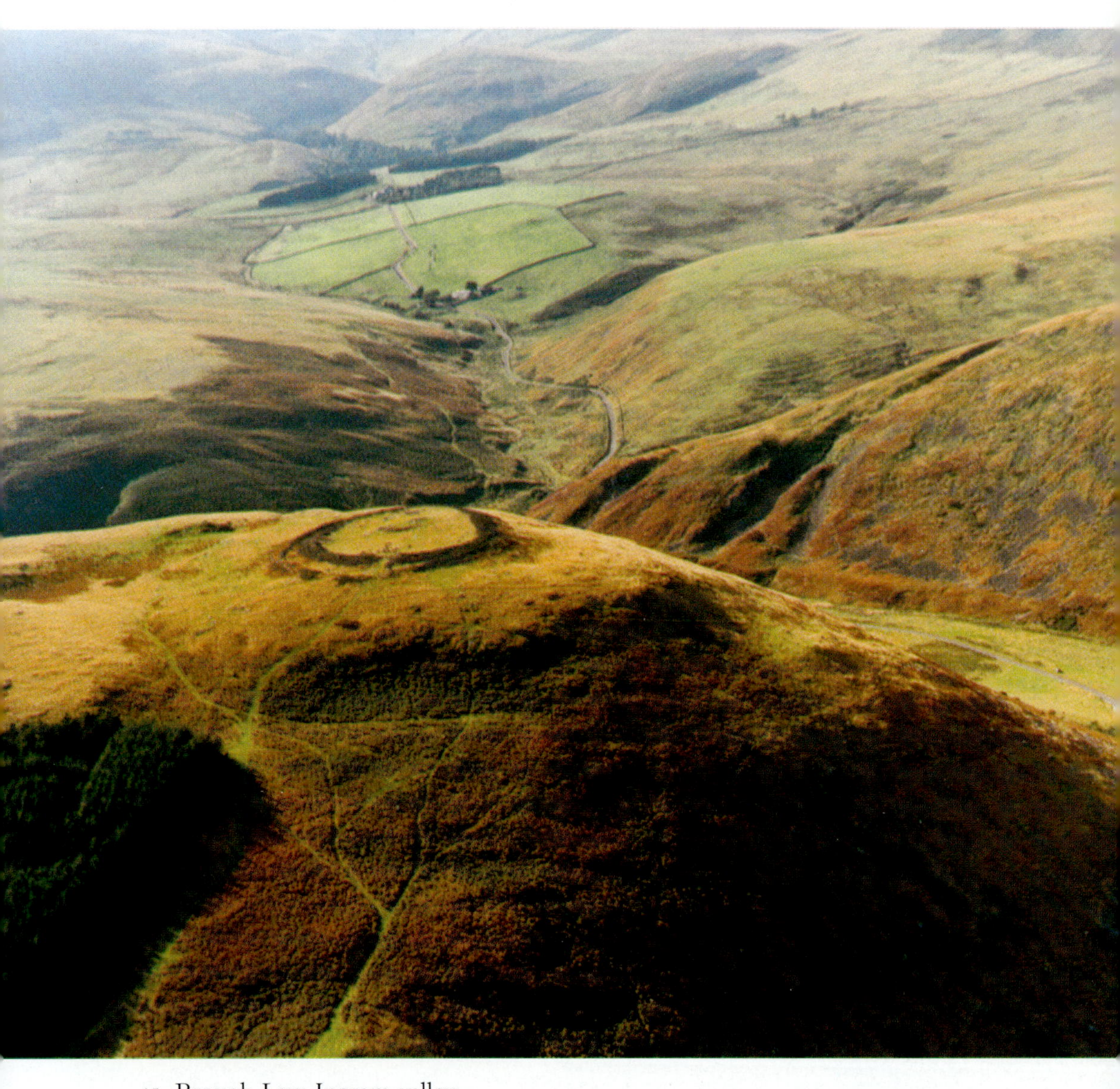

15 Brough Law, Ingram valley

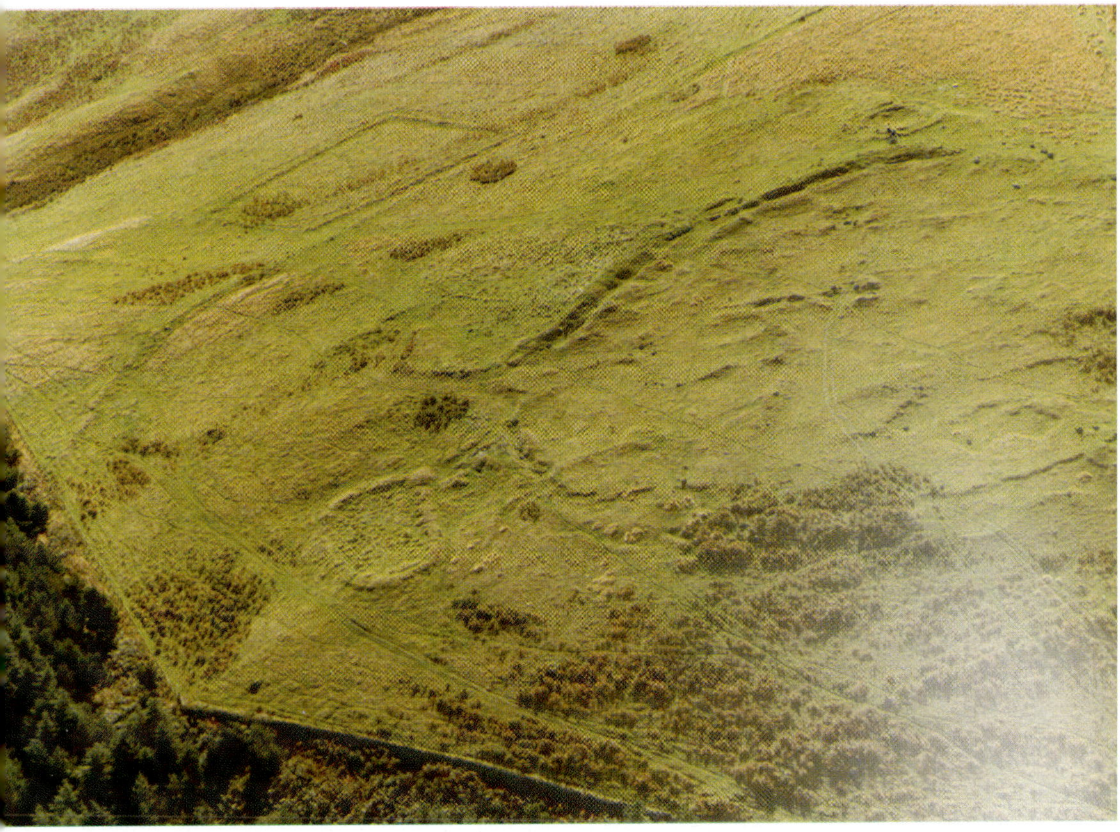

16 Chesters Burn, Ingram area

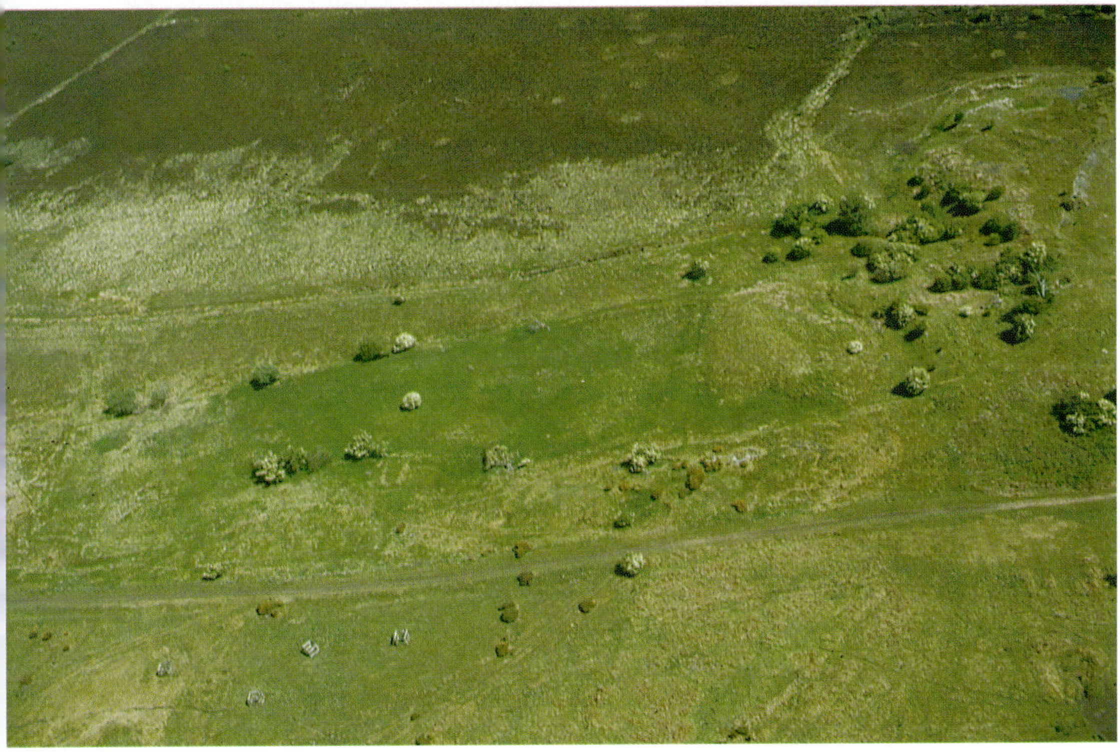

17 Ford Moss

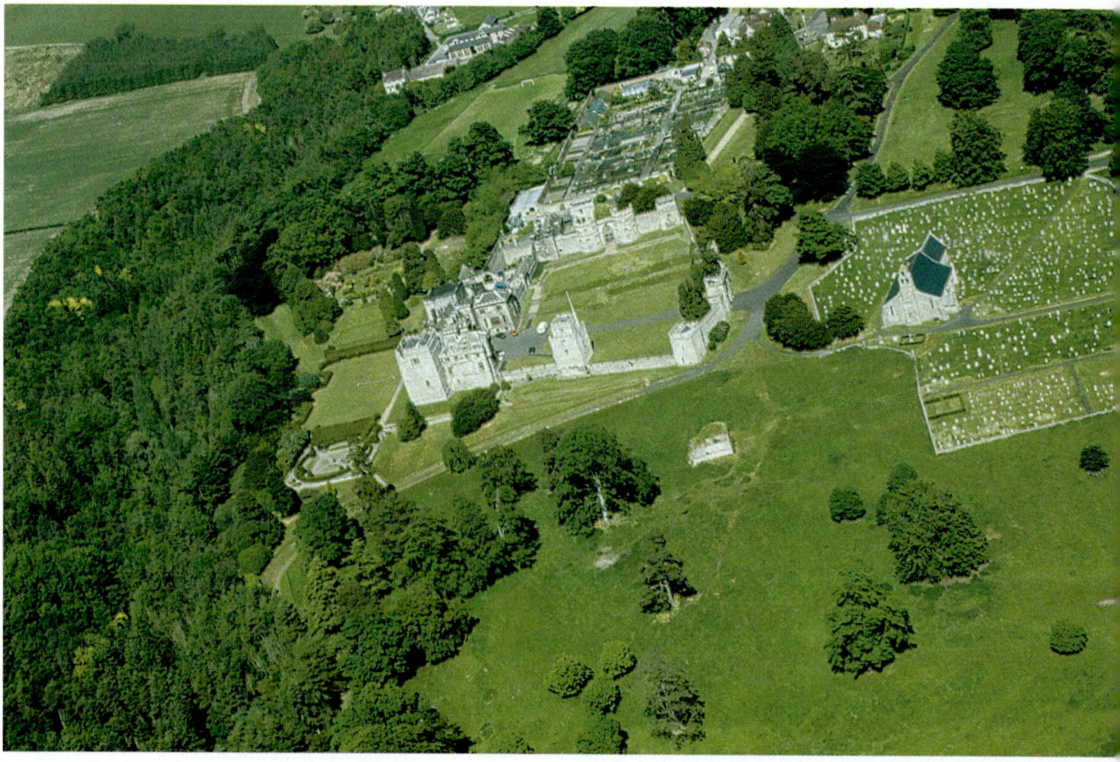

18 Ford

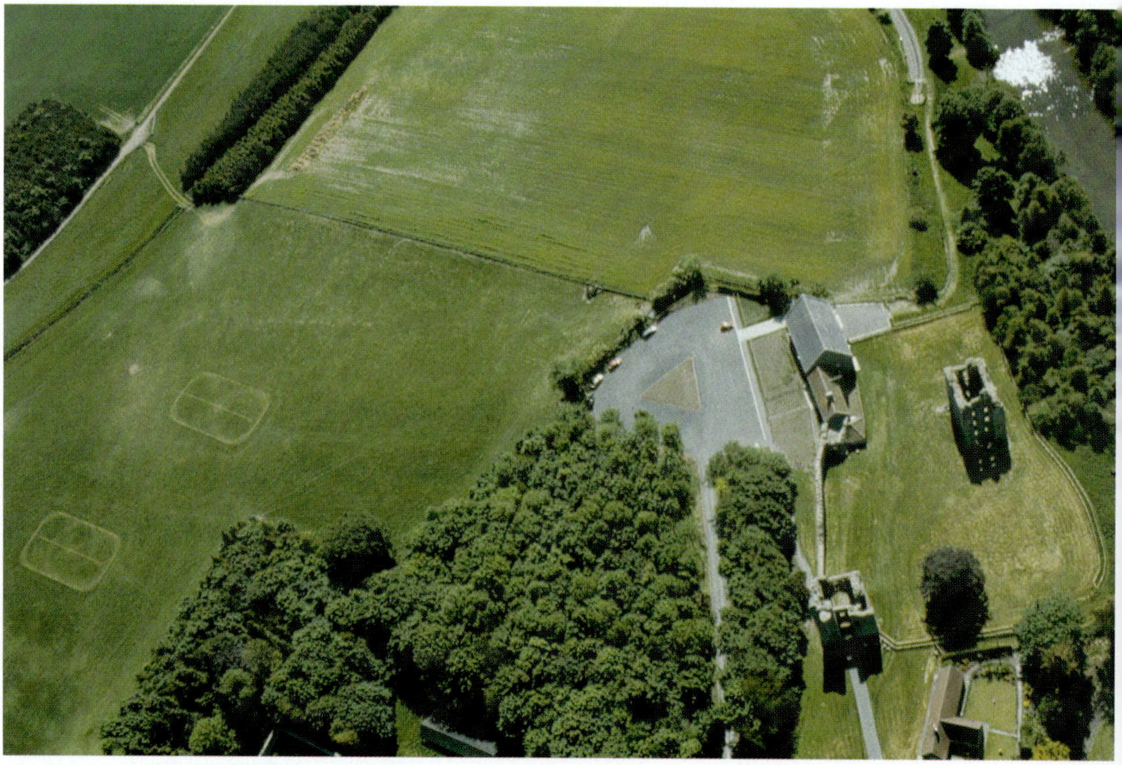

19 Etal

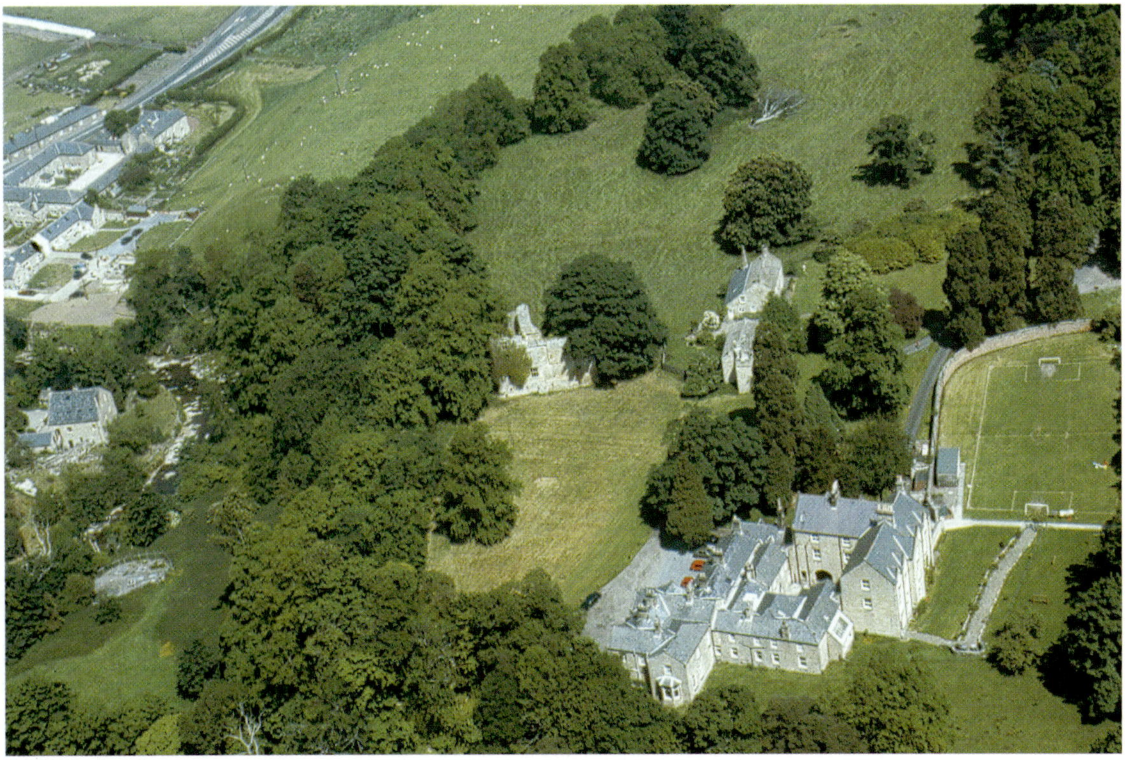

20 Dilston

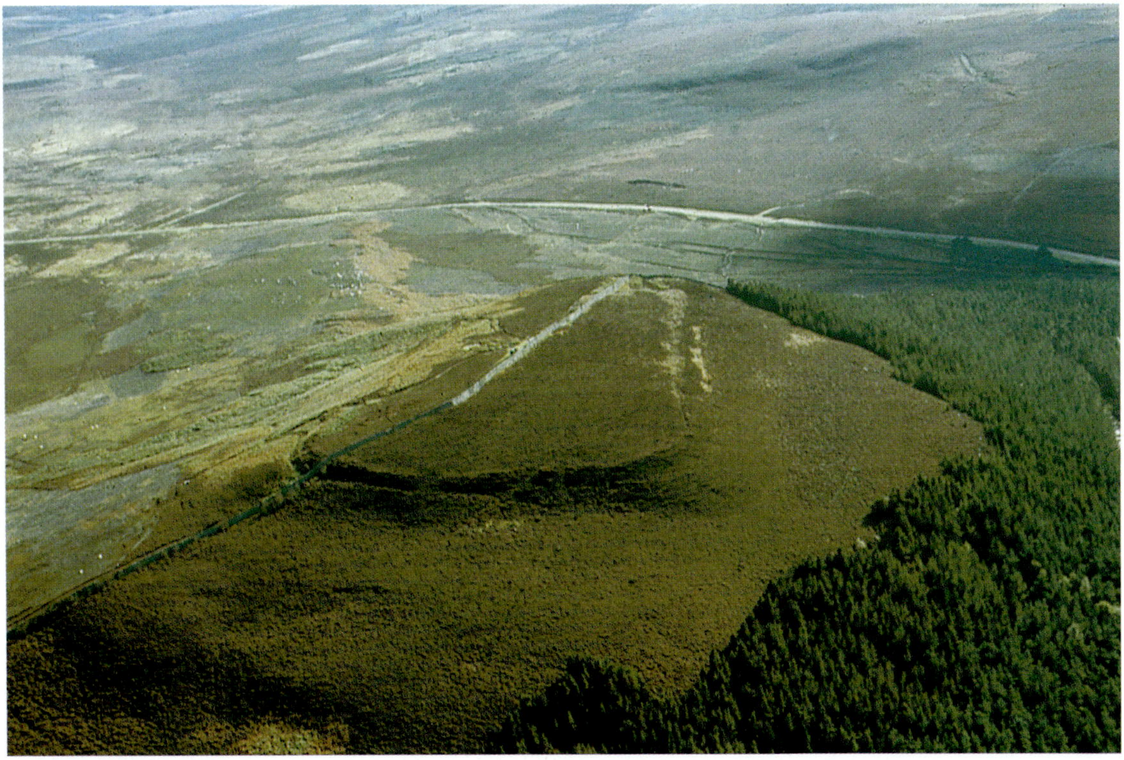

21 Ros Castle

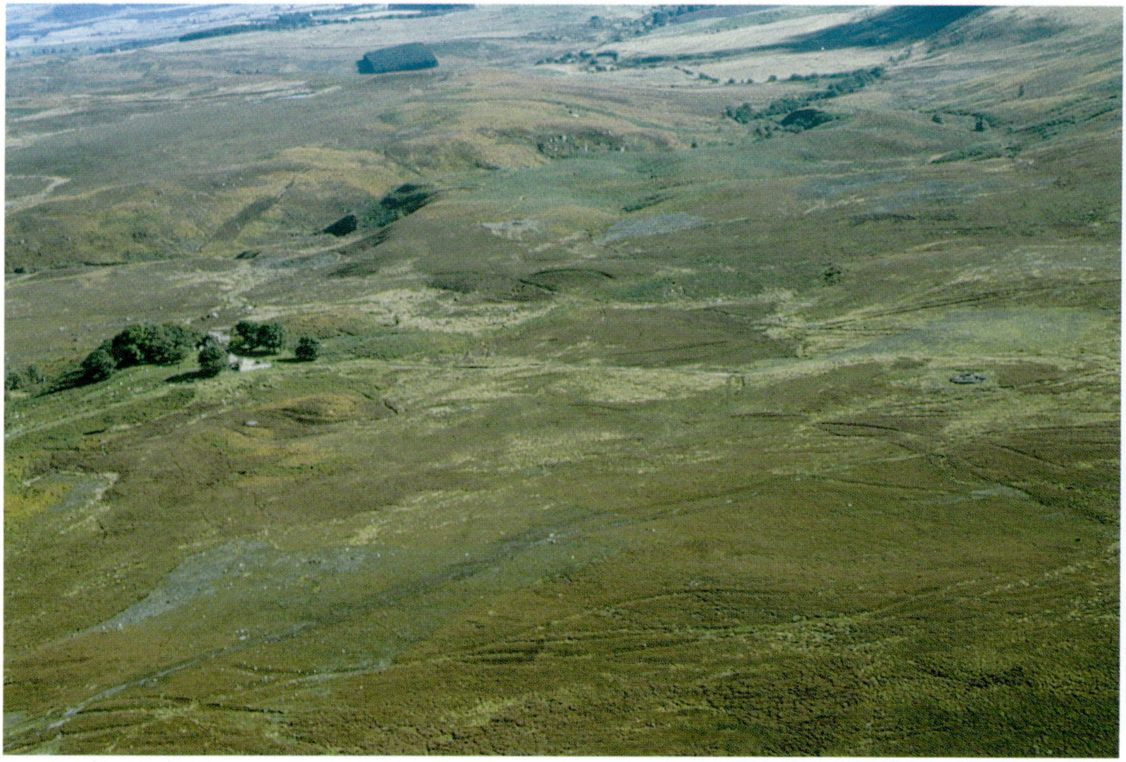

22 Old Bewick Moor (Blawearie)

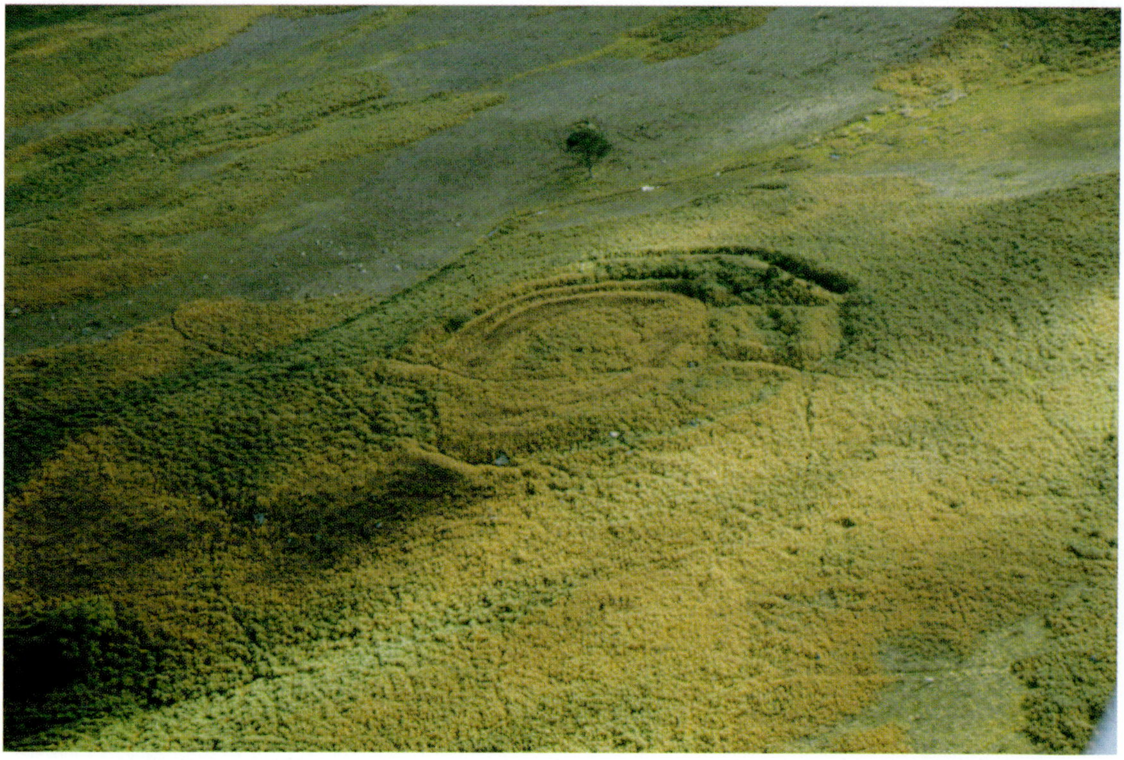

23 Beanley Ringses

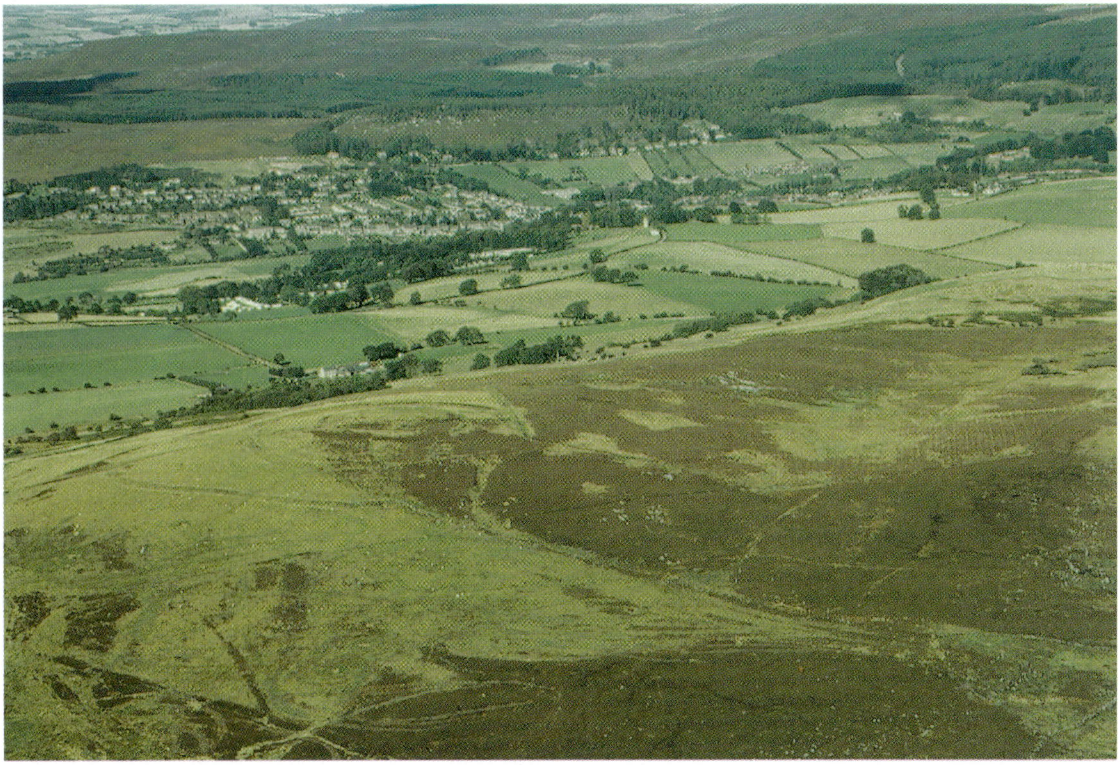

24 Lordenshaw

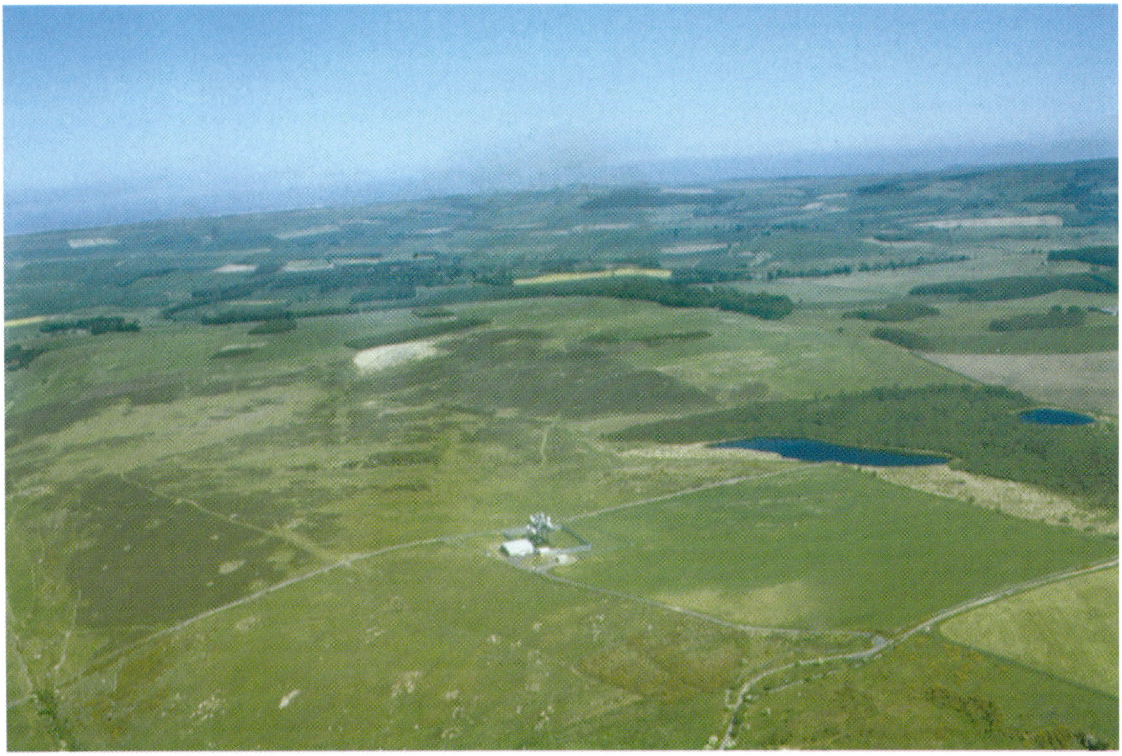

25 Coldmartin

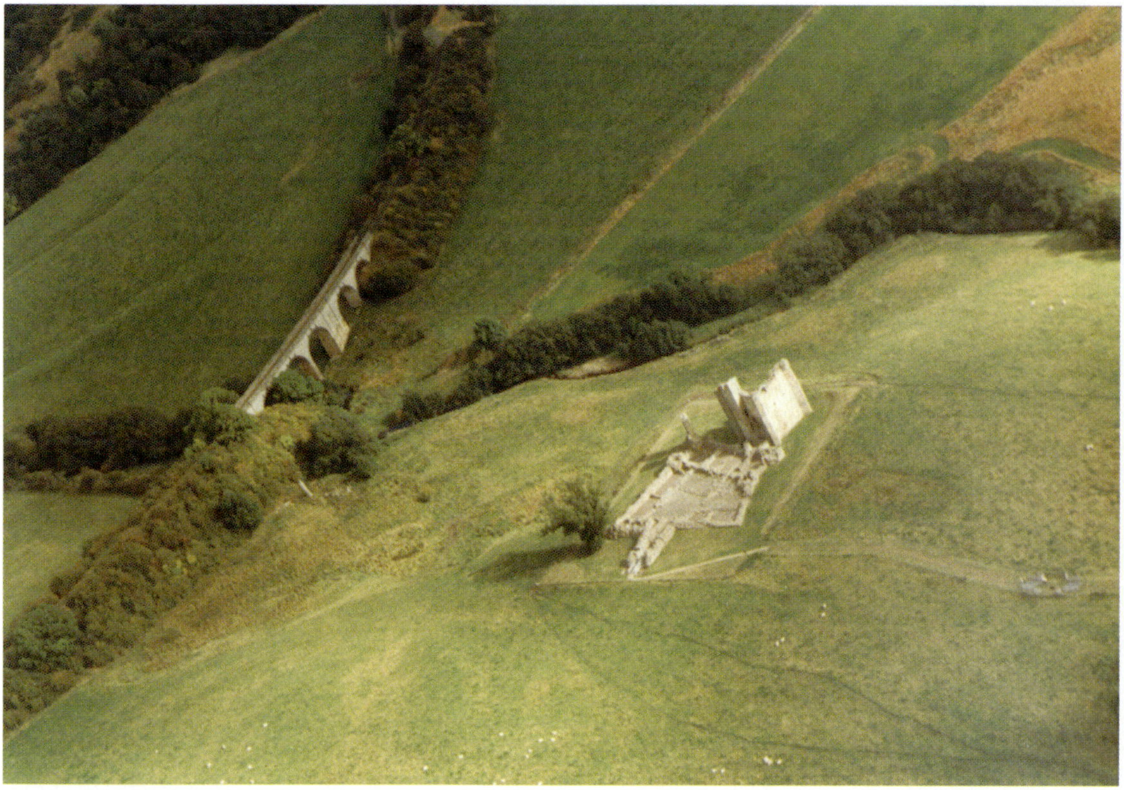

26 Edlingham

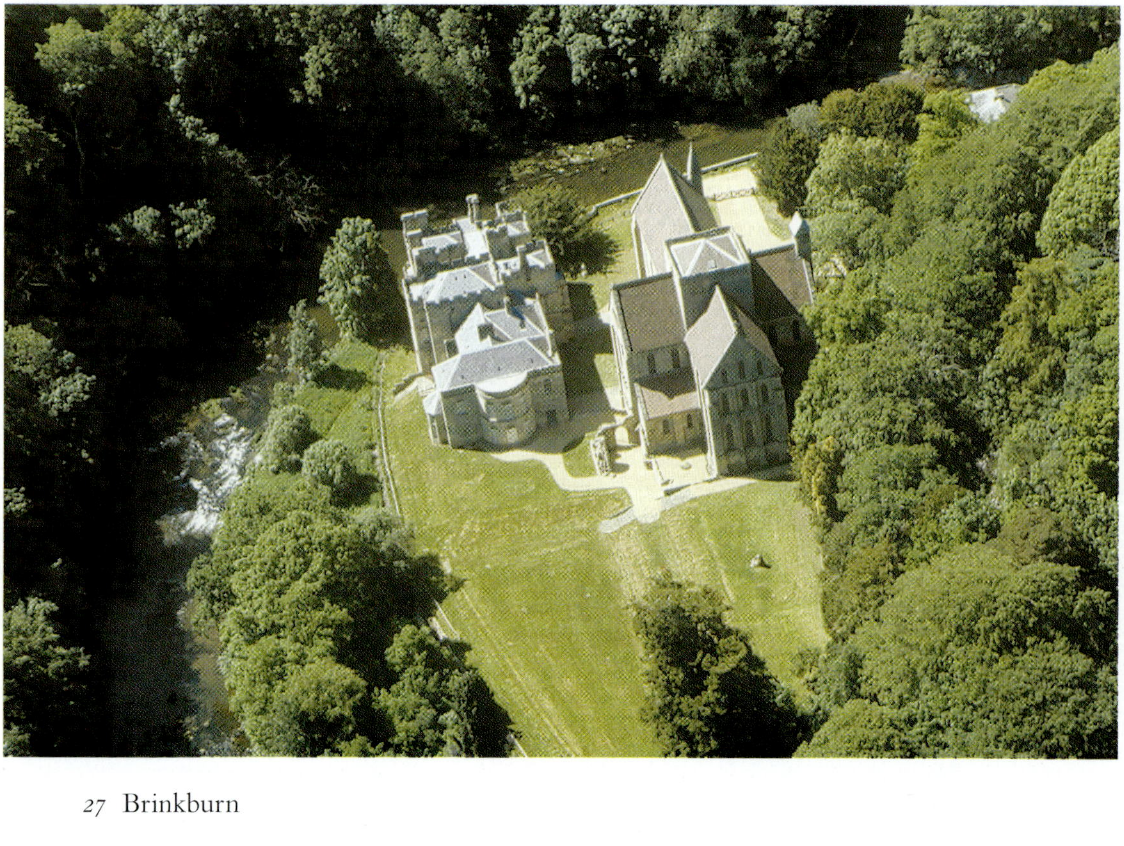

27 Brinkburn

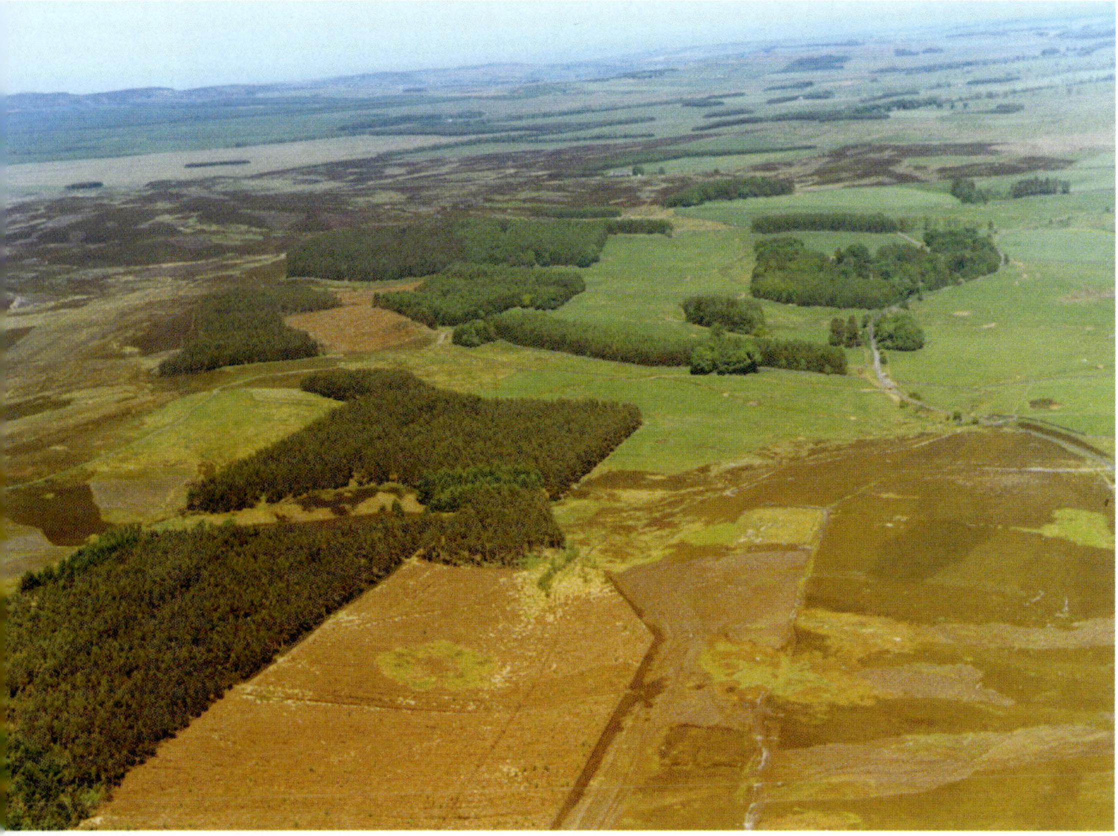

28 Ray Burn area

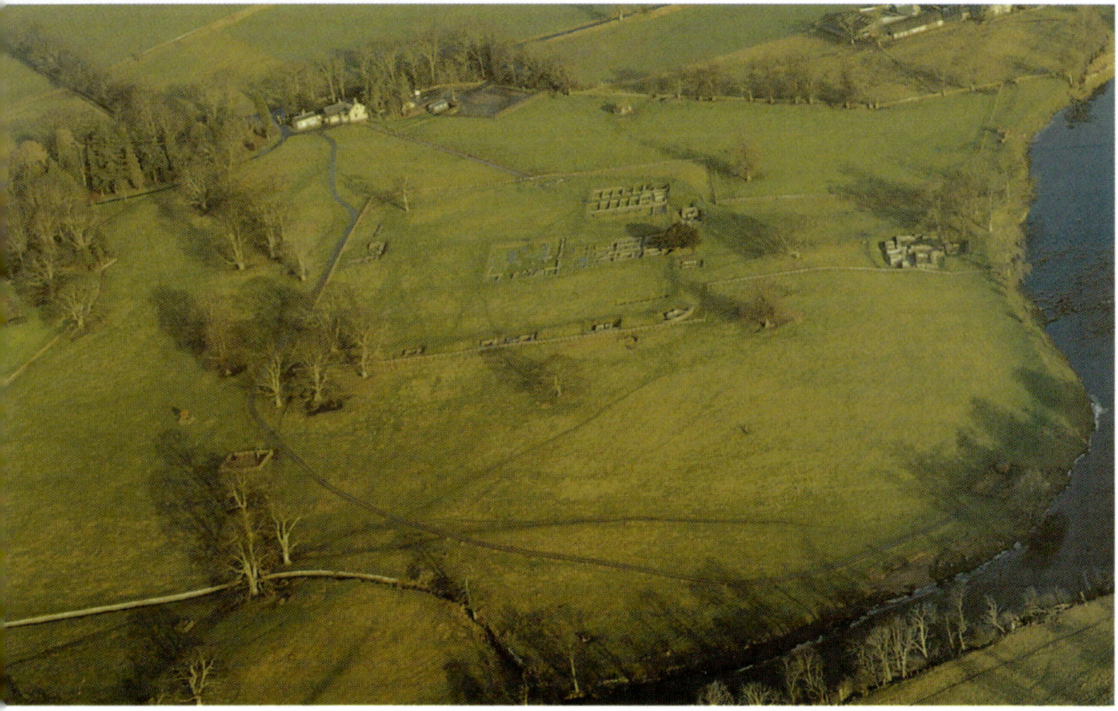

29 Chesters

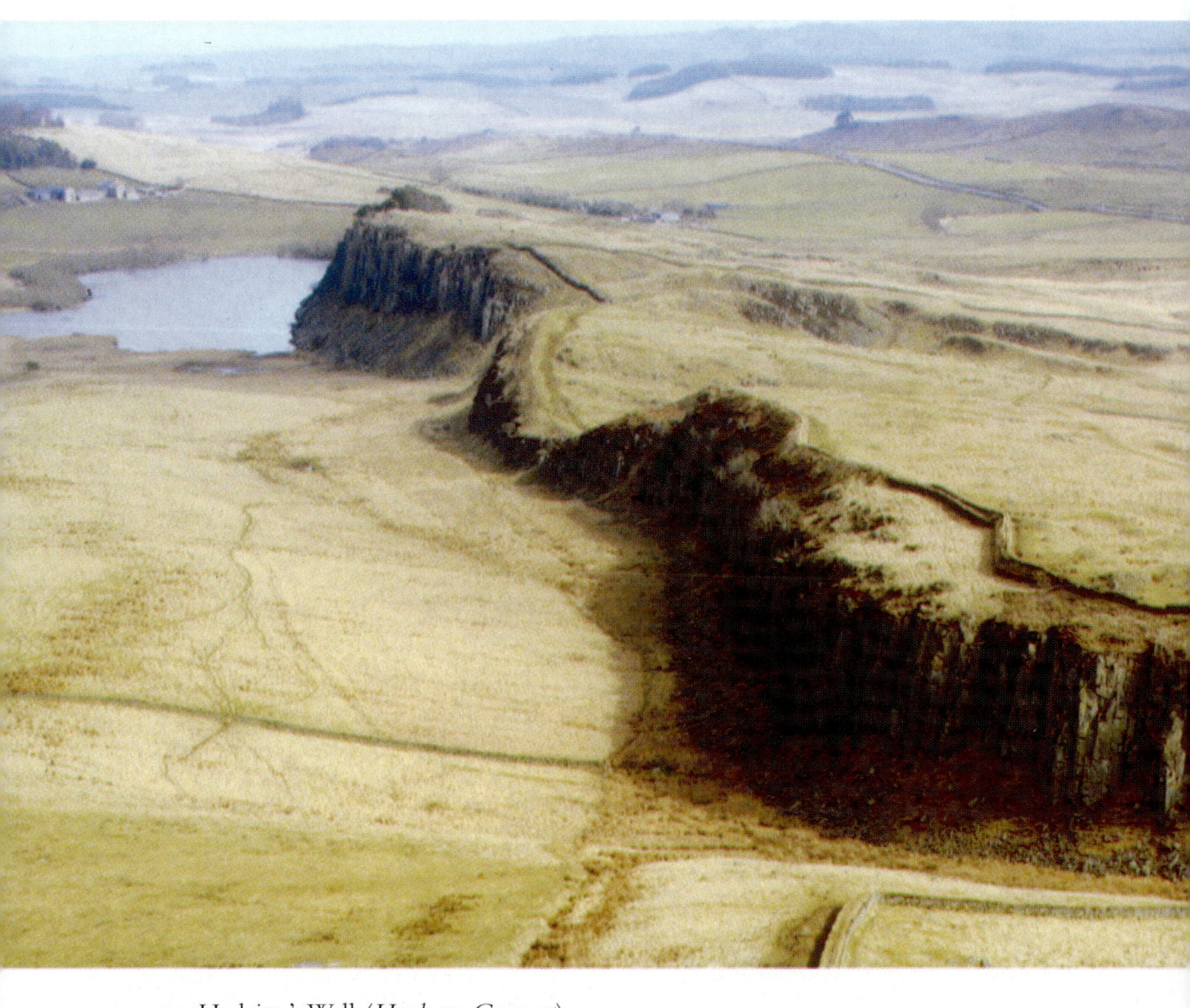

30 Hadrian's Wall (*Hexham Courant*)

7

MONUMENTS

Monuments encourage the persistence of memory. In a sense all relics of the past are monuments, though they may not have been built with that in mind. Two rare monuments are chosen here out of many, both henges.

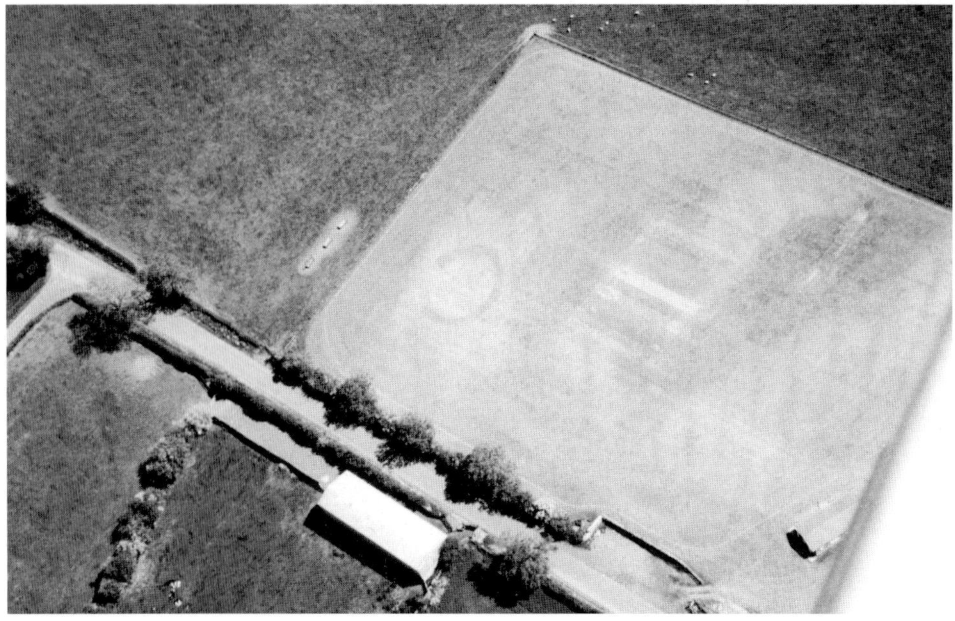

86 The Wooler Henge.

This shows the henge under the recently-mowed grass of the Wooler cricket ground, shaped like a necklace, along with the traces of rig and furrow ploughing. The henge is an area enclosed by a ditch, with one entrance in this case. It has not been investigated any further.

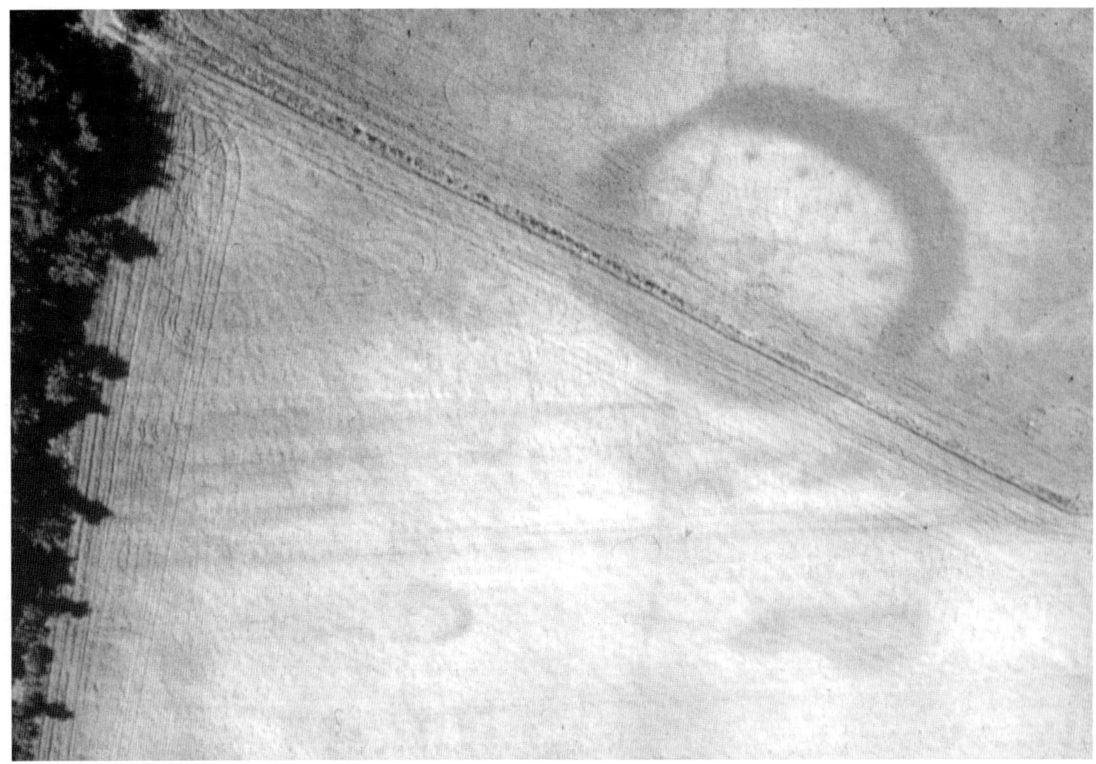

87 West Akeld Steads (NUM).

The value of infra-red photography is clear. The henge which contains a ring of post-holes is formed by a hidden ditch. The field area is flat, but the fertile soil concentrated in both ditch and post-holes allows them to be seen as crop-marks after over 4000 years. The Milfield Plain and Glendale have revealed many more of these structures, some of which have now been excavated. They are focal meeting places, not only parts of a sacred landscape, but of ordinary life. The name, obviously given hundreds of years later, means that it was on an oak-slope.

Gravel extraction on the plain has revealed an area rich in prehistory, adding significantly to what was already known of the Anglo-Saxon period, mainly from the air. We now know that the earliest use of the landscape was Mesolithic, some 8000 years ago, with hunter-gatherer activities extending into more settled agriculture and the building of small henges, burial sites and pit/stake alignments. These discoveries continue to be made.

8

FORTIFICATIONS

With the coming of the Roman army Northumberland became an outpost of Rome, the end of empire, even though there were still incursions north of what is now called Hadrian's Wall. The wall was never a line between England and Scotland: a popular fallacy, because the wall divided a 'civilized' Roman province from the *Brituncult* – the barbaric Brits. Before Rome, land had been divided up in prehistoric times among farmers for thousands of years, and part of this division included fortifications that could be used in an emergency or used as enclosures or meeting places.

As in the rest of the country, the Norman conquest over Anglo-Saxon tribes led to the establishment of numerous castles that kept the Normans in power as a warrior aristocracy, but the position of Northumberland on the front line of the Anglo-Scottish Border either led to the extension of these Norman strongholds or to building on new sites; there was also a rash of fortified towers at a more local level, necessary to protect communities who were prone to attacks.

Under James I there was a more peaceful period after 1603, when the old draughty and uncomfortable fortresses were abandoned or made more congenial.

This is largely the legacy we have, with the addition of war-time defences such as pillboxes, anti-tank blocks on the coast and airfields. It is clear that insecurity and ambition have resulted in much that we see from the air today, as the following examples will show. In some cases, the sites chosen are but a fraction of what can still be seen, but are representative of different periods.

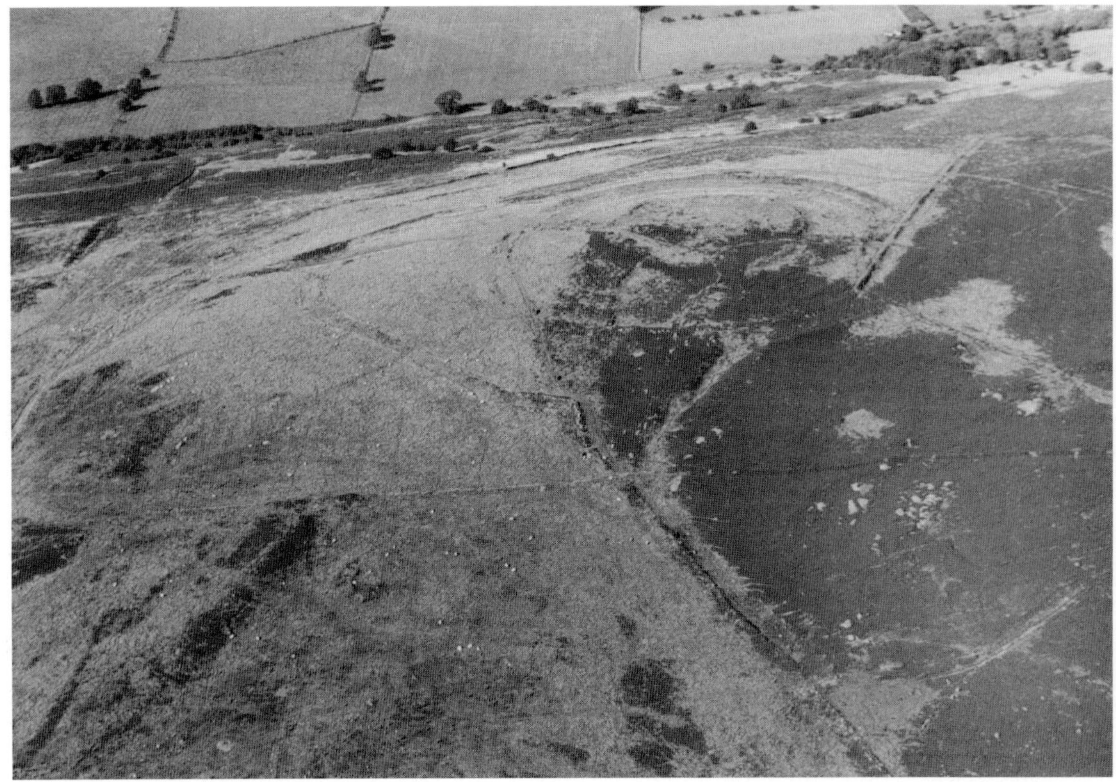

88 Lordenshaw.

Lying south of Rothbury, with easy car park access, this large enclosure, on a rise overlooking the Whitton Burn and Coquet valley, is one of the best prehistoric sites to visit. It bears signs of having been modified many times for different uses.

Central is the enclosure formed of walls and ditches, with entrances and internal round houses visible. Part of the ramparts has been levelled and round houses, perhaps of Romano-British times, laid down.

Much earlier are the prehistoric rock-carvings and cairns. There are unusual ancient but undated field systems in the same area, with large stones defining their boundaries; it is likely from their positions that they are of the Iron Age or the Romano-British period.

Fields to the left of the prehistoric enclosure have faint, parallel, close rig and furrow ploughing from later arable use. Old field walls are seen often as heather-covered; there are many of these.

At the top of the picture is the small valley of the Whitton Burn, a tributary of the River Coquet, flowing east.

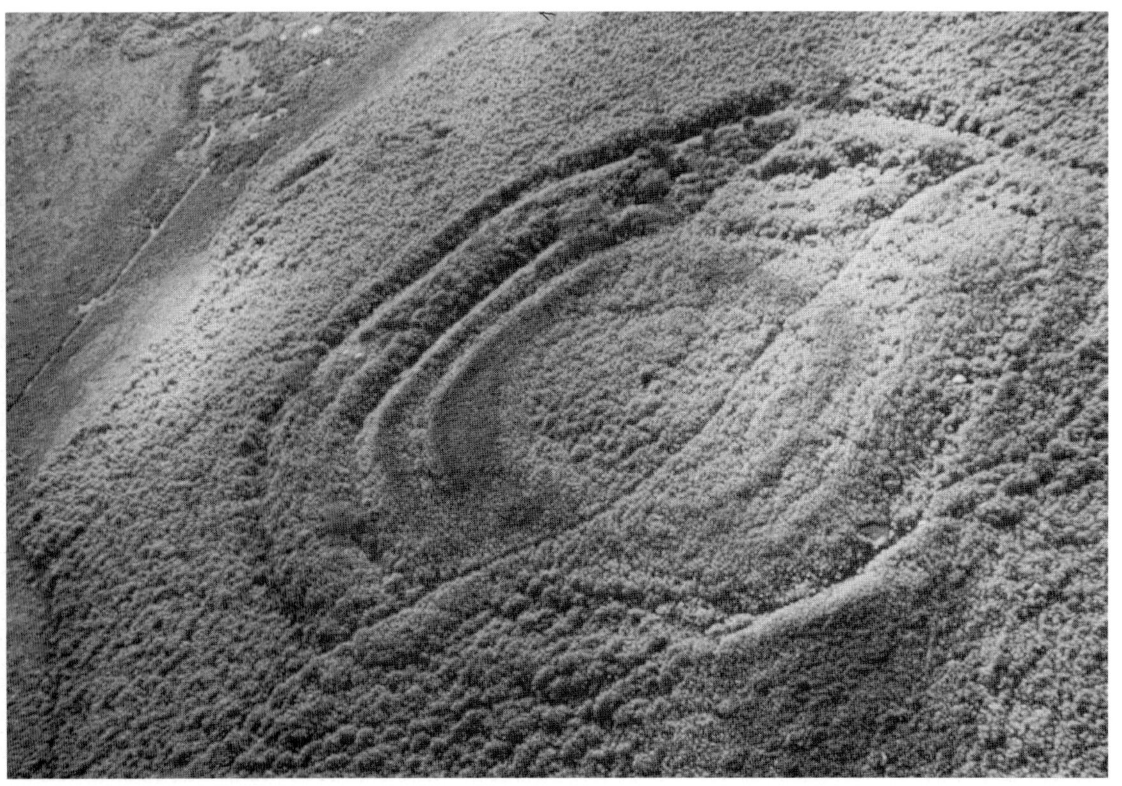

89 Beanley Ringses.

The bracken is just beginning to die off, helping to show more clearly the roughly-circular walls and ditches of a pre-Roman enclosure in moorland. The smallness of the area enclosed at the centre may mean that this was as much a status symbol as a defensive site.

As we see elsewhere in this book, prehistoric enclosures come in many shapes and sizes; the amazing thing is that there are so many of them in a good state of preservation, a result of the land not being used for arable farming later.

The spread of bracken on this site is characteristic of so many others. It grows extensively, burrows deeply and is not eaten by animals. Efforts to control it have not been successful. Its redeeming feature is the lovely golden brown that it turns to in the autumn.

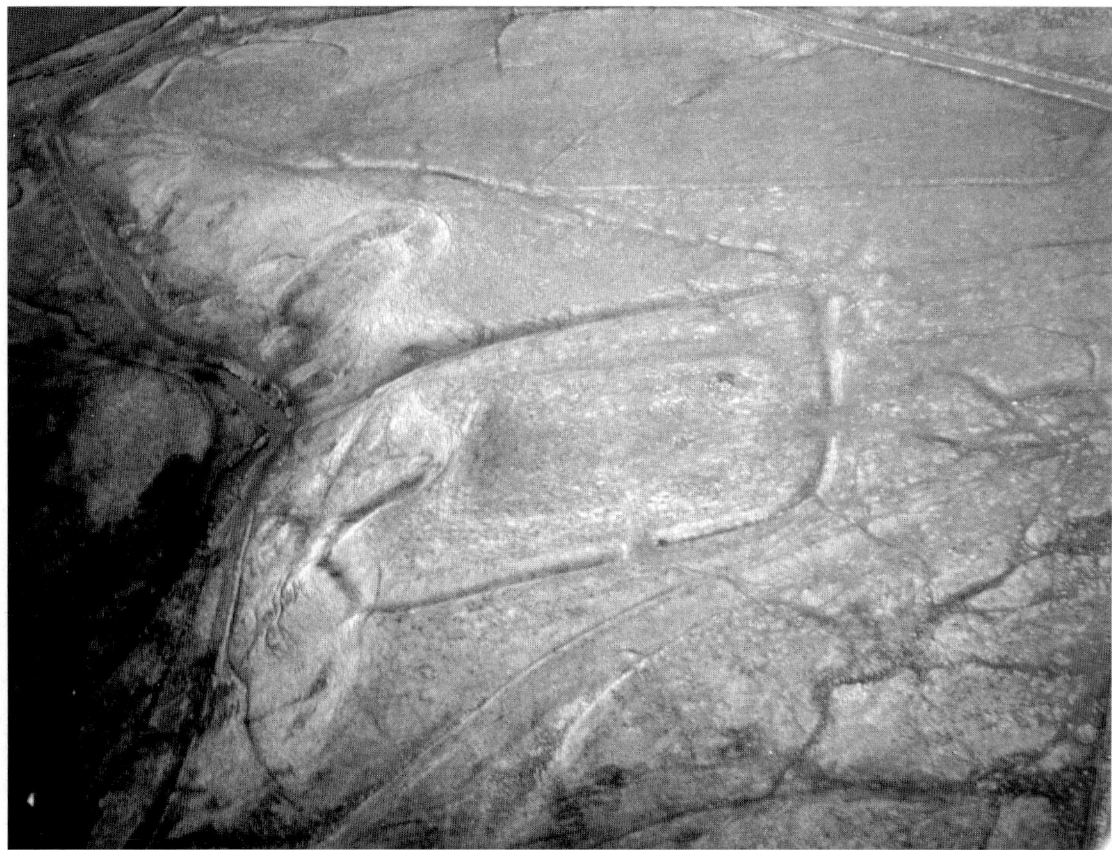

90 Haltwhistle Burn (Roman).

The regular outline of a Roman fortlet, with ditches and walls, sits beside the Haltwhistle Burn. The fort is south of Hadrian's Wall, as it is on the earlier Antonine frontier, with a road called the Stanegate linking it to others (below the fort). The fortlet, seen at the centre of the complex, covers about an acre and traces of buildings are visible inside it. Outside the fort is a large ditch that seems too far away to be exactly contemporary with the inner structure, possibly pre-dating it and made in preparation for a larger fort to be slotted in. Entrances appear to be from the south, east and west.

The large fields are now used as pasture for sheep and cattle. The road at the top right-hand corner leads to Cawfields, which is on Hadrian's Wall.

Haltwhistle means that it is a high place overlooking joined streams. Cawfields are crows' fields.

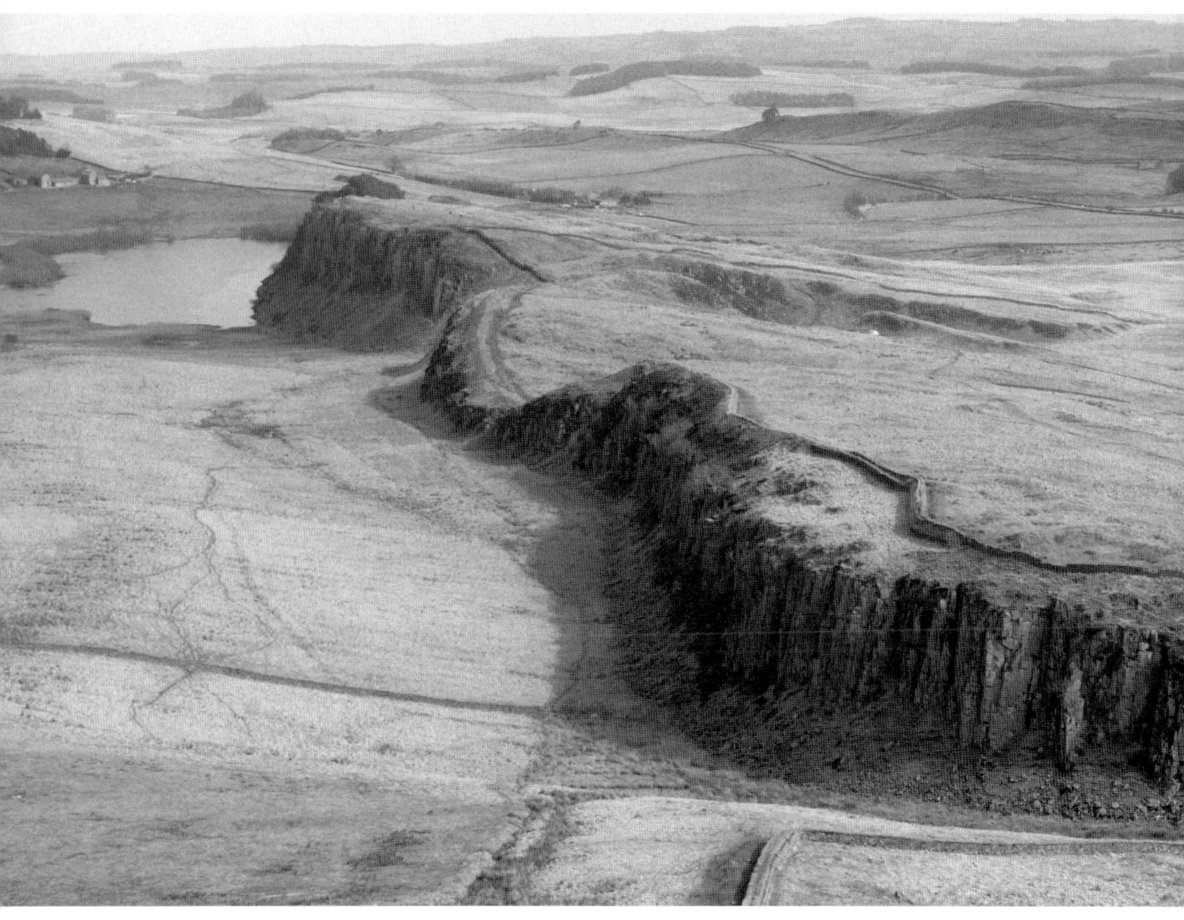

91 Hadrian's Wall (*The Hexham Courant*).

This central section of the Wall is one of the most famous, as the whinstone crags rise dramatically on a fault line, capped by what used to be a wall 15ft high with a lough at its base. The Wall trail now gives access to miles of very exciting countryside, and provides thousands of people with exercise and an interesting landscape.

The choice of frontier is obviously a natural one, not necessary as an insurmountable barrier, but as a clear line of demarcation between Romans and the 'Britunculi.' The natural lough, seen below the crags, would have been used for fishing or wild-fowling, and there would have been abundant wild life to hunt.

Beyond the wall on the crags is the military way, linking forts, milecastles and turrets.

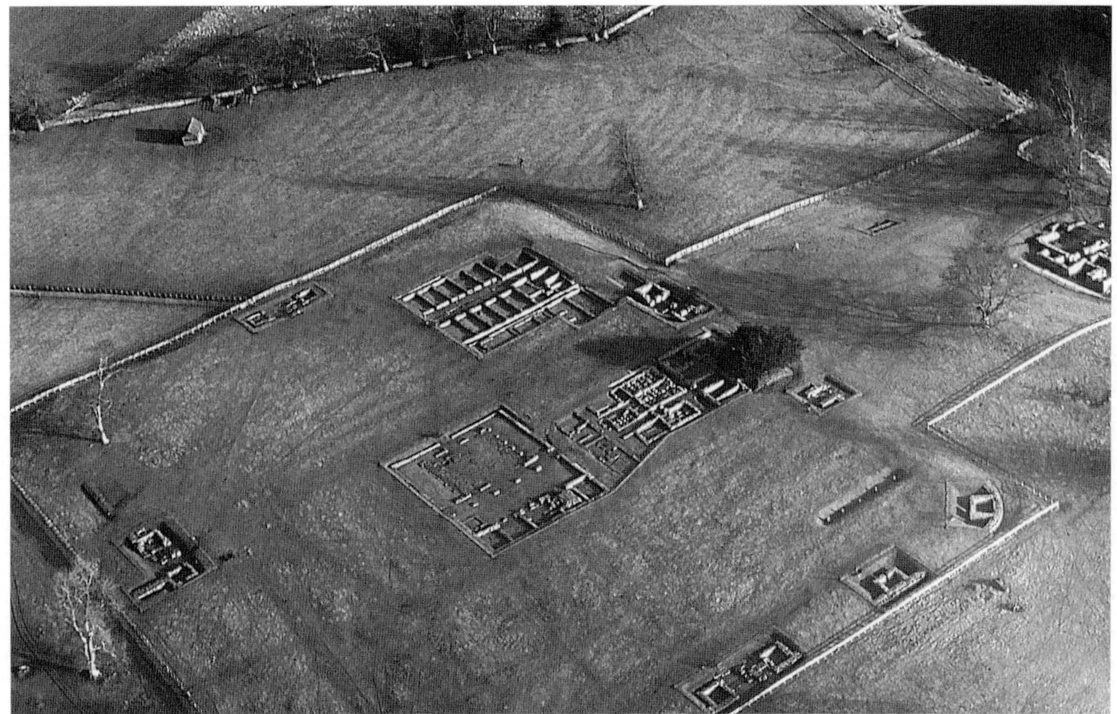

92 Chesters.

The Roman fort here has as its centre an excavated headquarters building, Hadrian's Wall leading in from the river crossing to the right. Outside the fort, in the top right-hand corner, is the bath house. The unmistakable plan of a Roman fort, with its straight lines and right angles is echoed many times along the Wall. It was intended as a launch-pad for attacks, but for most of its time it was a place to live and work. 'Chesters' comes from 'castra/ceaster', meaning that it was fortified.

The picture shows that the interior of the fort has been ploughed since its abandonment, and tonnes of stone have been removed for buildings and roads locally. The sweep of rig and furrow above the fort towards the River North Tyne shows that the land has been ploughed for crops.

Other forts, notably and spectacularly Vindolanda (south of the wall), are revealing a wealth of information about life on the Roman frontier.

ELSDON MOTTE AND BAILEY

Two photographs show detail of the motte and bailey castle and its larger setting. The name was 'Eledene' in 1236, meaning 'Elli's valley'.

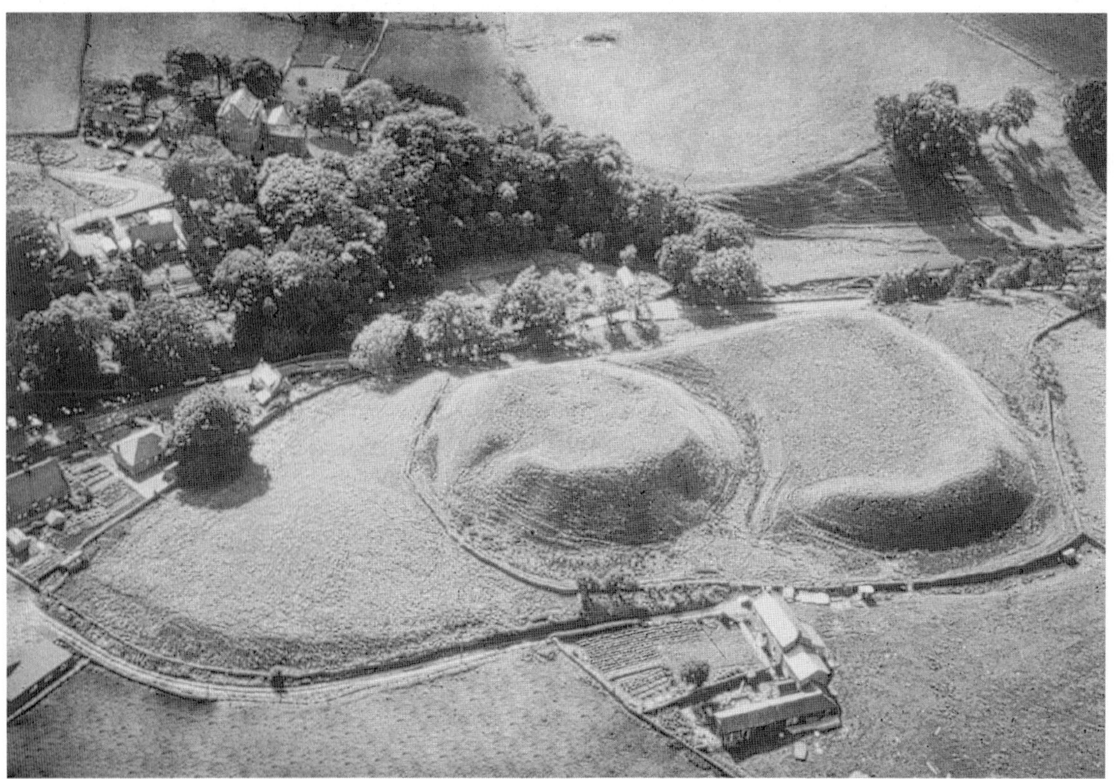

93a Elsdon Moot Hills (NUM).

The plan of a Norman motte and bailey castle has been preserved because the earlier timber buildings on it were not replaced in stone, and the site was abandoned. The 'motte' is the central mound, built largely by digging a ditch around it. To the right is the main bailey, an enclosed area created by another massive earthwork. At the top is the natural defence formed by the steepness of the burn valley.

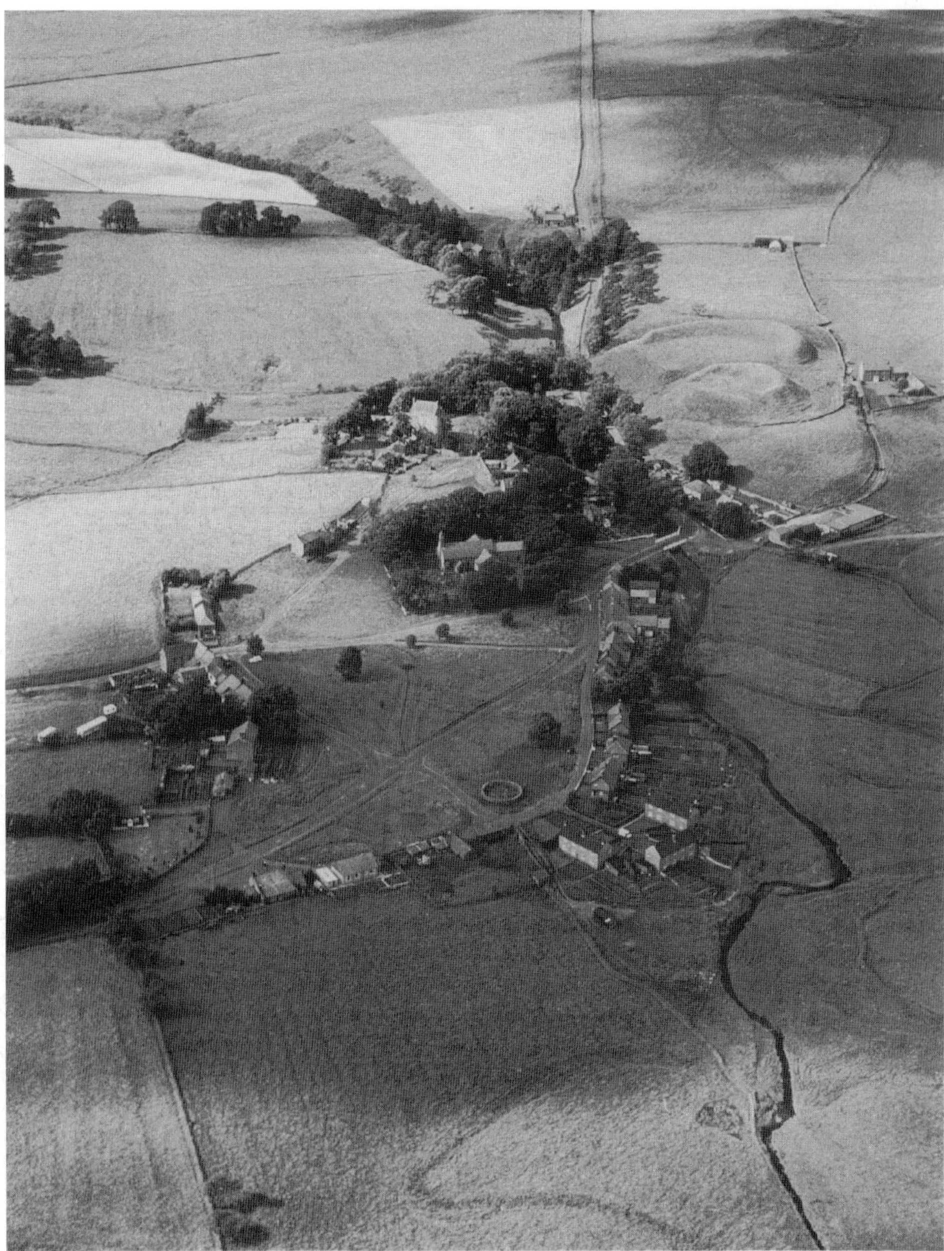

93b Elsdon village (NUM).

The castle site is seen here with the rest of the village of Elsdon, its large village green being a place to which drovers brought cattle on their way south from Scotland to the fattening pastures and markets of England. The importance of the village is emphasised by its strong defensive stone tower and church. Some of the buildings around the village green have ancient foundations.

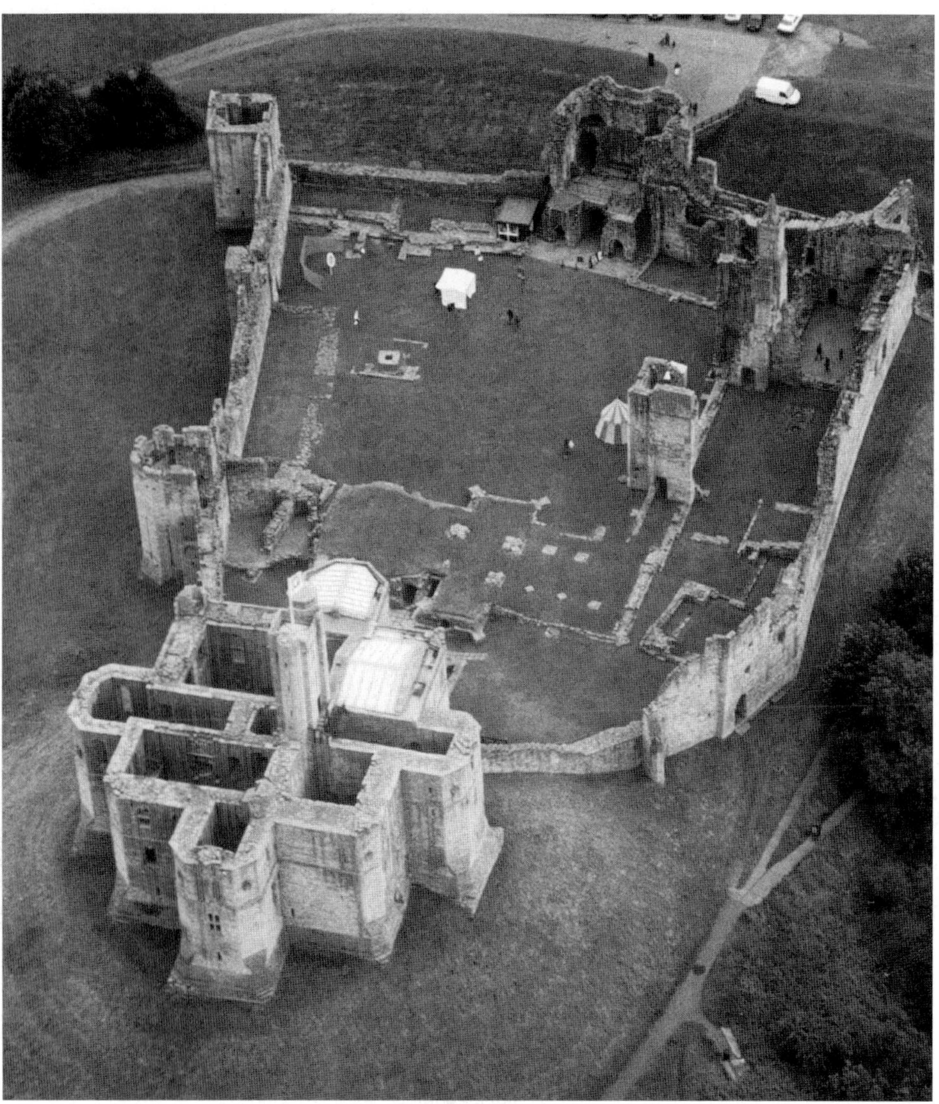

94 Warkworth Castle (Gordon Tinsley).

Castles and other defences figure prominently in this book in a wider context, and here I take Warkworth Castle as a good example of a choice of site and its fortification. This print, from 1998, shows the motte (round mound) at the bottom with the elaborate keep built on it; one of the finest pieces of castle architecture in Britain, removed in many ways from the grim fortress. The walled area above, the bailey, has strong towers and a gateway. The interior has a range of domestic buildings, including hall and kitchens, and the foundation of a church built above a crypt.

A ditch at the top cuts off the promontory on which the castle and town are built from the south, running from river towards the sea.

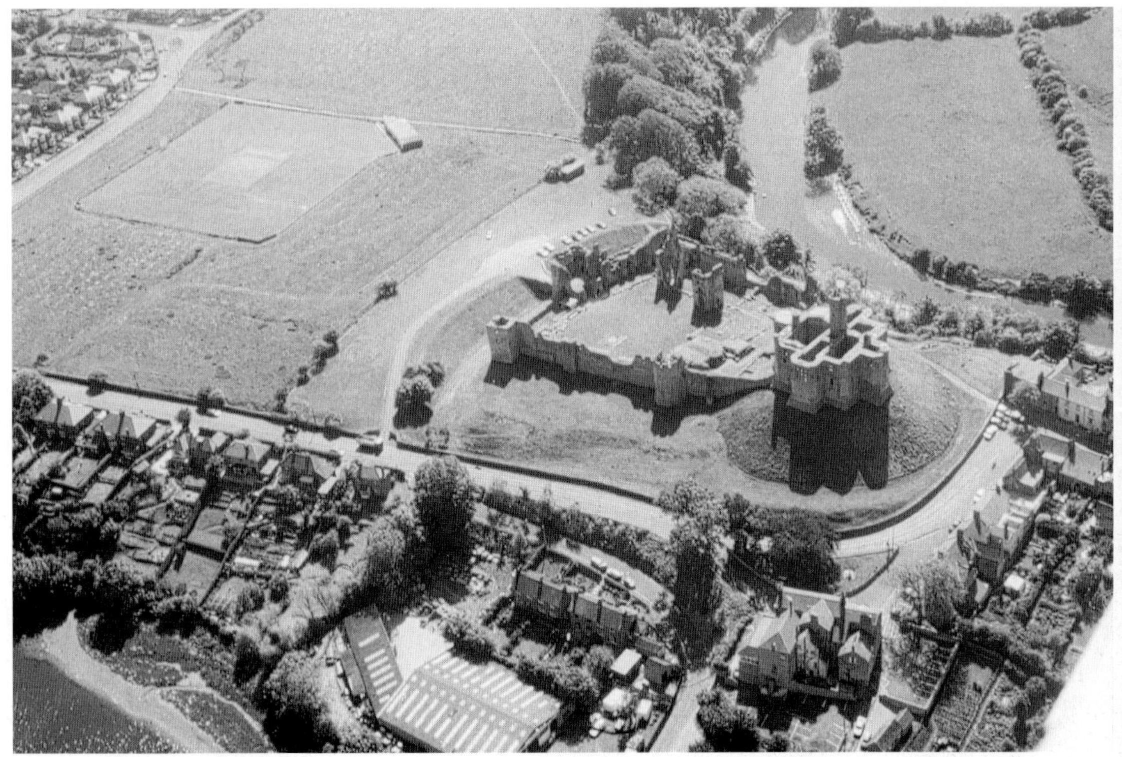

95 Warkworth.

The moat which is cut from river bank to river bank stands between the castle and the cricket ground.

This view from the east shows an interesting feature in the development of the castle plan: running parallel to the east wall is a fainter wall beneath the grass, possibly an early timber construction, later to be replaced by a stone wall.

The small square corner tower is called the Amble or Montague Tower, and the northern polygonal tower is Grey Mare's Tower, typical of the thirteenth century.

Despite some encroachment of housing from the south (left), the cricket field and pasture provide a lovely open view of the castle gateway.

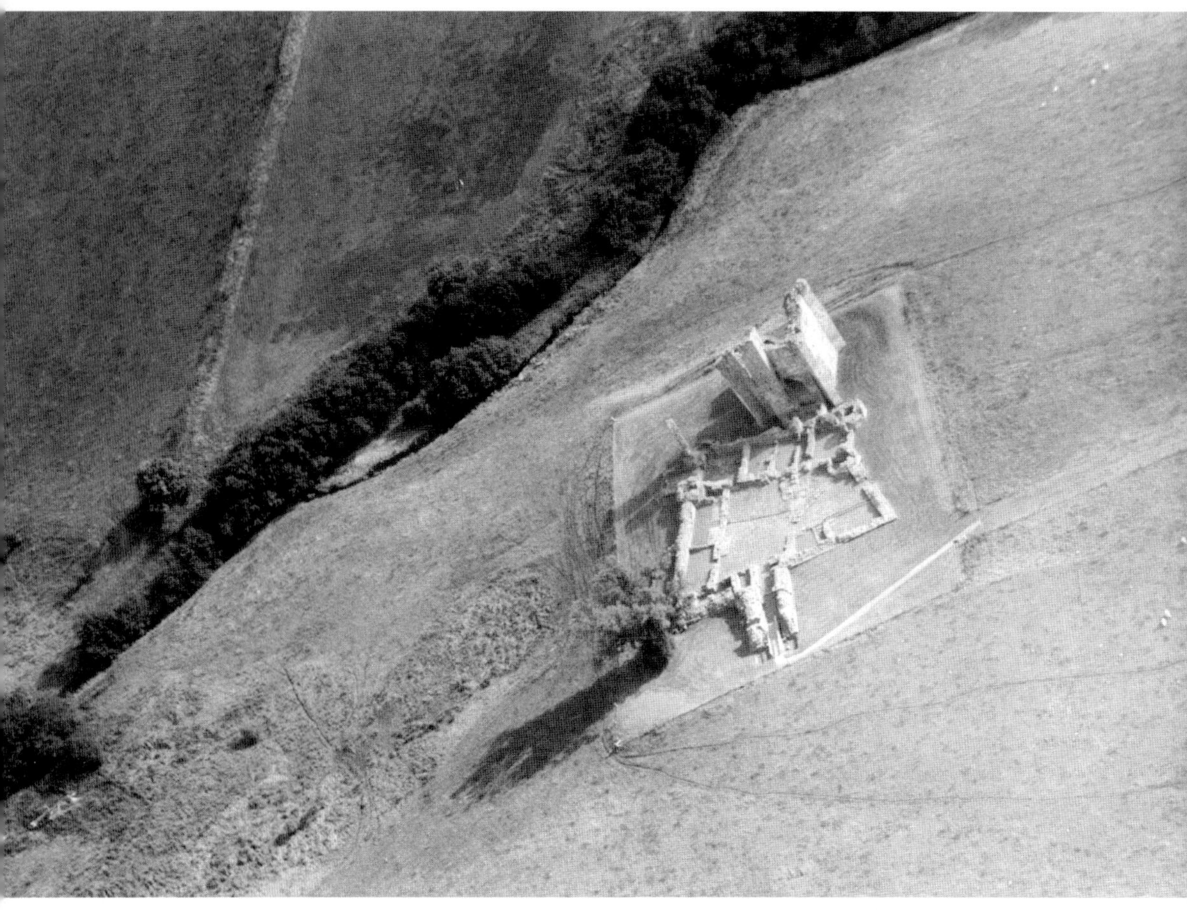

96 Edlingham Castle.

Not many years ago a large part of the castle was covered with a large grass-covered mound. Detailed excavation from 1978-82 has revealed what we see in this picture: a small, complex castle beginning as a moated enclosure around 1250 and developing into a rectangular hall house with octagonal towers at one end, a gatehouse leading to it, a courtyard with flanking buildings and a large tower. The excavation has been very valuable in leading to an understanding of how such a building has developed (see also picture 71).

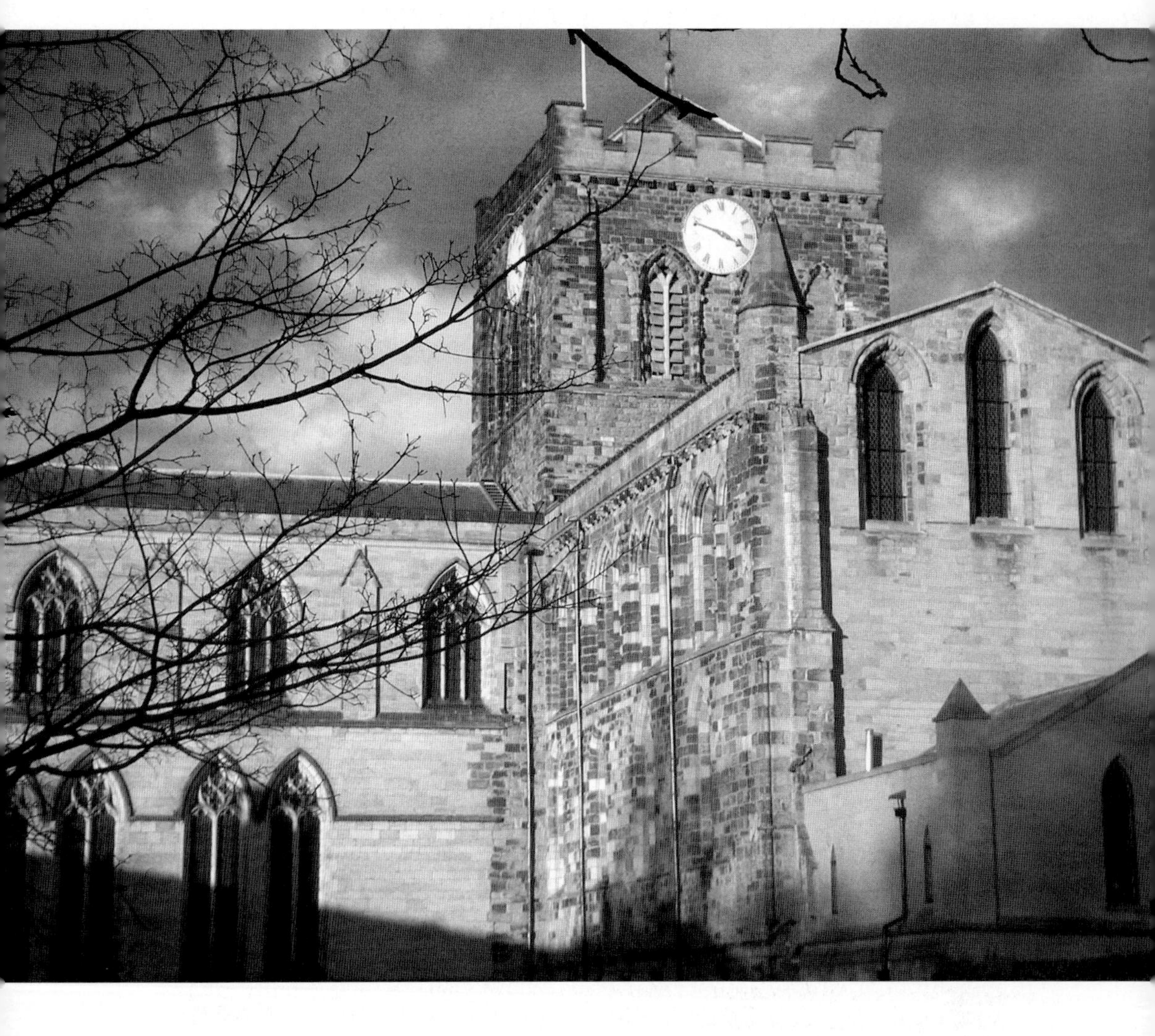

9

CHURCH AND MONASTIC SITES

Despite the turbulence of the Border, there are many fine churches. There are also many chapels of a later period when such movements as Methodism reached the parts that the established church could not, such as mining communities. The Dissolution of the Monasteries made land and buildings available to those who benefited from Henry VIII's policies. Whereas some monasteries almost disappeared, others were modified and allowed to exist fairly well intact, especially the monastic churches, because they continued to serve the local communities. Examples of these follow.

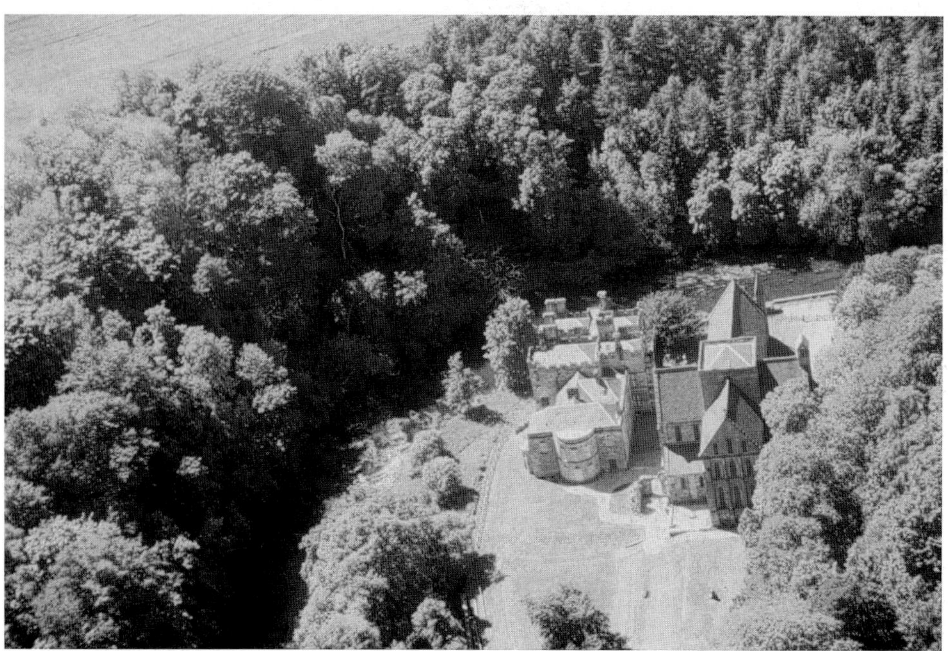

Previous page 97 Brinkburn Priory.

The Priory is situated on the bend of the River Coquet. This north bank location is overlooked by high ground which has a prehistoric enclosure beside the car park. The water was used to power a mill, and the river would have produced an abundance of fish and game. When the Priory was 'dissolved' part of it was used to construct a domestic building. The Cadogan family restored it in the mid nineteenth century. The Priory church, transitional Norman-Early English in style, has been splendidly preserved, and is used for concerts and services. It is cared for by English Heritage and open to the public.

The river provided water with sufficient flow to operate a cornmill, first recorded in 1535, the present building being early nineteenth century.

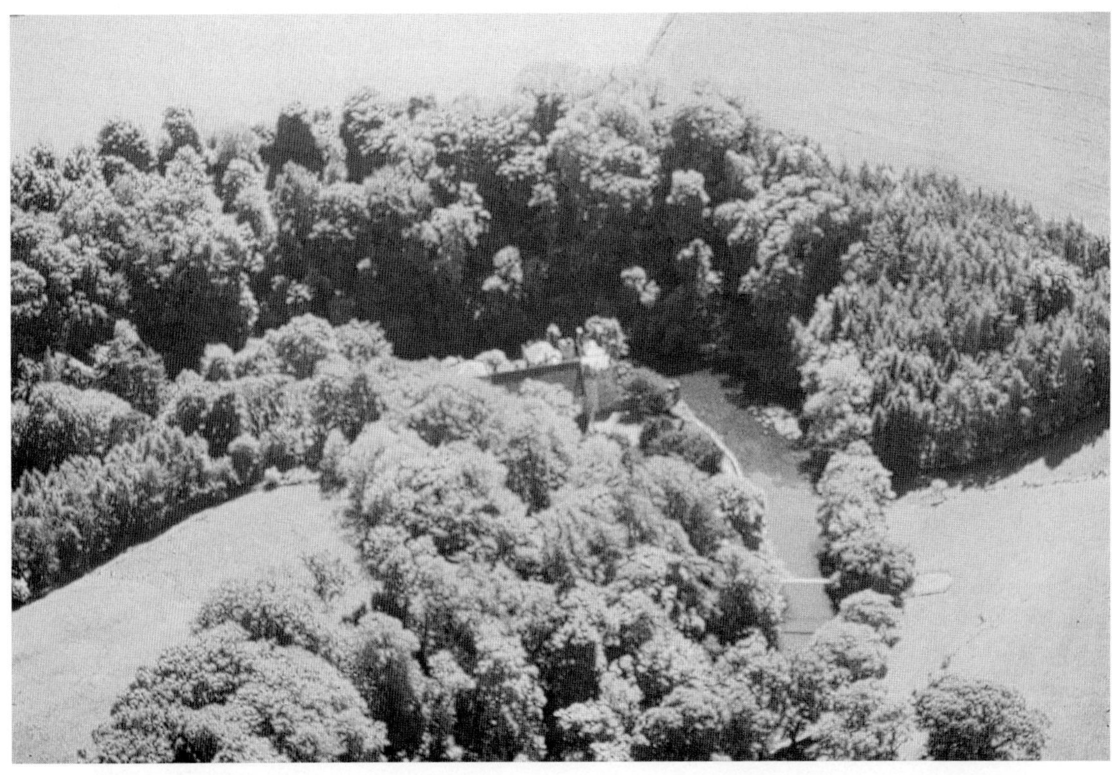

98 The Priory in a wider context.

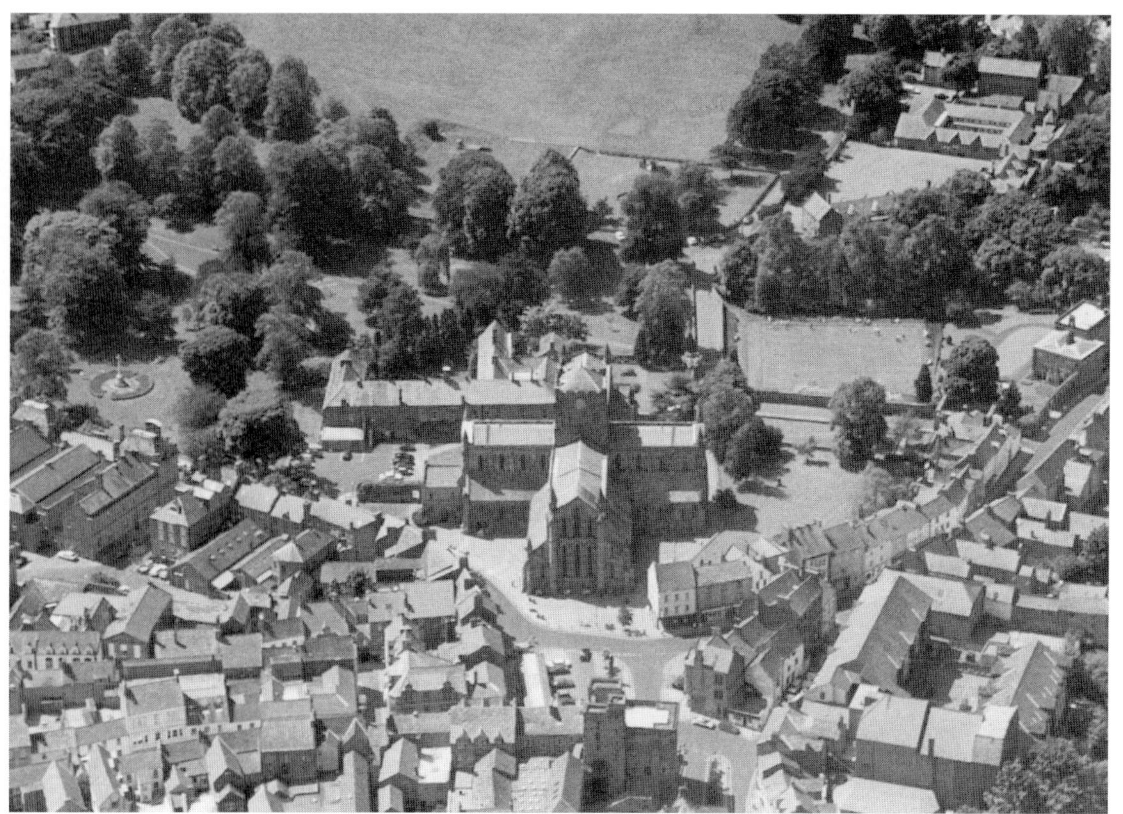

99 Hexham.

Built by St Wilfrid and regarded as one of the finest churches north of the Alps at the time, what we see today was constructed over an Anglo-Saxon crypt. Some of its buildings around the cloisters were swept away so that Beaumont Street could give access to the market place from the south-west in the nineteenth century, when the east end was demolished and the new chancel built by Dobson. In the early twentieth century the nave, in ruins for centuries, was rebuilt. Symbolically, what used to divide the church from the town has also been swept away, so that a paved area brings the market place right up to the Abbey walls. The Priory grounds were surrounded by a wall, the curved course of which, bottom right, can be traced and the parkland to the top is now called the Abbey Grounds. The Abbey is dedicated to St Andrew.

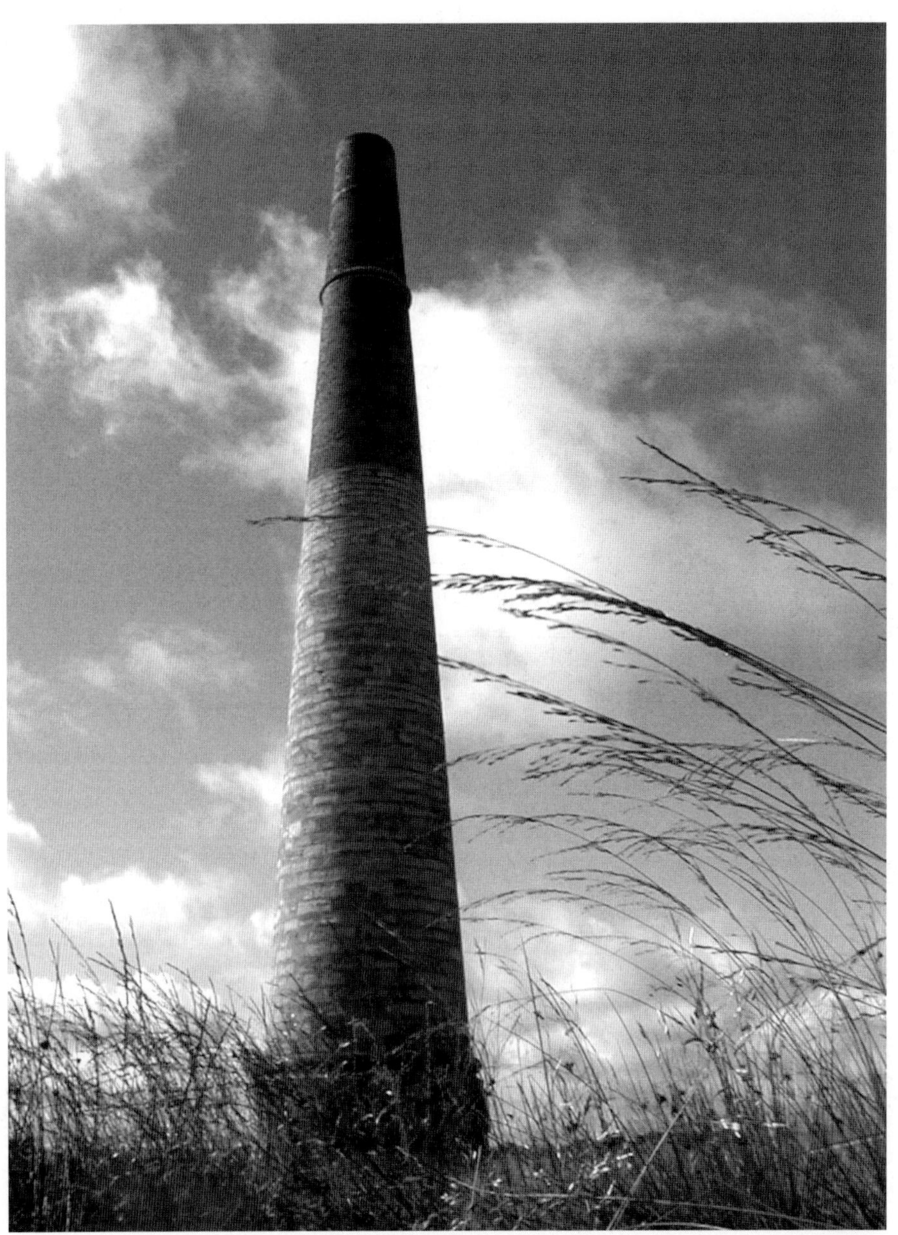

10

INDUSTRIES

The most important industry of Northumberland was agriculture, until the vast deposits of coal, iron and lead ore placed the county firmly at the head of the Industrial Revolution. Small-scale mining and quarrying had always been important, but now the countryside was opened up as never before, with a network of railways which today are ghost tracks. Old towns were enlarged, but the increased population mainly concentrated near to the south-east coast, where new towns sprang up, such as Ashington. In many cases the landscape was completely transformed.

Quarrying whinstone for road-building is important. Other quarries extract 'aggregate' and the gravel which now covers many gardens, and sandstone for building.

There are many mineral sources, two of the most important being coal and galena (lead ore). There are sources of sandstone of different kinds, some fine-grained 'freestone' and others coarse grits. The pictures that follow give glimpses of these industries.

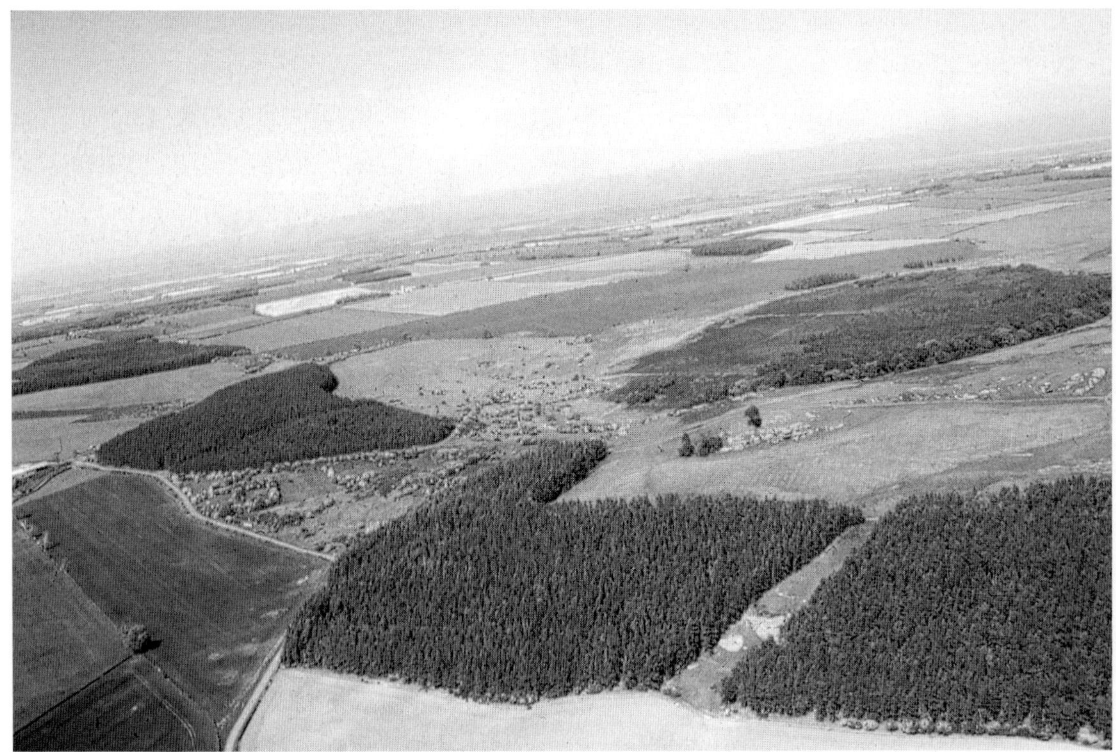

100 Ford Moss colliery site.

The abandoned mine at Ford Moss, so close to the Ford Castle Estate, is seen from the edge of the Milfield Plain, where thick clay soils can be seen at its edge. The view is extensive, as far as the North Sea. At the bottom, where there is a gap in the forest planting, the intermittent sandstone cliffs known as Dove Crags begin.

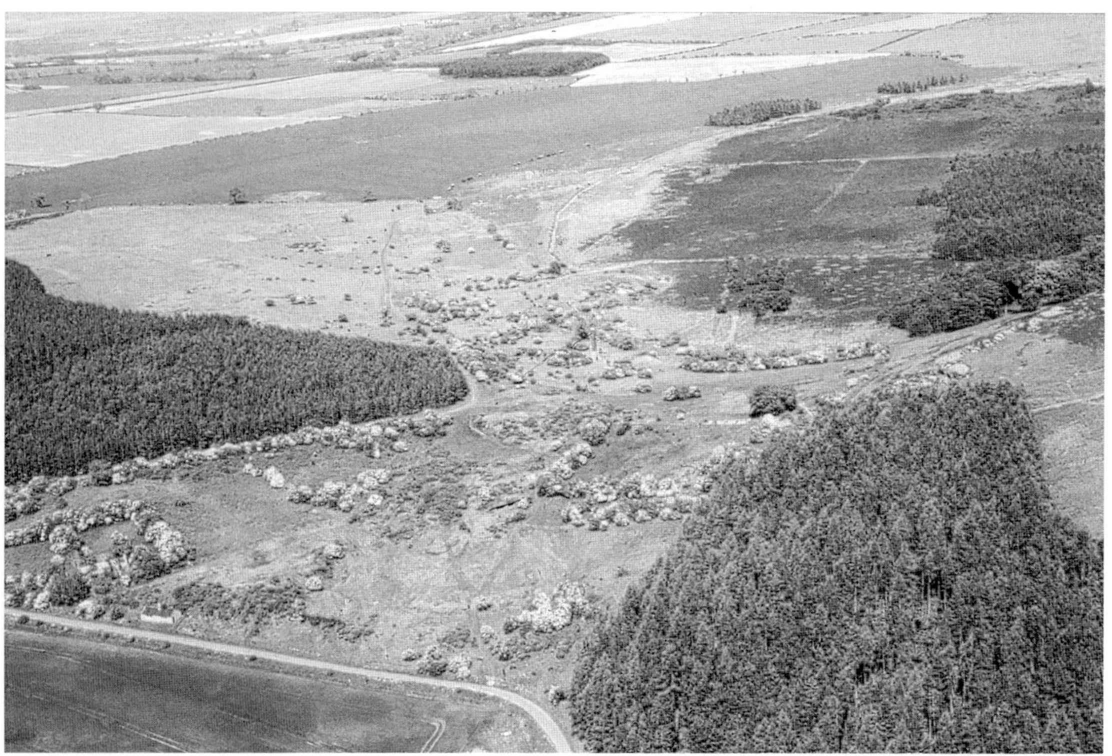

101 Ford Moss village and mine area.

The dark ground leading to trees at the top of the picture is the 'moss' – a Site of Special Scientific Interest for its plant life. The area below that is the site of Ford Moss Colliery, which abandoned the extraction of coal using the bell-pit method for deeper and more complex mining. Here the living quarters and gardens of the miners can be seen, with hawthorn hedges in flower in June 1994. Although engine houses pumped out water from the mine, it was abandoned, not being able to compete with the coalfields along the south-east coast. The coalfield had its own quarry for freestone nearby, with workings still visible.

BUTTERWELL OPEN-CAST MINE

The coal deposits of the coastal plain have been abandoned as deep mining, but are still being exploited by open-cast methods. The scene at Butterwell shows an earlier open-cast mine. Others are being opened up and more applications are being made.

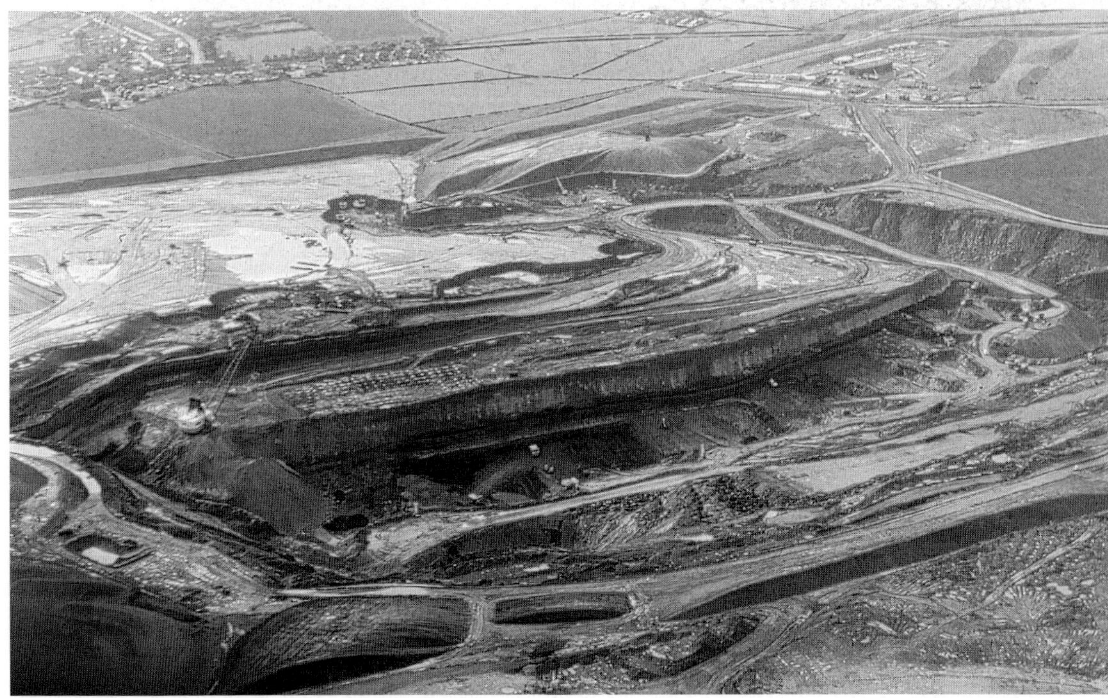

102 Butterwell open-cast mine.

This view gives the whole geological structure of the coal deposits and the method of extraction.

Among the machines is 'Big Geordie', to the left, a huge excavator that leaves pad marks in the ground when it is moved along. These open-cast mines are filled up afterwards and restored to large fields.

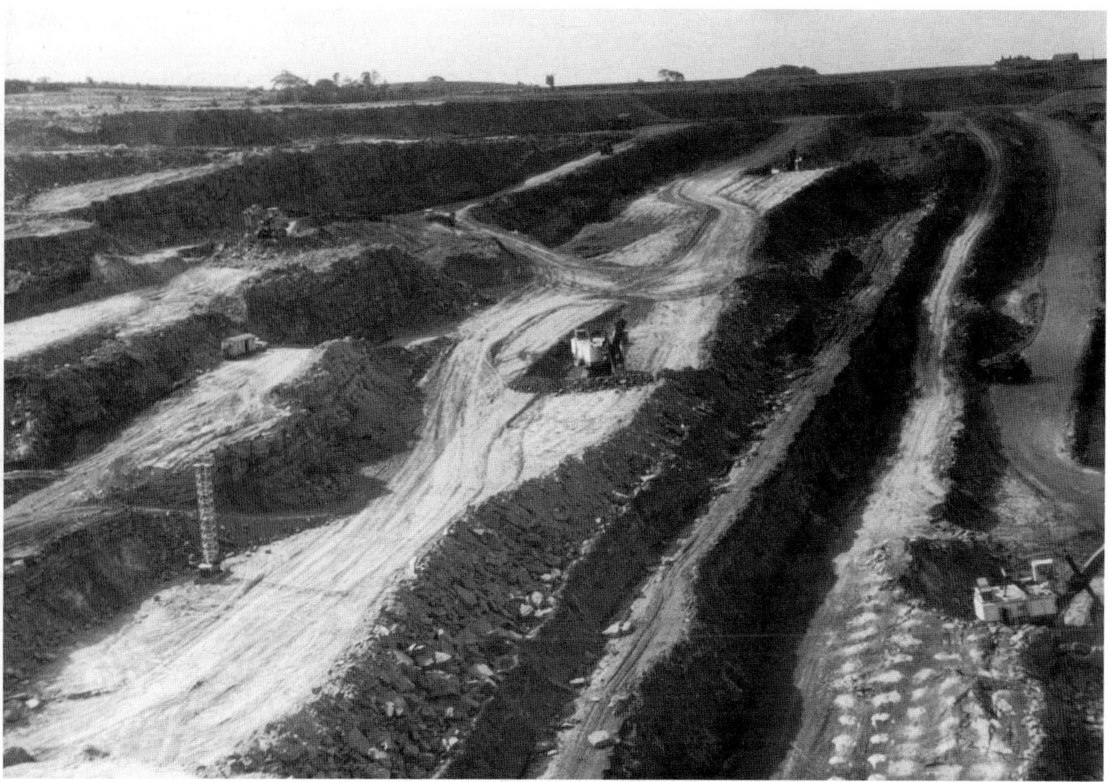

103 Butterwell open-cast mine detail.

A closer view adds more detail to this method of extraction. Three great excavators stand in line among the terraces from which the coal is extracted.

About a quarter of Northumberland's coal reserves are still underground and under the sea, and may be called upon in future, with new technology, to help solve an energy crisis.

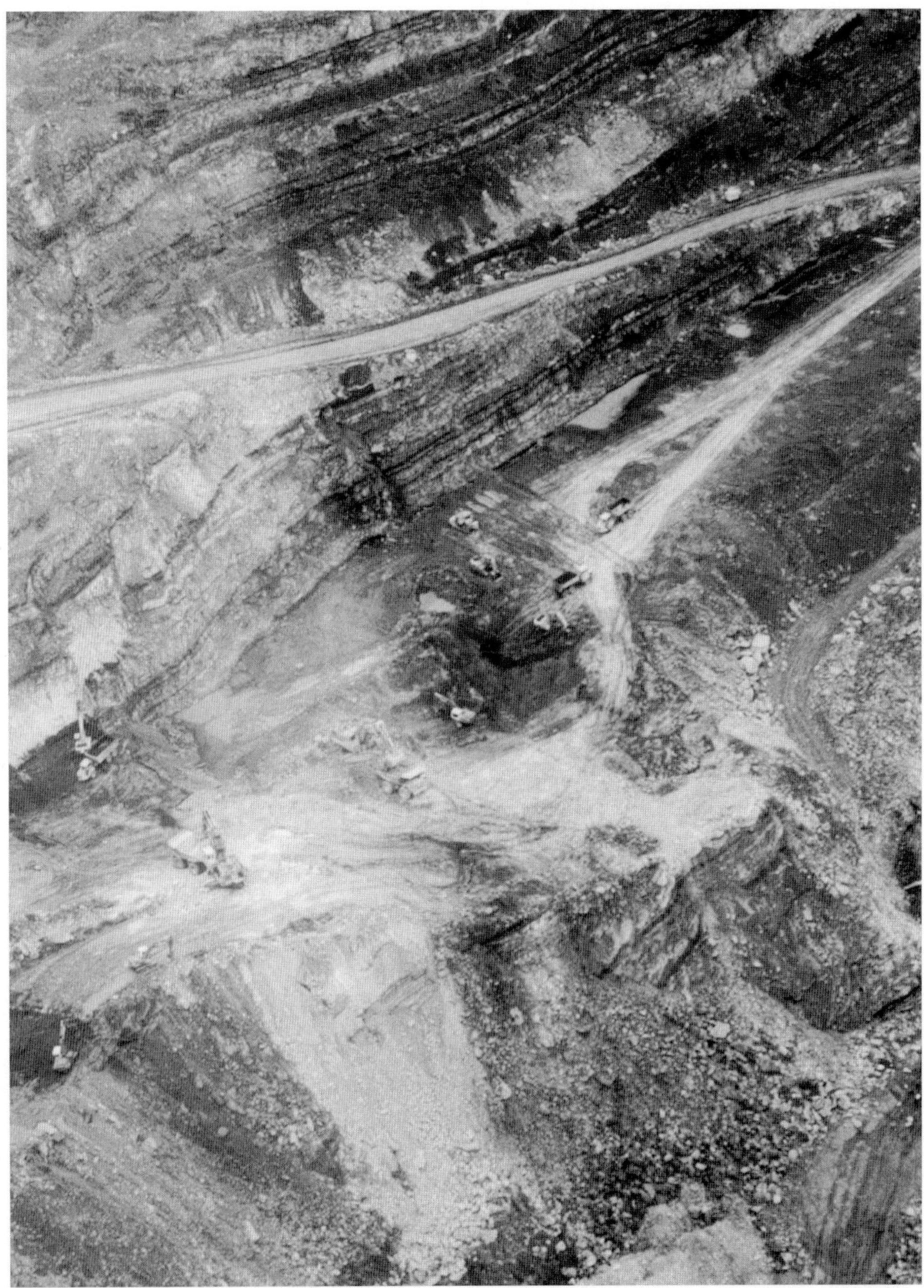

104 Stobswood open-cast mine (Gordon Tinsley).

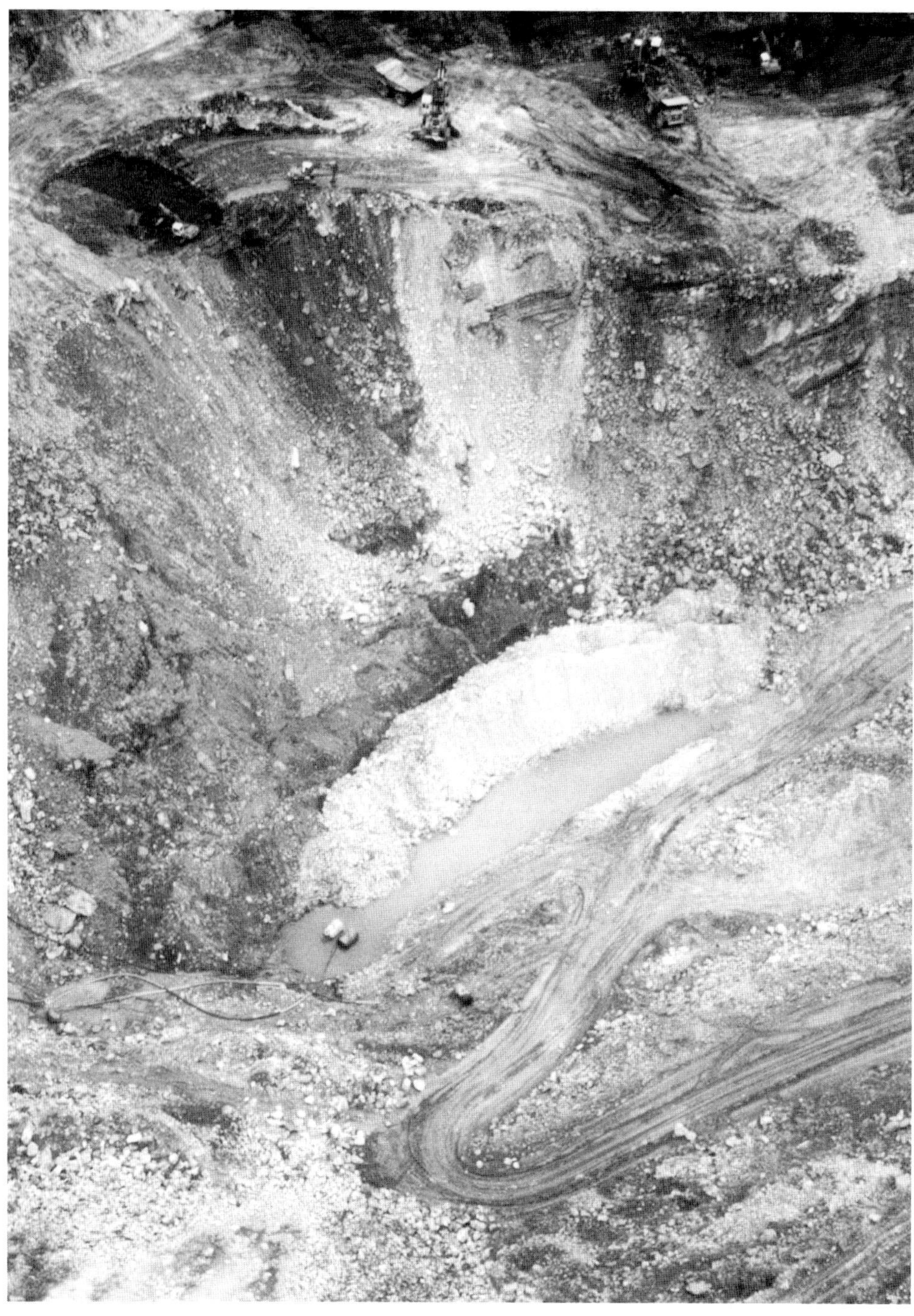

105 Stobswood open-cast mine (Gordon Tinsley).

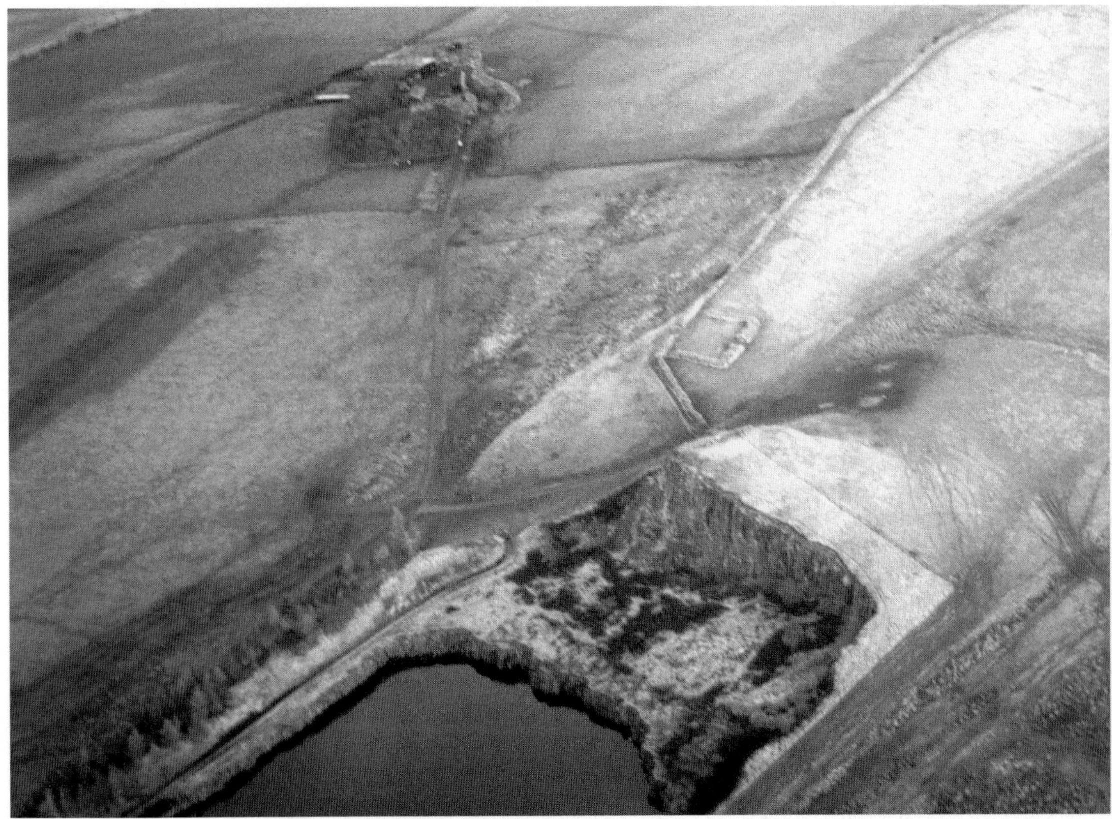

106 Whinstone quarry on Hadrian's Wall (1993).

The Wall comes in from the top right-hand corner of the picture along a natural ridge to a 'milecastle', and then is cut off by a quarry for whinstone.

The picture shows what a considerable amount the Cawfields quarry has taken out of Hadrian's Wall, leaving it in mid-air with a lake beneath it.

The exploitation of dolerite has ended here and such destruction of a now-protected monument in unlikely to happen again, especially as the Wall is a World Heritage site. There are many other quarries at 'dykes' crossing the county which provide valuable aggregate and roadstone. This also used to be exploited for an extensive local rail network.

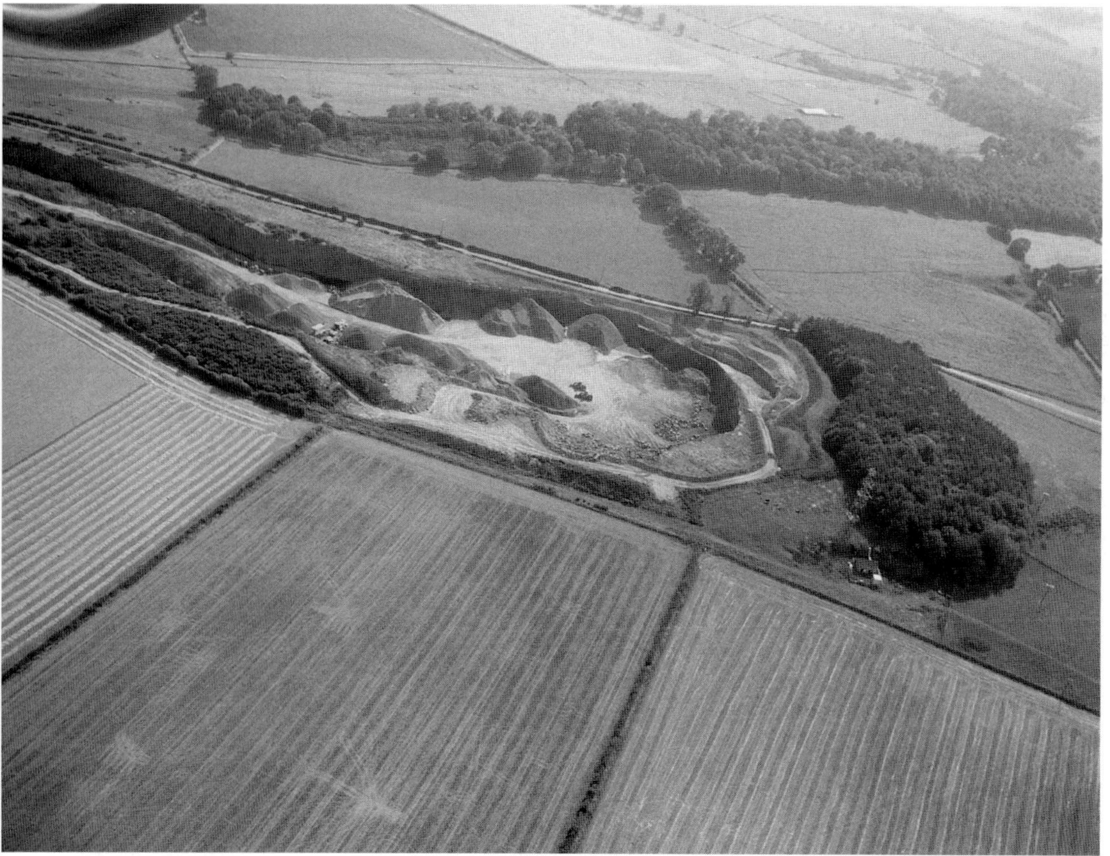

107 Quarry, near Longhoughton.

This type of quarry exploits many sources of stone for road building, aggregate and building stone.

PRUDHOE INDUSTRIES

The expanding industries of Prudhoe along the Tyne valley stretch below the green belt of the castle grounds. They include unique chalkland, spread out as waste ('The Spetchels') from an ICI factory that flourished during the Second World War, producing agricultural fertiliser. The works was replaced by the SCA Hygiene factory; since then many other industries have been established.

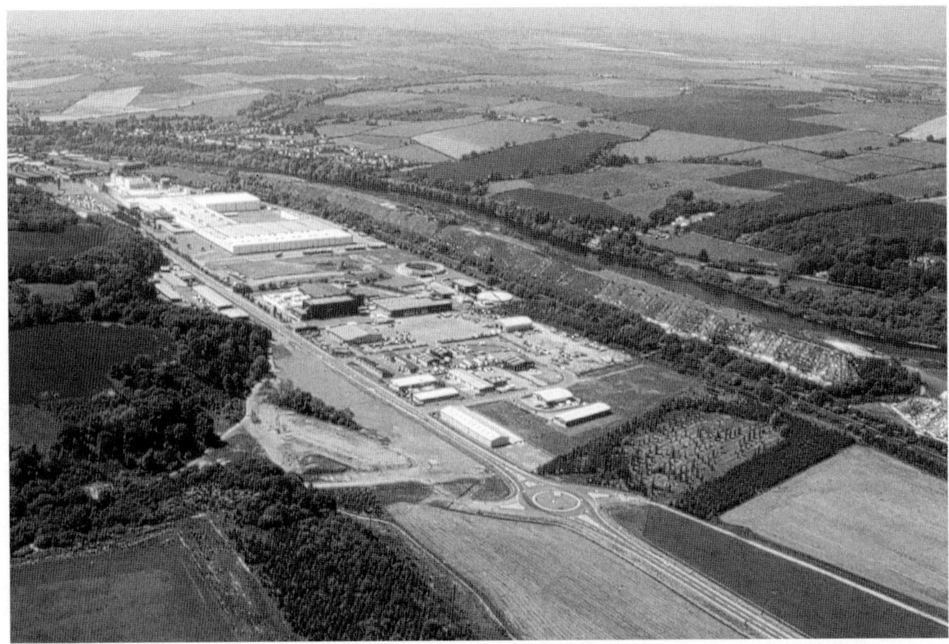

108 Prudhoe. This view is from the east, taken in 1994.

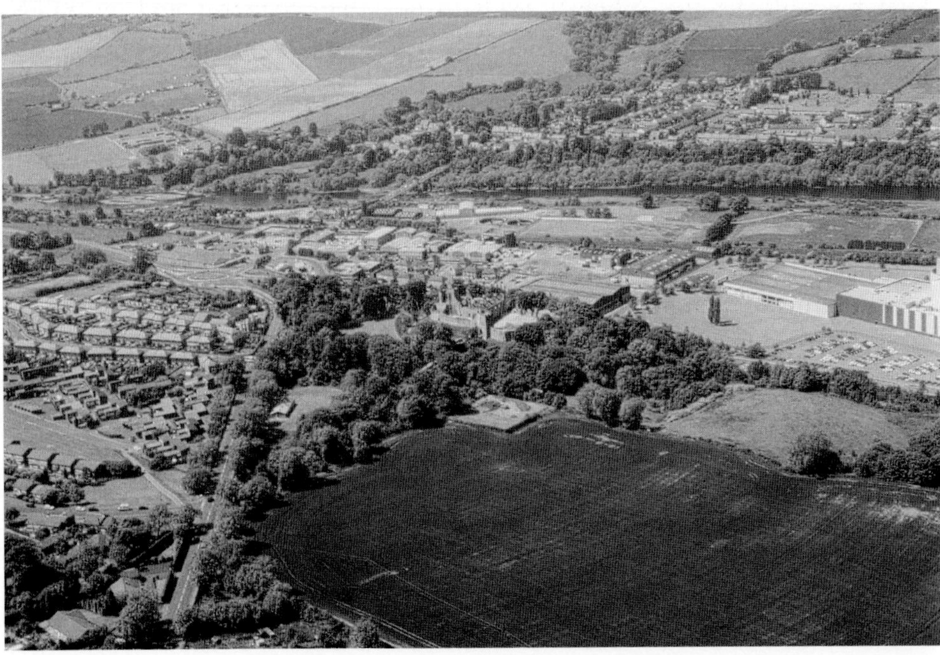

109 Further west, the relationship of industries to town and castle is seen. Across the river, the village of Ovingham, recorded in 1238, named after Ofa, has a church with Saxon workmanship. It is linked by bridge to Prudhoe.

11

COMMUNICATIONS

The long coastline and good harbours have made the North-East an important maritime province, particularly in its shipbuilding facilities and its capacity for trade. Rural Northumberland has small ports which, as in the case of Alnmouth, have become disused, although the boom in leisure has turned some into marinas, like Amble.

Elsewhere the land was crossed by tracks, often using ridgeways, but the Romans built the first efficient roads to link their fortresses and settlements. These were essential to the control of the frontier. After the Romans left, roads would have continued to be used, but not repaired and many eventually became buried. Drove roads, trackways hollowed out by the frequent passage of cattle from Scotland, enjoyed a long life, until other means of transporting beasts were found in the age of road building and railways. Many of today's roads, mostly small ones, follow old paths. In the case of the Alemouth Corn Road, the landowners would enclose areas and drive straight roads through them, but these are interspersed with the older routes that skirted land holdings and fields.

A feature of 'modern' Northumberland is that all the routes through the county to Scotland are mainly single carriageway, and this causes great concern to local businesses. There is a strong and justified feeling that the south of England is favoured and the North-East neglected.

There is also the need to maintain and expand the railway network as an alternative to the use of private and commercial road vehicles.

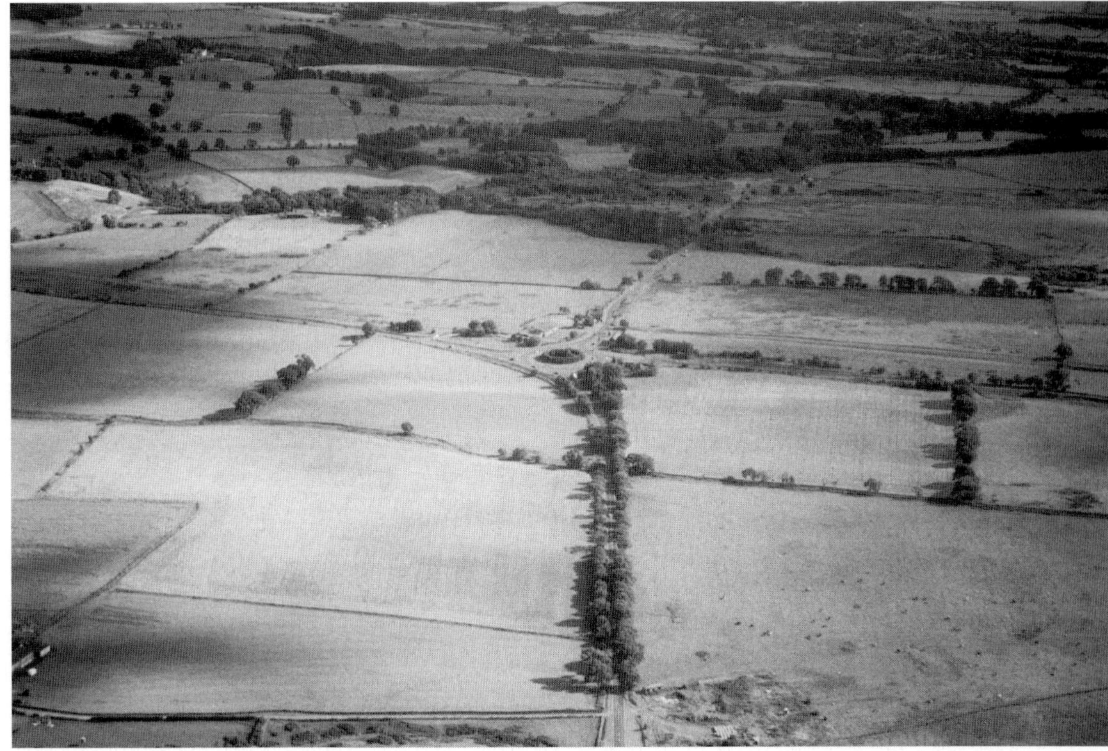

110 Dere Street Roman road (Matthew Hutchinson).

The Roman road here runs from Coria (Corbridge) via Stagshaw Common from the south (top) to meet at the centre of the picture the ditch, vallum and Hadrian's Wall at a place called Portgate (the gap through which the road passes). It then runs north past a derelict mine, seen at the bottom of the picture as a rough patch of ground.

The A68 runs alongside, over, or near Dere Street, as the Roman road is called, for many miles. The earliest roads were laid out by Agricola or his successors, the one in this picture going south via Corbridge to York, crossing the Tyne by an impressive bridge, the southern end of which has just been excavated and reinstated.

Many visitors find the switch-back ride on this road exhilerating, but at times perilous, when its staightness makes them forget that there are many steep dips.

The building of Hadrian's Wall placed the Roman east to west route north of Agricola's Stanegate.

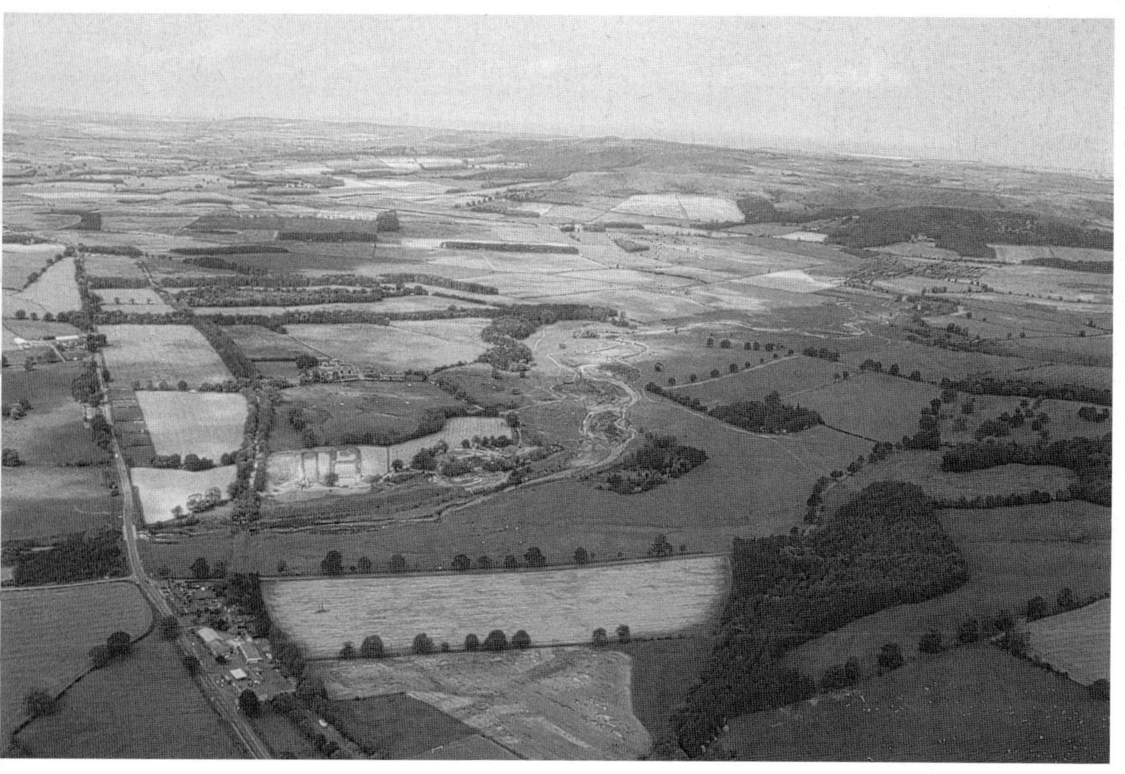

111 The A697 at Lilburn, south of Wooler.

There are few major roads in Northumberland. The A697 single carriageway road, seen here to the left of the picture in 1995, is on its way to Wooler. It has reached Lilburn, which in 1170 probably meant 'Lilla's burn'.

In parts, the Alnwick to Cornhill railway, now abandoned, runs alongside or crosses the road, and some of its fine stations are still visible and used along this road.

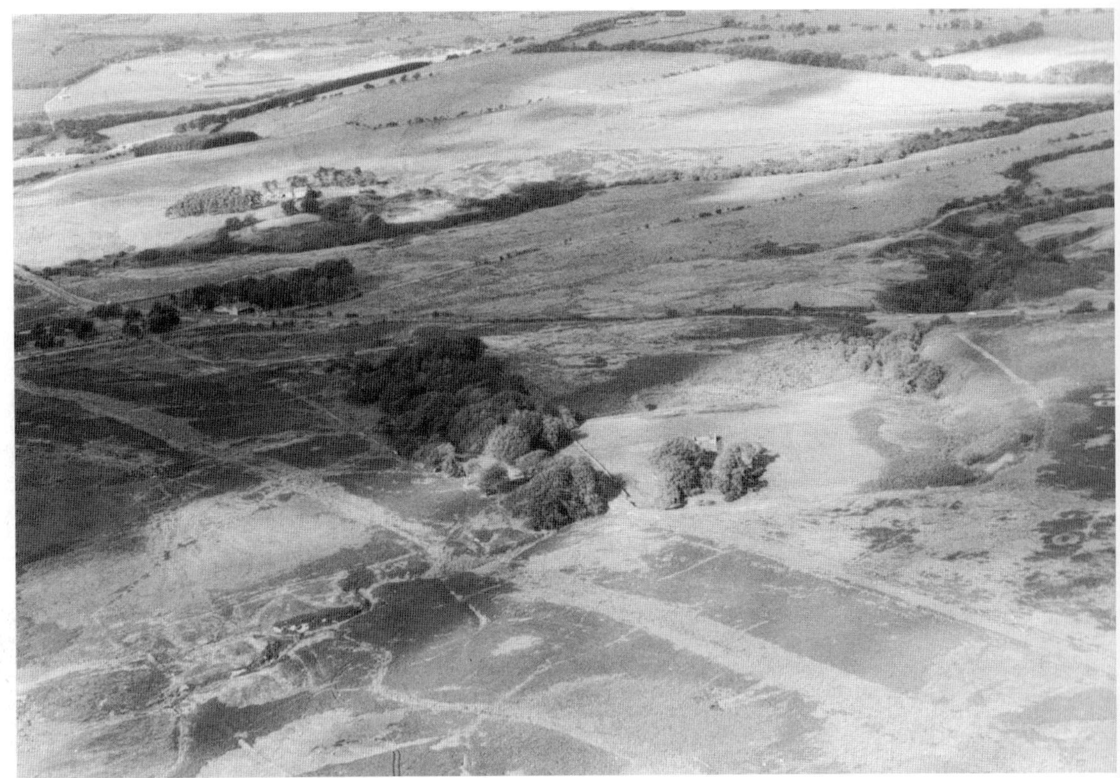

112 Newmoor crossroads.

The same road is seen here further south; it is a modern road that has replaced part of the old stagecoach road from Newcastle to Edinburgh. The old highway is seen above the gas pipeline excavation (at the bottom of the picture) passing through the clump of trees at the centre of the picture. Between this and the main road, scarcely visible, is the route of the Devil's Causeway, a major Roman road.

At the centre left edge there is a house on the A697 which marks the crossroads where the 'Alemouth Corn Road' from Hexham to Alnmouth intersects. Its route can be seen obliquely at the top only as a faint trace, but it gives views of some of Northumberland's finest country.

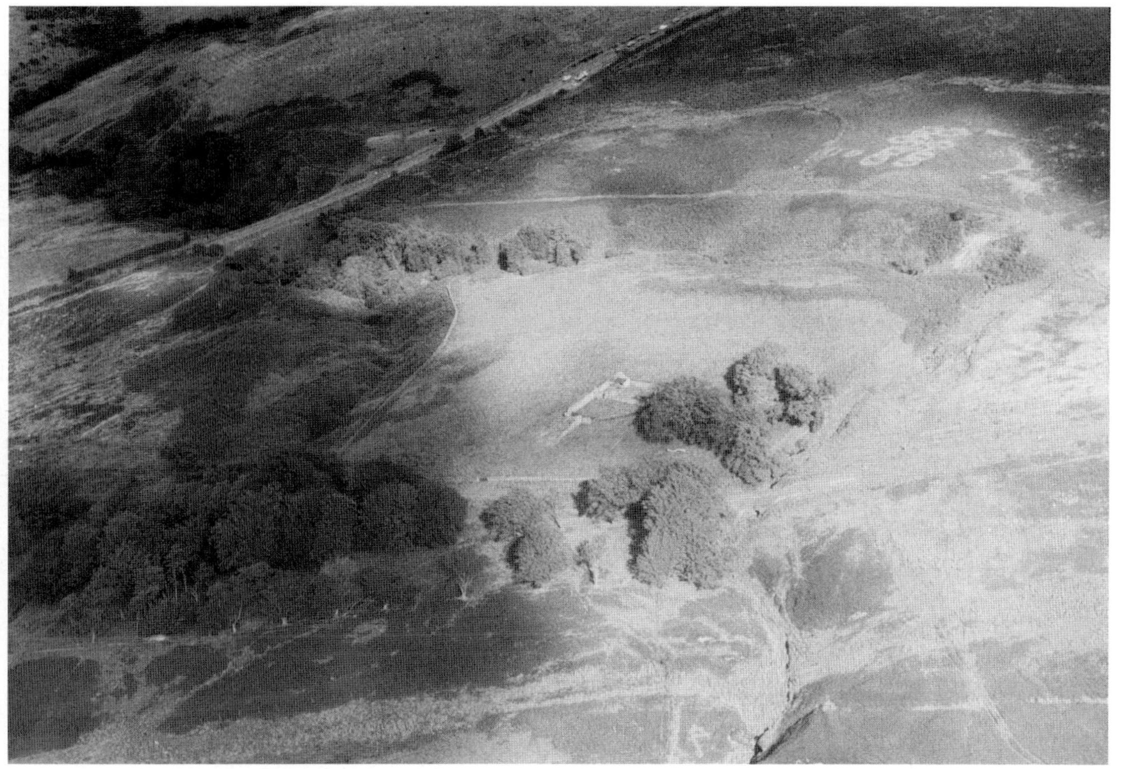

113 Newmoor Inn.

The inn which served the coach travellers is seen as a ruin in these pictures. The green-covered substantial surface of the coach road goes through beech plantings which covered some rectangular walled fields that would have had horses in them for the change-over. The old track reaches the turnpike road, the 'Alemouth Corn Road' near the Newmoor crossroads, then continues visibly on its way to Whittingham.

The position of the old inn is high above the landscape, giving splendid views to the north-east along the scarp which includes Caller Crag and Corby's Crag. Perhaps here, though, the thoughts of stagecoach travellers would have been more on keeping warm and getting a good meal than on the scenery. In the field around the ruined building are many sherds of white glazed pottery unearthed by moles and rabbits which give some idea of the quantity of crockery used here. Below the house, among the trees there are also considerable quantities of dark green bottle glass.

The position of the gas pipeline trench is seen again at the bottom of the picture. The A697 cuts obliquely across the top left corner, a road which replaced this older one.

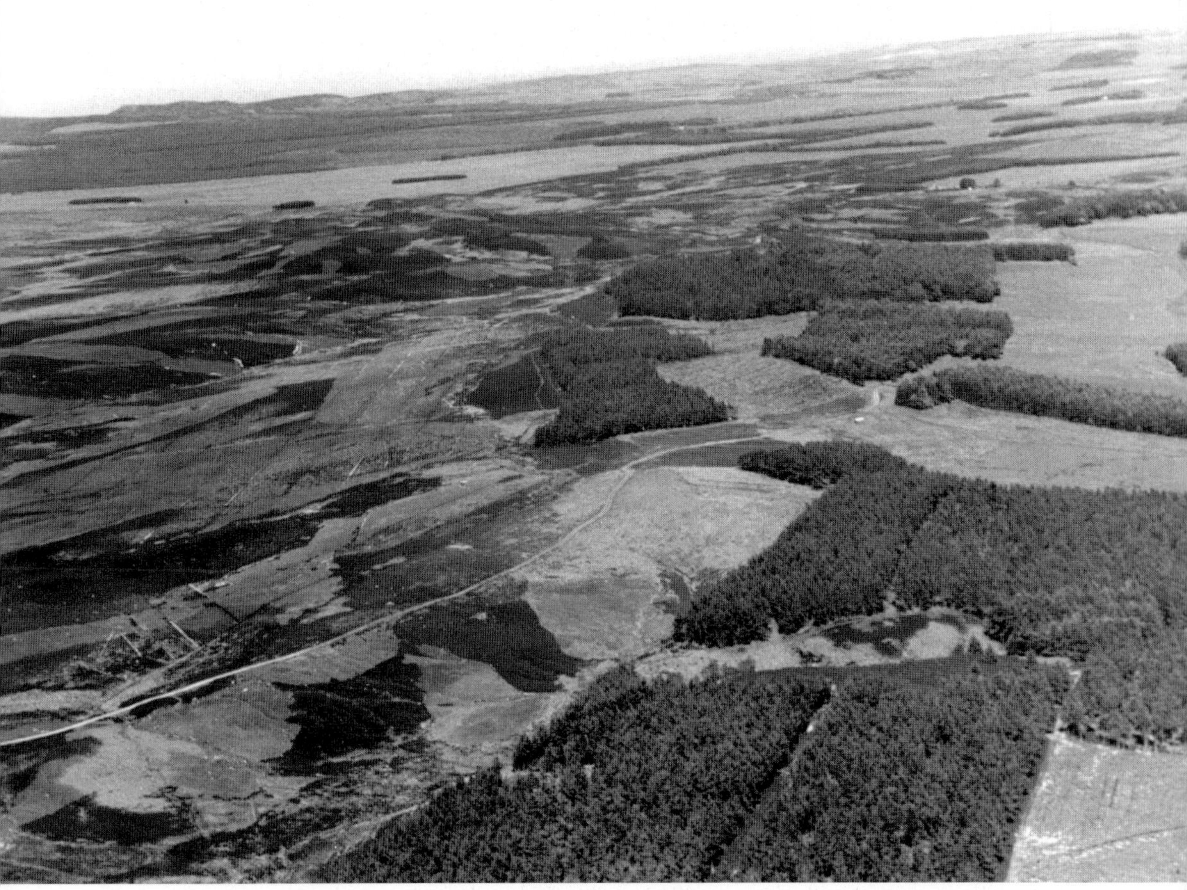

114 Railway at Ray.

In this picture there is an abandoned curved railway track that shows just what an extensive system had been created in the nineteenth century. The rails have been taken up, but the bed remains. Often these are used by hikers to gain access to the countryside, but are often blocked. Although the area seems remote today, it has evidence of many prehistoric enclosures and burial sites.

Recorded as 'Raye' in 1300, it may mean a nook or landmark.

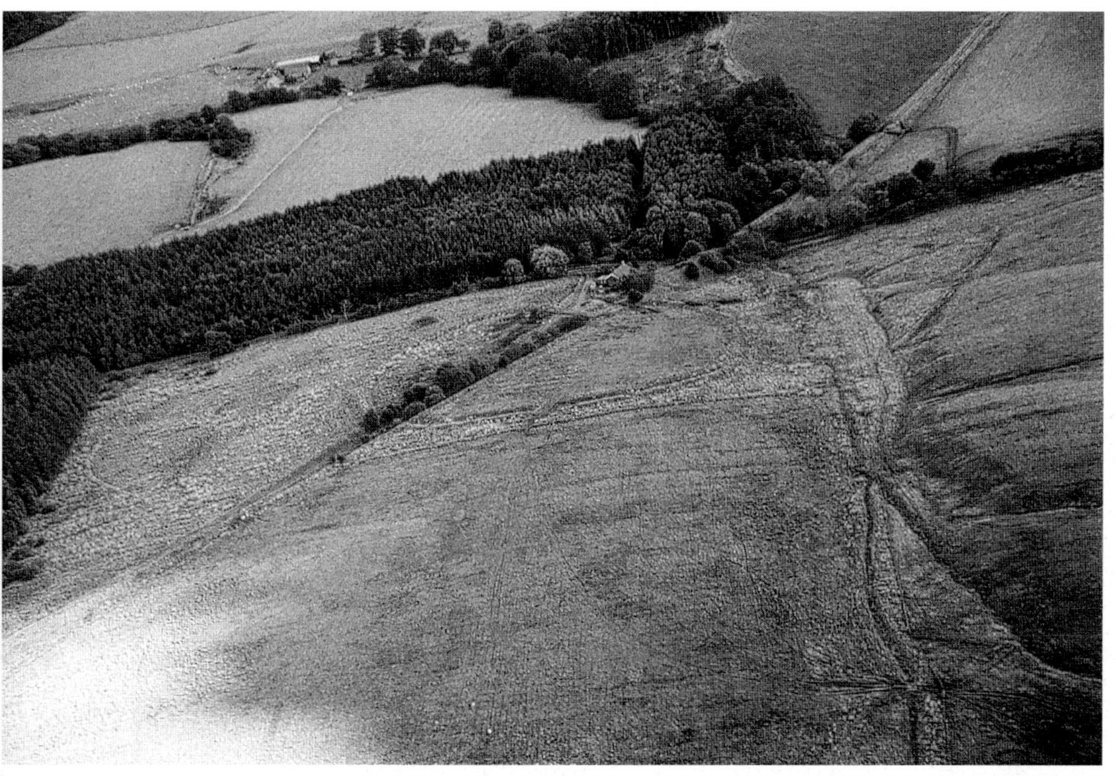

115 Ewesley.

Part of the 'Wanney Line', this track took no heed of the prehistoric enclosure (possibly a henge) through which it cut. Perhaps it was not recognised as such.

Recorded as 'Oseley' in 1286, it means 'blackbird wood'.

ESHOTT AIRFIELD

Much of the wartime airfield has been reconverted for agriculture, but a base for small private planes, including microlights, remains – a great advantage to the author. Called 'Esseta' in 1186, it means 'an ash grove'. Now it has been partly reclaimed from its use as a military airfield; runways, dispersal points and other features are still visible.

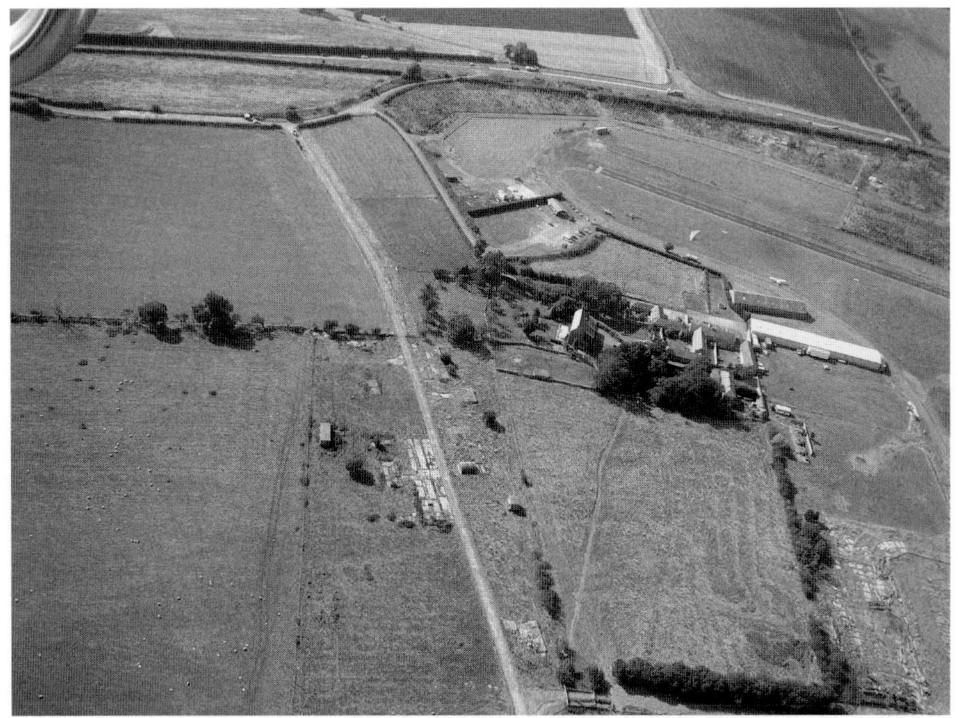

116 Bockenfield House and airfield.

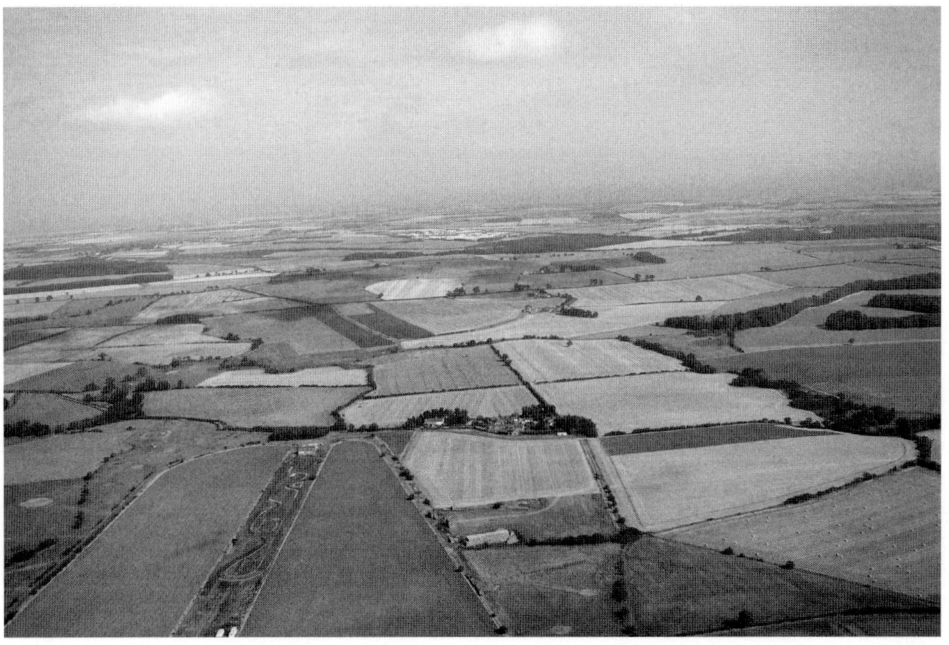

117 Eshott to Acklington.

12

LAND USE

Arable field-systems are largely on a regular 'enclosure' pattern, flat when farmed in modern times, but ridged by medieval and later ploughing. High ground tends to have thinner soils not suitable for growing crops effectively; they are easily exhausted. Sour and thin soils, however, can be used for forestry, especially for coniferous trees. Native deciduous woodland survives naturally in river and stream valleys that no one wants to use for anything else. There is a great demand for timber and at Hexham the Egger plant for making chip-board is one of the largest and most modern in Europe. The long-term plans for the timber industry are clear from the air; forests are felled, cuttings left to encourage minibeasts and the land is then planted again. There has been a reaction against drab, dull coniferous woodland and more varieties of trees have been introduced, especially on the margins. Quarrying has always made a big impact on the land, and this has its own section in the book.

Other land use includes sites for settlement, for industry, roads and water supplies. Again, these may be dealt with separately, but all are linked as 'land-use'. Other less-obvious impacts on the landscape are being made by the erection of masts and by the possible spread of wind-farms.

Leisure needs have also claimed much land, such as golf-courses and caravan sites. A few examples follow.

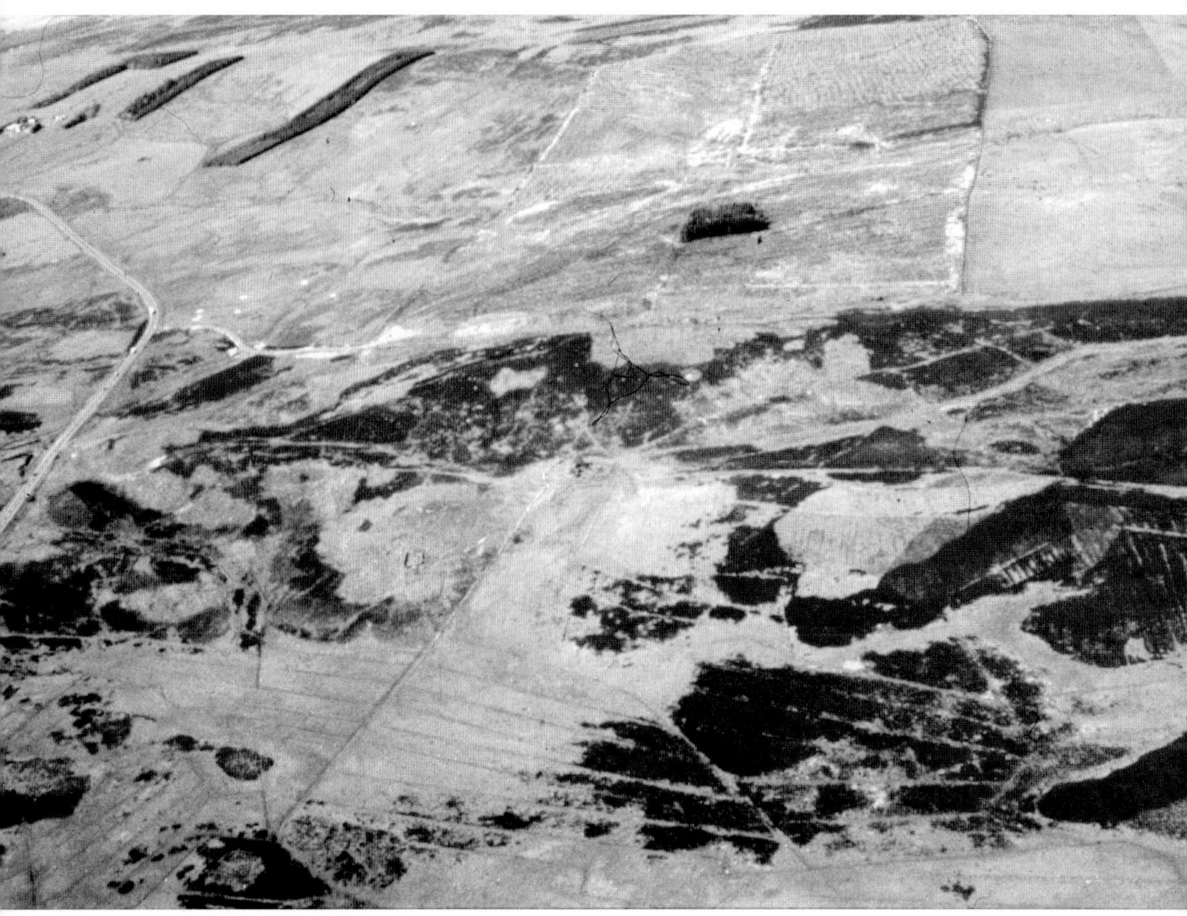

118 Tod Crag/Ottercops Moss.

At the top is a large rectangle of recently-felled forest. In the foreground are outcrops of sandstone, some quarried, and clear signs that part of the area has been drained. The rough grassland is used for sheep and cattle pasture. A 'tod' is a fox.

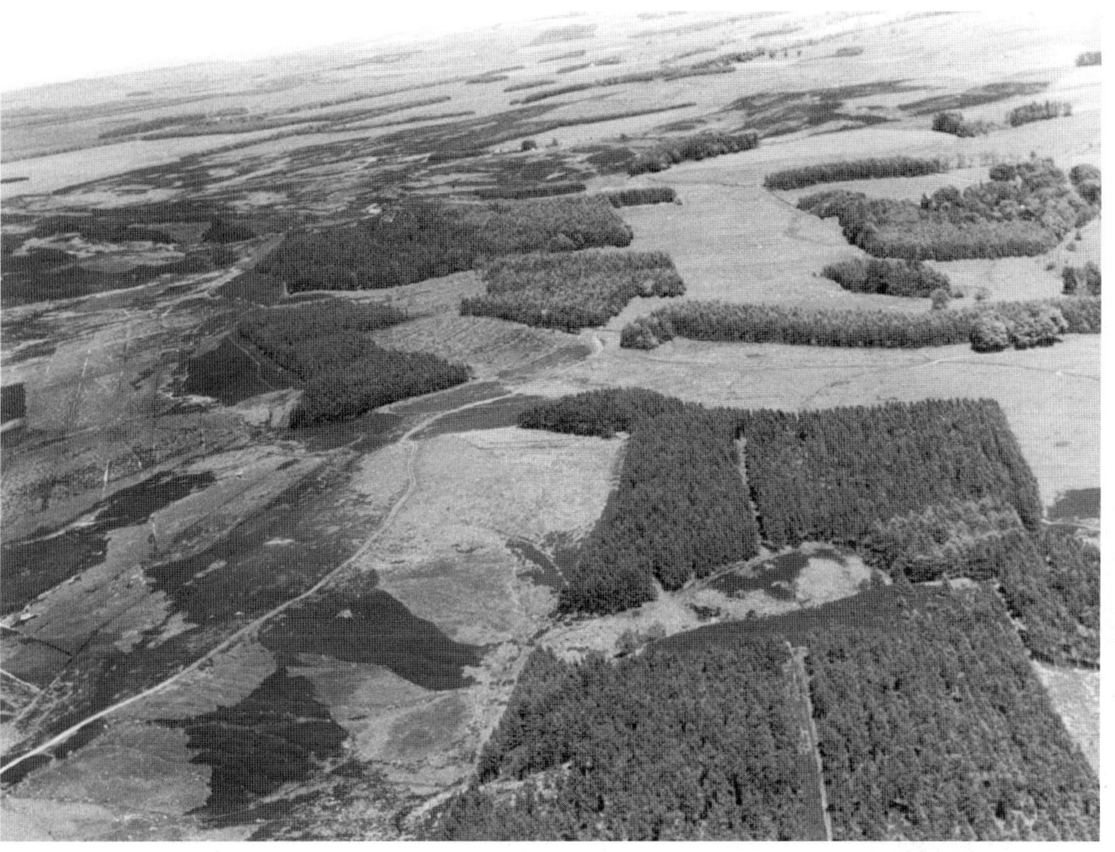

119 Wanneys.

This is a 'managed' forestry site with old, new and recently-felled plantations and moorland, all in a regular pattern.

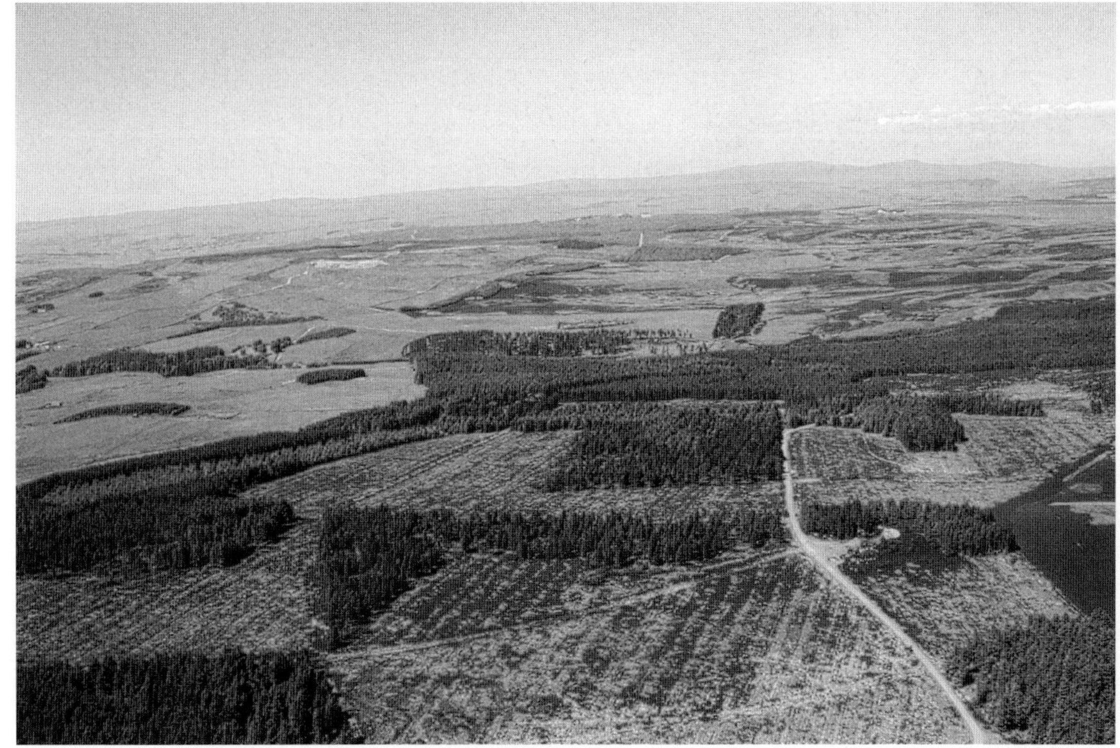

120 From the Wanney Hills to the Cheviots.

The extent of use of moorland is seen here; the view covers a large area of north-west Northumberland. Like many other sites in Northumberland, the Wanney Hills are being considered as possible wind-farms, but there is considerable local opposition to the destruction of such places of remote beauty and history.

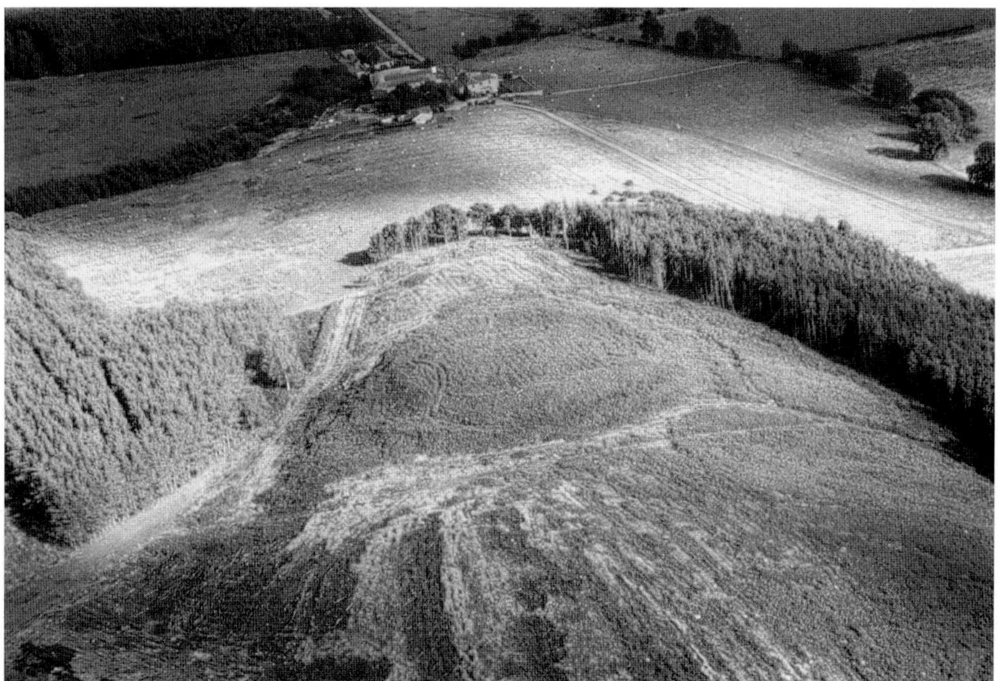

121 Titlington Pike.

Management of ancient sites has become a priority. Here we see the careful felling of woodland that had been planted over a prehistoric enclosure on a hill. According to records of 1123, it was originally settled by Tytel or Tytta.

The enclosure is one of so many in this county; it is built on a contour plan, with near-circular parallel ditches from which material was thrown up to build the walls. It would have been one of many in use in pre-Roman times and possibly later, although we have no dating evidence for this.

Recent excavations concentrate not only on structures, but on buried environmental evidence of what was growing or living there. Although this site has been disturbed by afforestation, there is still great potential for such discoveries using more sophisticated techniques than were available to antiquarians.

The choice of site was a good one: a down slope, with the land falling away on three sides, although it was vulnerable to attack from the west (bottom).

GOLF COURSES

Golf courses have made a significant impact on the landscape, as these three examples show. They are part of the growing demand for more space for leisure facilities.

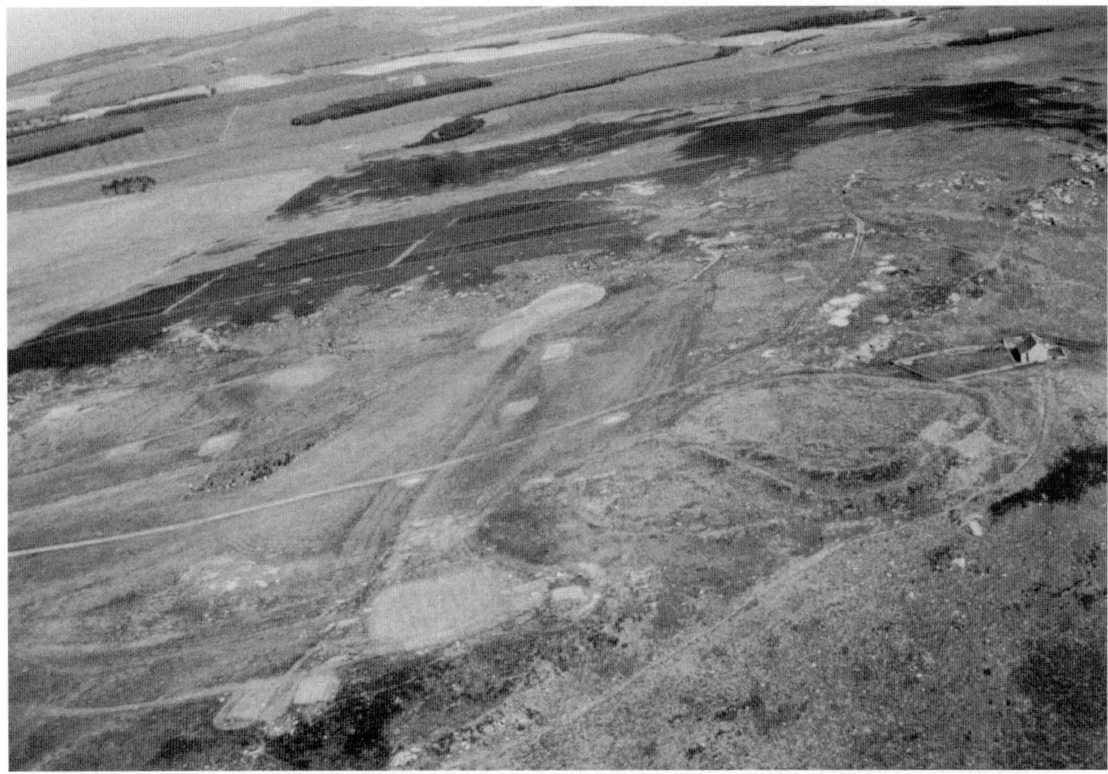

122 Dod Law golf course.

In the foreground is the scarp slope on top of which the ring ditches and walls of a pre-Roman enclosure can be seen. The rest of this hill is now used as a golf course, and nearby is an important sandstone quarry, used occasionally.

In the far distance is another line of scarps, before the dip slope takes us gently to the sea.

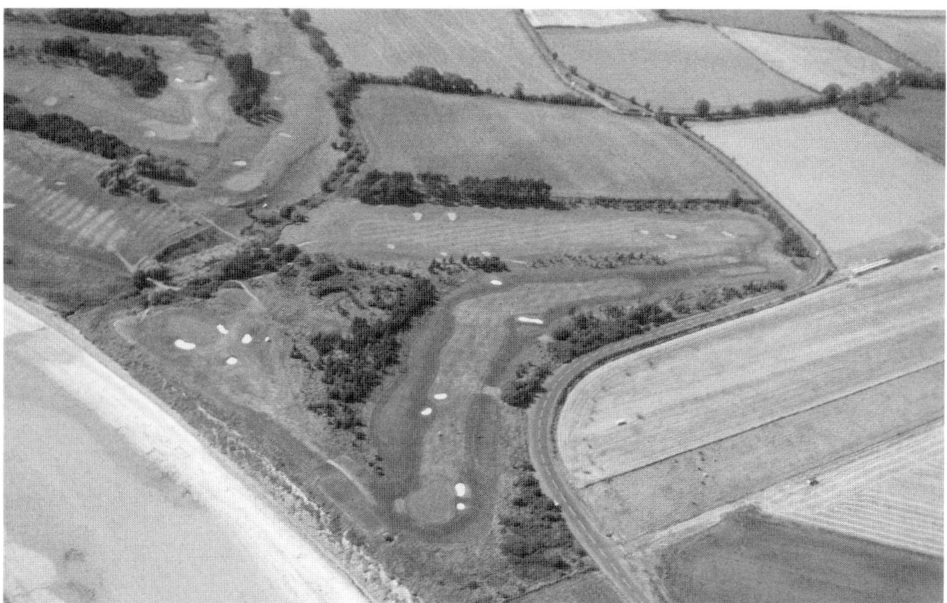

123 Foxton.

This borders the sea, close to and north of Alnmouth, which already has one of the earliest courses in England.

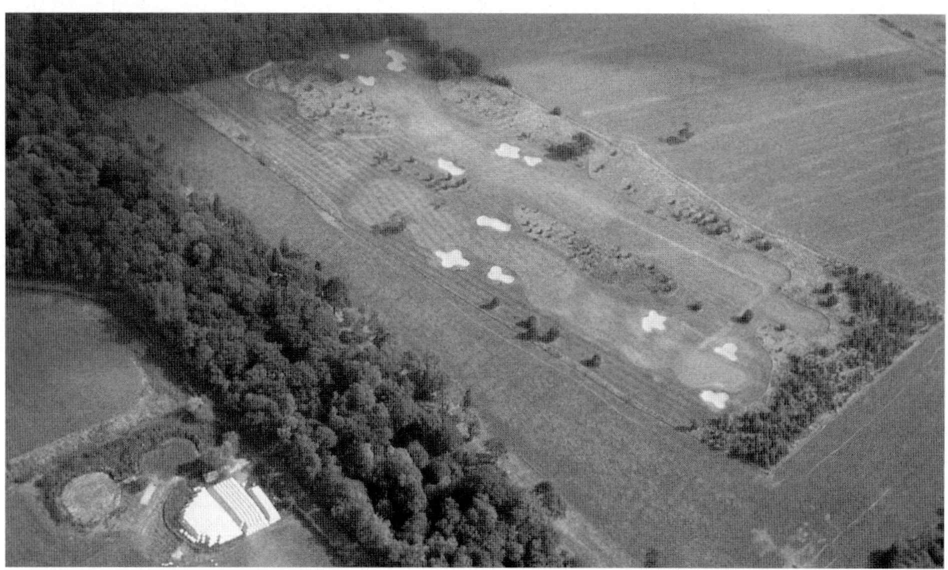

124 Burgham.

Between the old A1 near Felton and the A697, there are now two small golf courses.

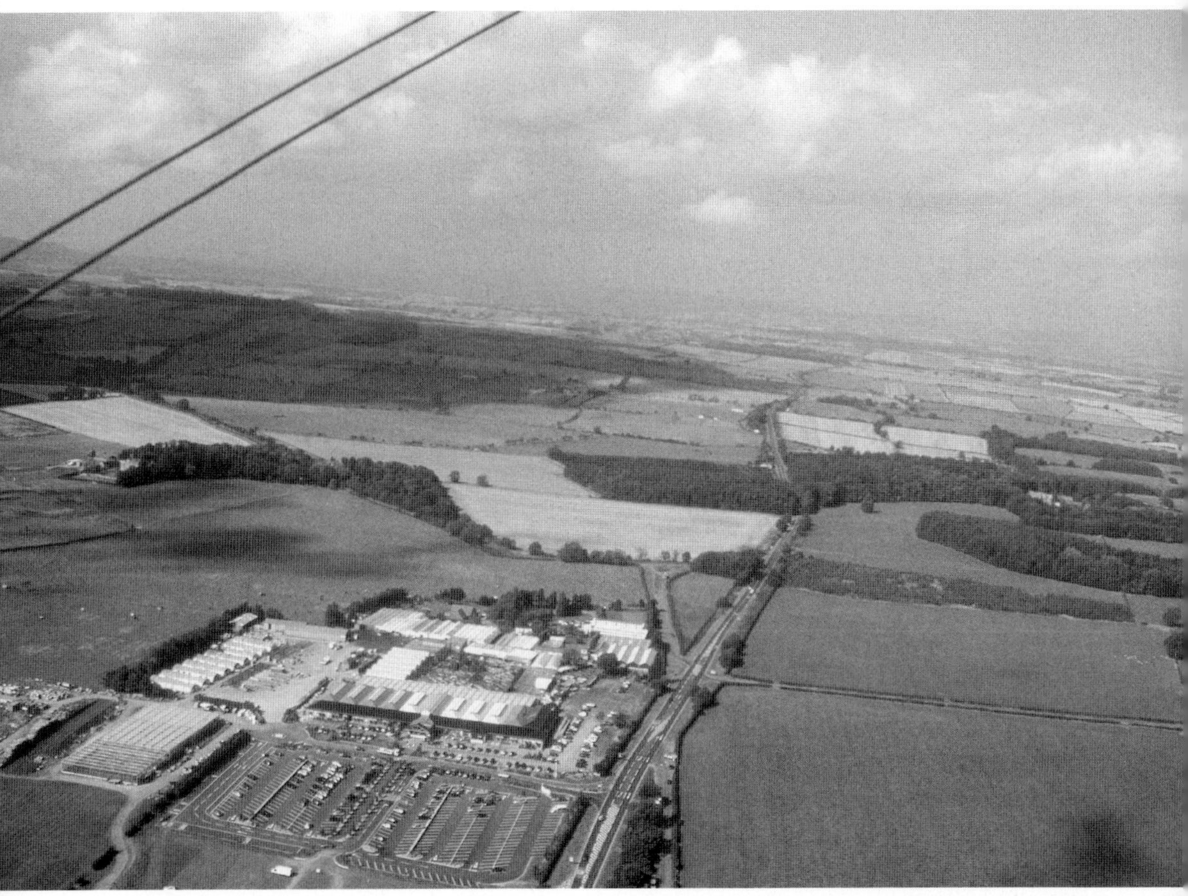

125 Heighley Gate Nurseries.

Garden centres have also become popular and now cover substantial areas. This one, just north of Morpeth and on the A697 has expanded rapidly to incorporate many retail outlets not necessarily linked to gardening, including cafes, gifts, bookstores and stationery. The car parking to the south and the provision of a children's playground has added to its use of space.

The expansion of such centres may be attributed in part to television gardening programmes, but one finds many people visiting for part of a day out and a meal or snack. There is also an increase in the number of retired people and leisure time.

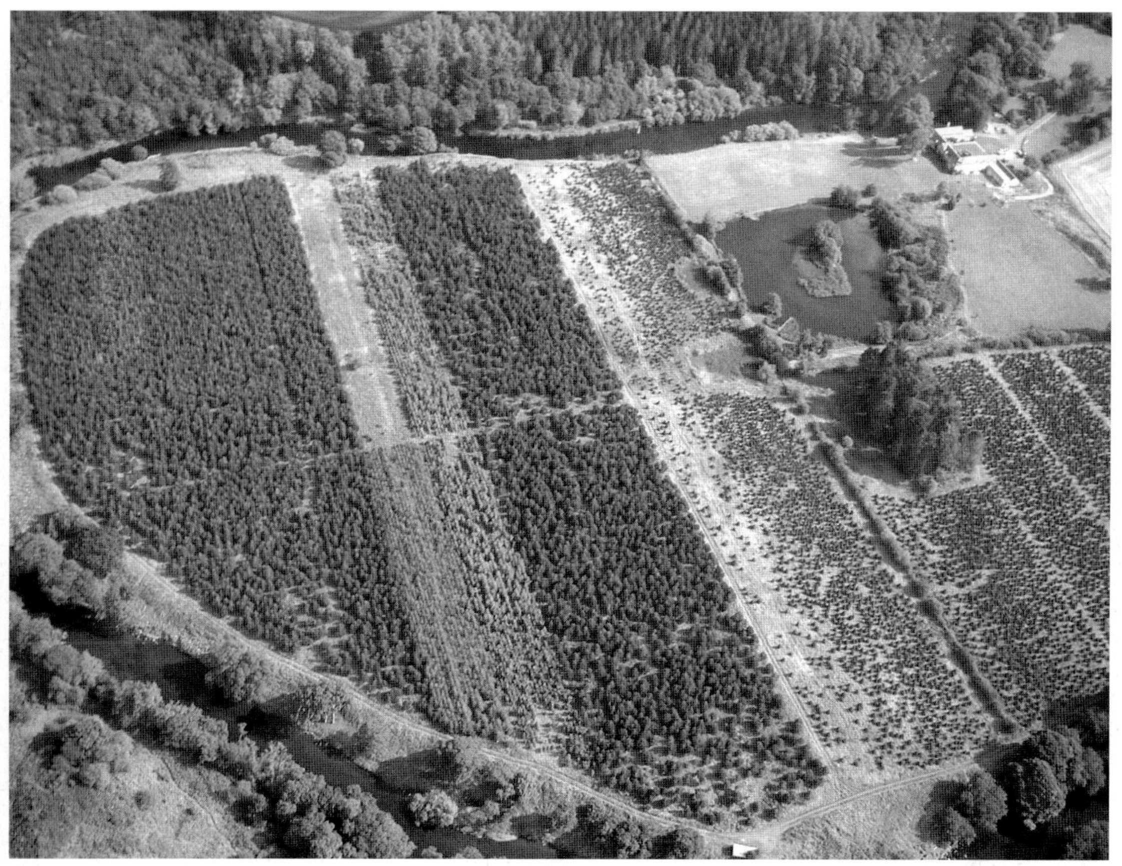

126 Shothaugh.

The haugh is alluvial land in the bend of the River Coquet west of Felton. A 'shott' or 'furshott' was a division of the old medieval field system of ploughing, another name for a furlong in which the strips of land all ran in the same direction. Clearly, its use is no longer for arable crops.

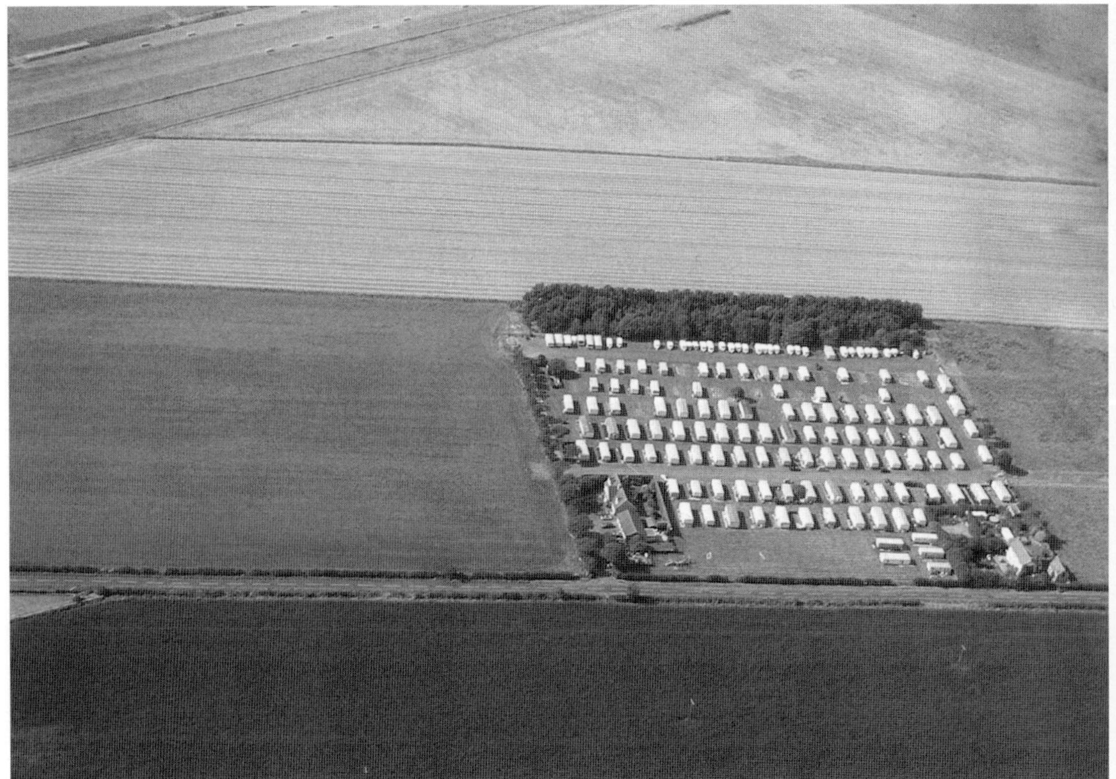

127 Caravan site at Seaton Vale, near Boulmer.

Caravan sites provide relatively inexpensive holiday homes, either long-term or temporary. Sometimes they disfigure the countryside to which people are attracted. Others may be more discreetly sited. Either way, they attract tourism, which has become a very important Northumberland industry.

13

WATER

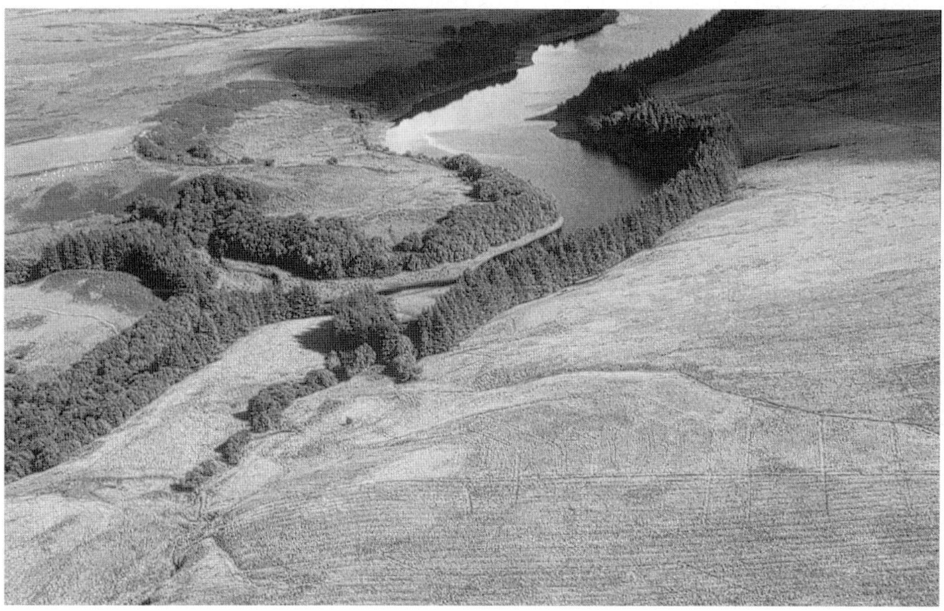

128 Fontburn.

Fontburn reservoir is a major source of stored water south of the Simonside Hills. A number of small valleys created by streams has watered the land and divided it up, and there are prehistoric sites of various periods on the land so formed, not all of which have been eliminated by later farming and small-scale mining.

This picture shows the Fontburn in its wooded valley. The large field (below) has many drains etched into it, and a large circular earthwork there may be of Roman or pre-Roman date.

The reservoir is fed by the Fallowlees Burn and the 'River' Font.

In a landscape where there are few buildings, it is notable for the survival of prehistoric burial cairns, enclosures and a large table of rock art. There are also many quarries.

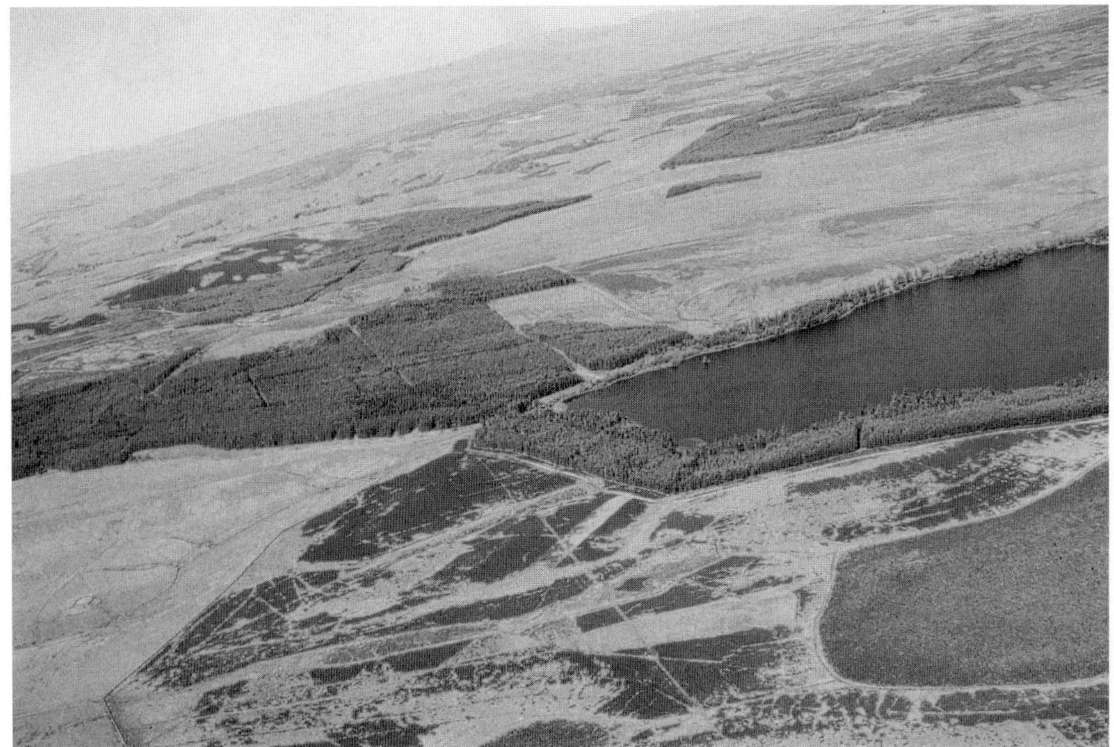

129 Sweethope Lough.

A 'managed' landscape of moorland, grass and forest includes this reservoir, with the dam wall to the left. Many of these small reservoirs have been completely dwarfed by the building of the huge Kielder Reservoir, the largest artificial lake in Europe, but are still used for water supply and fishing.

The lough is fed by several small streams and has been dammed to retain water. It is fringed by woodland and is reserved for fishing. South of it, lower right, is Sweethope Moss, wetland. The Wanney Crags are visible near the top left corner, above the planted woodland.

14

ESTATES

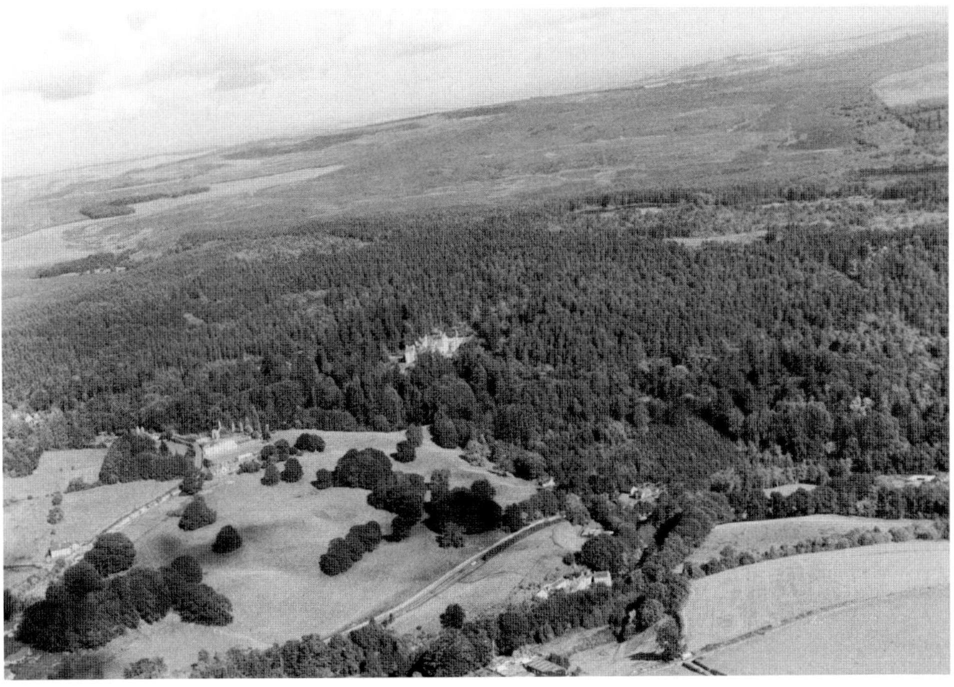

130a Cragside.

Cragside, now a National Trust property, lies at the centre of the picture of planted woodland and artificial lakes. At the top, the open moorland of Debdon Whitefield and Longframlington Common, with heather, bracken and grass, must have been the kind of landscape in which Lord Armstrong chose to build his estate. His money came from industry, and the transformation of this landscape shows that what can now be done to reverse the tree-felling of the past. At the bottom is the River Coquet with Thrum Mill, the road from Rothbury to Brinkburn, and the line of the old railway to Morpeth. Left, among the grass, is the Cragside glasshouse.

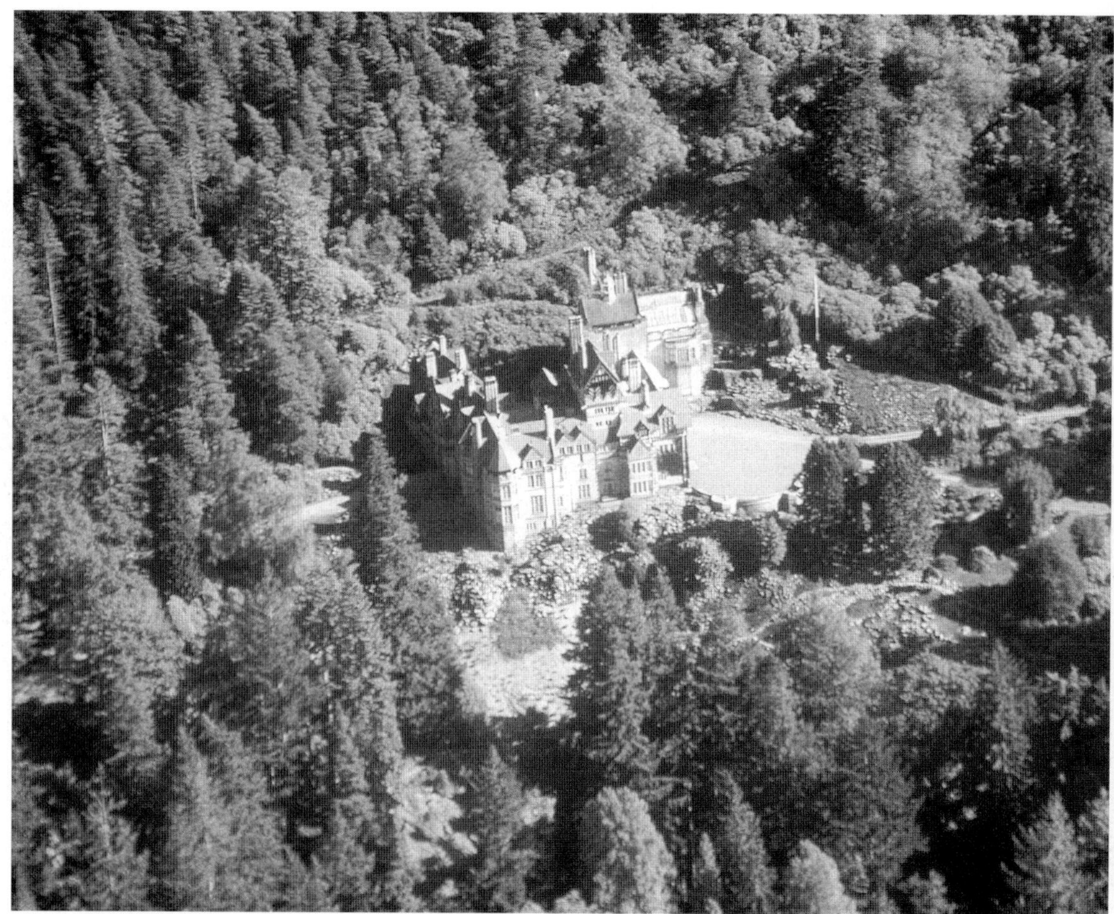

130b A close-up of Cragside house.

Cragside house and its landscape are a nineteenth-century creation, the house having been built on a platform formed by removing quarried stone from the crag, and developed over a number of years to suit the taste of the owner, Lord Armstrong. All the trees and the plants have been planted on what used to be moorland.

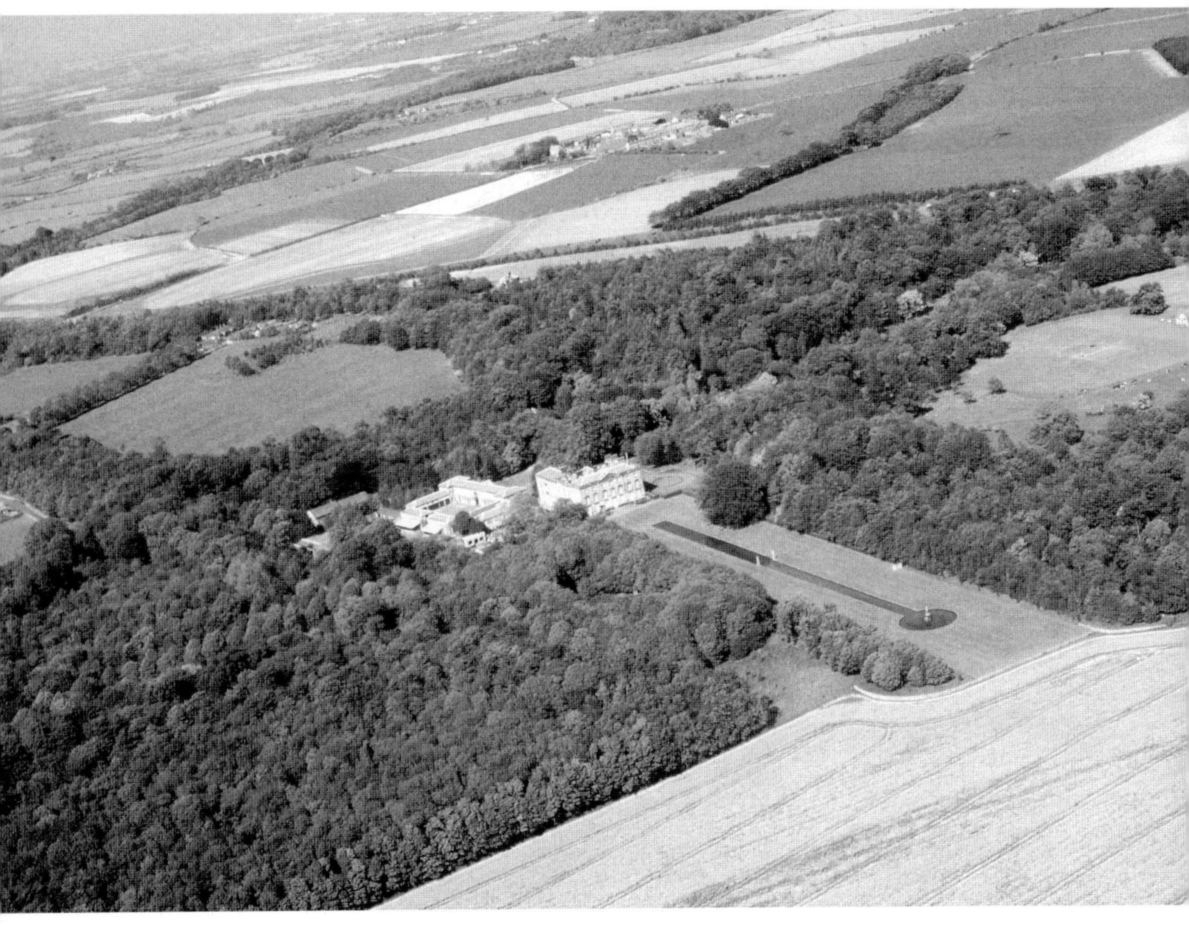

131 Blagdon Hall.

Taken on an approach to Newcastle airport in June 1994, the picture shows that the large field of oilseed rape gives way to the landscaped setting and woodland of Blagdon Hall, begun in 1735 and remodelled later in that century, with a lodge and stables added. The gardens, completed in 1938, were partly modelled by Sir Edwin Lutyens. It is the seat of the Ridley family. The name means 'a black valley'.

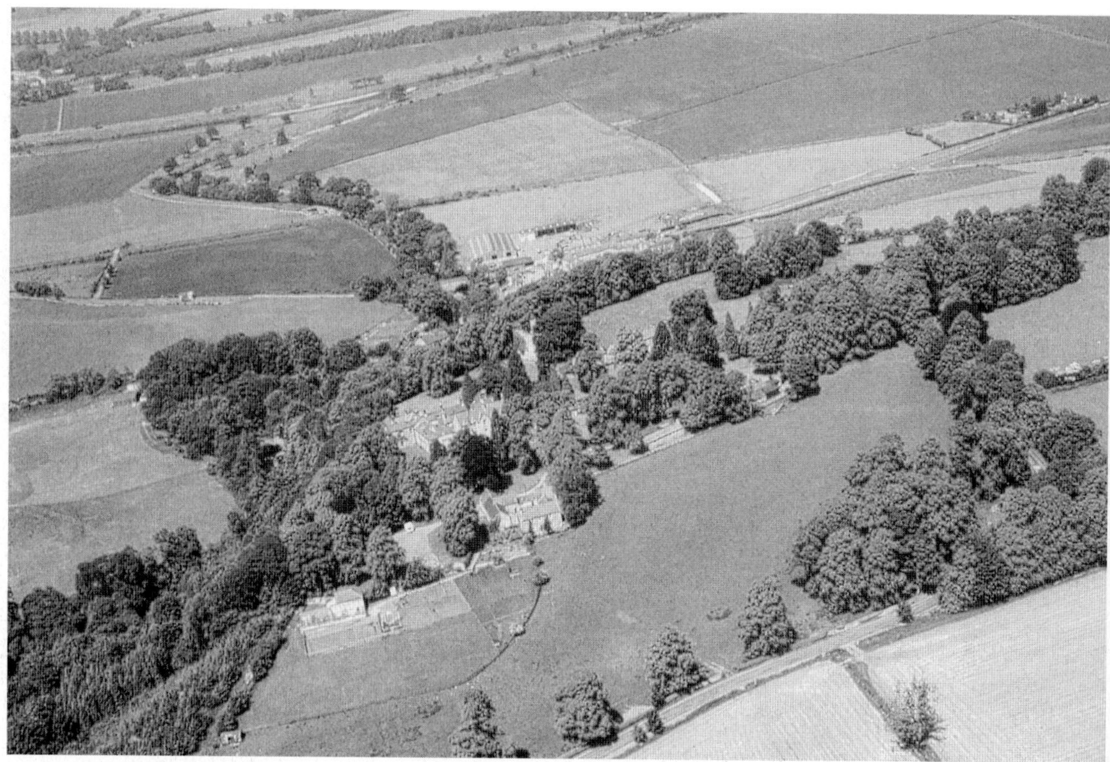

132 Dilston.

Woodland encloses the grassed area where there are the remains of a small castle and chapel. Below is Dilston College. This was the centre of the Earl of Derwentwater's estate, which included many other parts of Northumberland. Situated on the south bank of the Tyne where Devil's Water enters as a tributary, the estate included a mill and houses for farm workers. Excavation is beginning to piece together the early history of the site. Of great importance is the rich alluvial land, the 'haughs' on either side of the river. The maps of the Greenwich Hospital Commissioners, who were responsible for the administration of the estate after the earl's execution, are particularly fine pieces of recording. The name means 'the settlement on Devil's Water'.

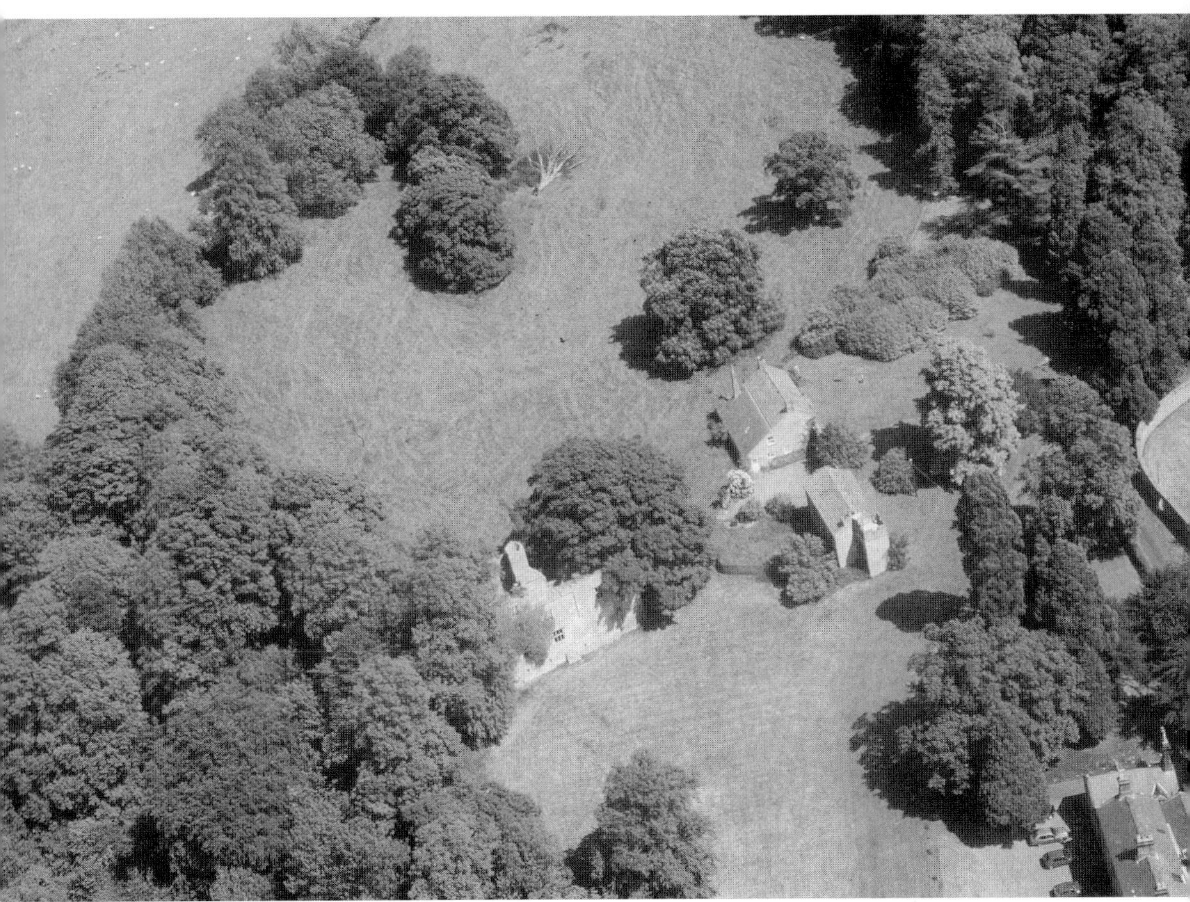

133 In the field to the east (top) of the castle the house of the Earl of Derwentwater once stood; it was dismantled after the unsuccessful Jacobite rebellion and the Earl's execution, the land handed over to Greenwich Hospital to administer. Beneath the field are the foundations of his hall, faintly visible, and some village houses must have been there too.

Those who demolished the hall left the stone tower house that had been there for centuries without a roof. It was L-shaped in plan when it was incorporated into Dilston Hall and has now been made safe. It lies at the lower centre of the picture, with trees around it. To the right (south) is a chapel, built in the early seventeenth-century as a place of worship for the Catholic family.

The Earl's estates were taken over after his execution and the death of his son, by Greenwich Hospital trustees, who have left an outstanding series of maps, with details such as field names and acreages.

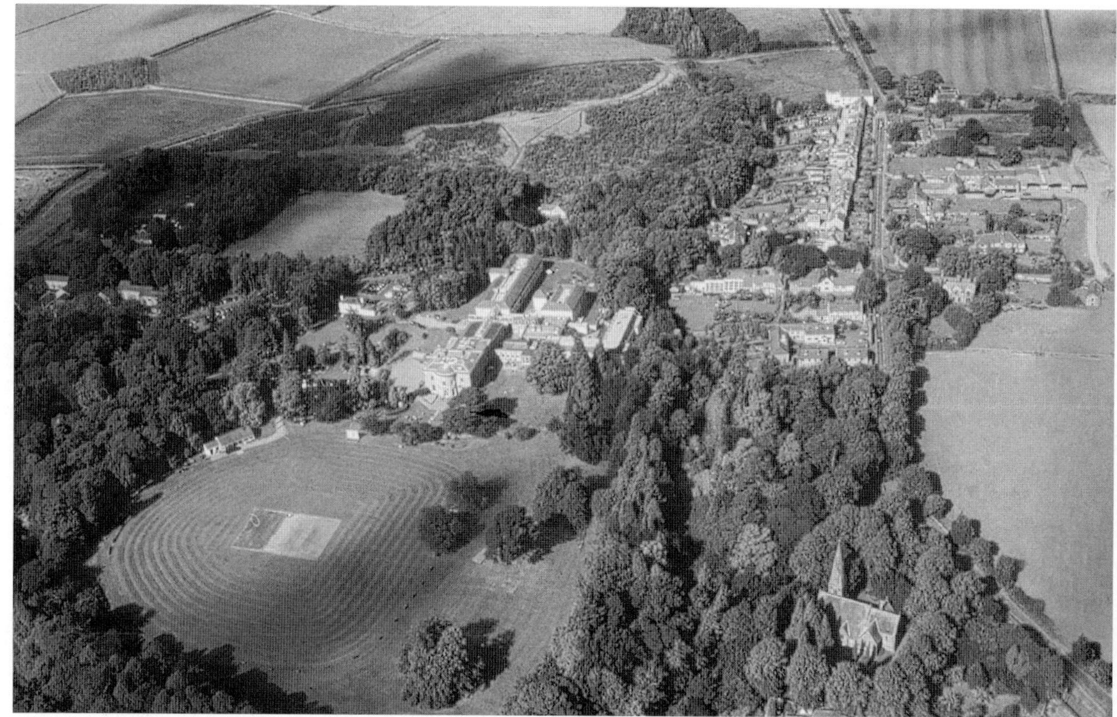

134 Longhirst Hall.

It appears as 'Langherst' in 1200, meaning 'the long wood' or 'wooded hill'. We see from the south a church (recent) in the wood, bottom right, with the straight main street and its ribbon of houses, a fine estate village, lying on the Longhirst Burn. Longhirst Hall is the centre of the picture. The estate has been reordered and is now used for leisure pursuits and as a conference centre. Originally it was built by Dobson; one outstanding feature was a central oblong hall with a circular glass dome. The house has conservatories and a walled garden.

Deciduous woodland is much in evidence, with arable fields all around, covering many filled-in mine workings. Pegswood open-cast mine has continued to exploit the same seam of coal.

15

DESERTED VILLAGES

Northumberland has many abandoned settlements of many periods, deserted for many reasons such as conversion of arable land to pasture, disease and less demand for agricultural labour.

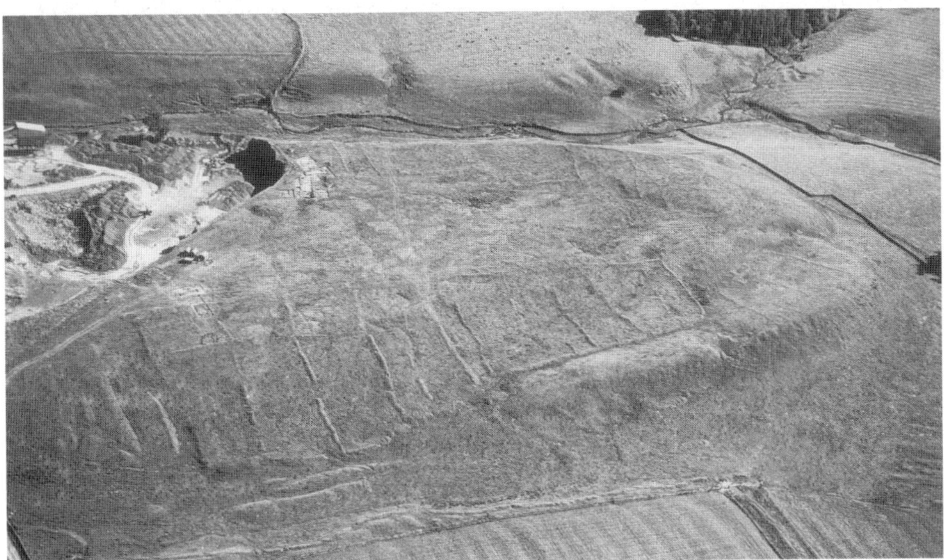

135 West Whelpington (NUM).

This is a classic site, with strips of land for cottages and gardens lying on either side of the road, and prominent rig and furrow ploughing in fields around. The hill is also being quarried, as it is an outcrop of whinstone. This prompted an excavation that revealed not only its late medieval history, but its early pre-Roman settlement. The later village had long houses in terraces; they were long houses in two parts, a living room and a byre, facing a broad green. It was Whelp's people's settlement in 1176.

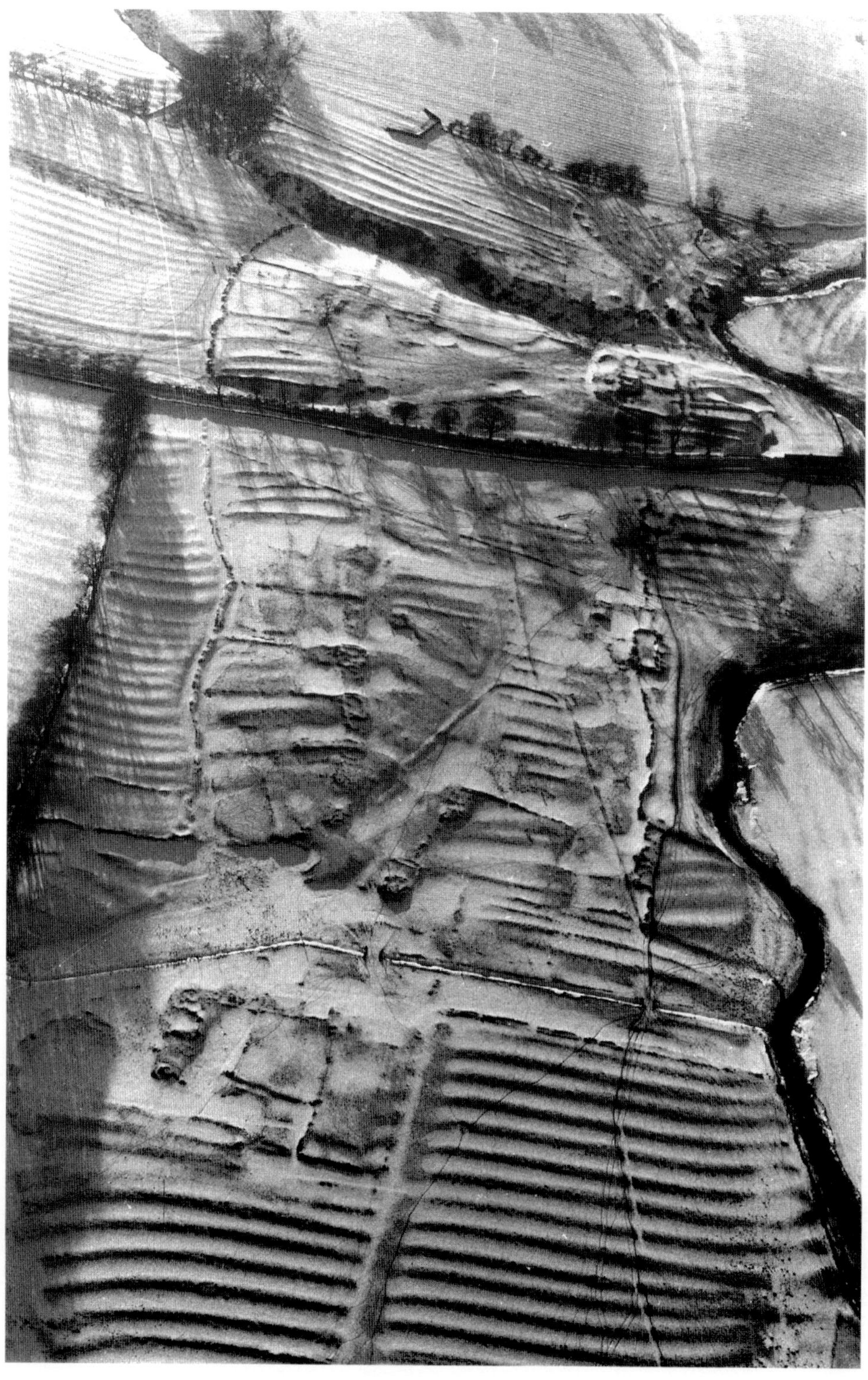

opposite 136 South Middleton (NUM).

The view from the east (bottom) shows that the settlement is now cut by a modern road (top).

All around the house sites and gardens, seen as little squares with rectangles attached, are deep rig and furrow systems of ploughing which either flank the village or (where they are later) encroach on it. All these features are highlighted by blown snow.

Houses have crofts/gardens attached for vegetables, a cow and other animals. To the north (left) of these plots was the village green, common land. West of the road (top) is a different group of houses that seem more randomly-placed, perhaps added later.

A few people were still living here in 1635 in four of the cottages. To the right (north) is the River Wansbeck.

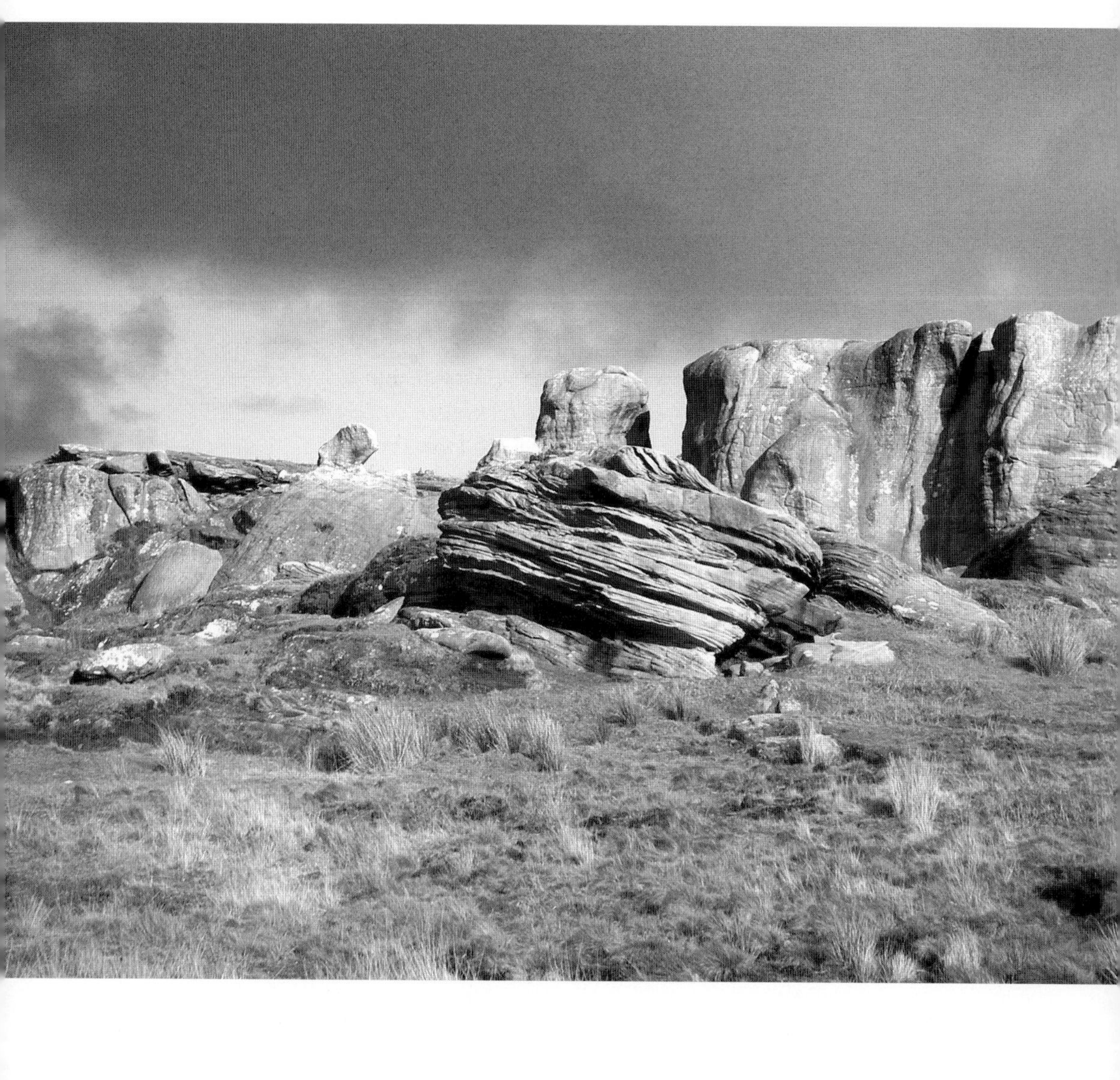

FURTHER READING

Aston M., (2003) *Interpreting the Landscape from the Air*, Tempus
Beckensall, S. (2001) *Northumberland: The Power of Place*, Tempus
Beckensall, S. (2003) *Prehistoric Northumberland*, Tempus
Beckensall, S. (2005) *Northumberland: Shadows of the Past*, Tempus
Beckensall, S. (2006) *Place names and field names of Northumberland*, Tempus
Beckensall, S., (2007) *Hexham: a history and guide*, Tempus
Frodsham, P. (2004) *Archaeology in Northumberland National Park* (CBA)
Frodsham, P. (2006) *In the Valley of the Sacred Mountain* (Northern Heritage)
Jones, G.B.D. and Wooliscroft, D.J. (2001) *Hadrian's Wall from the air*, Tempus
McCord, N. (1991) *North-East History from the Air*, Phillimore
Pevsner, N. (1992) Second edition. *Northumberland*, Penguin books
Wilson, D.R. (2000) *Air Photo Interpretation for archaeologists*, Tempus

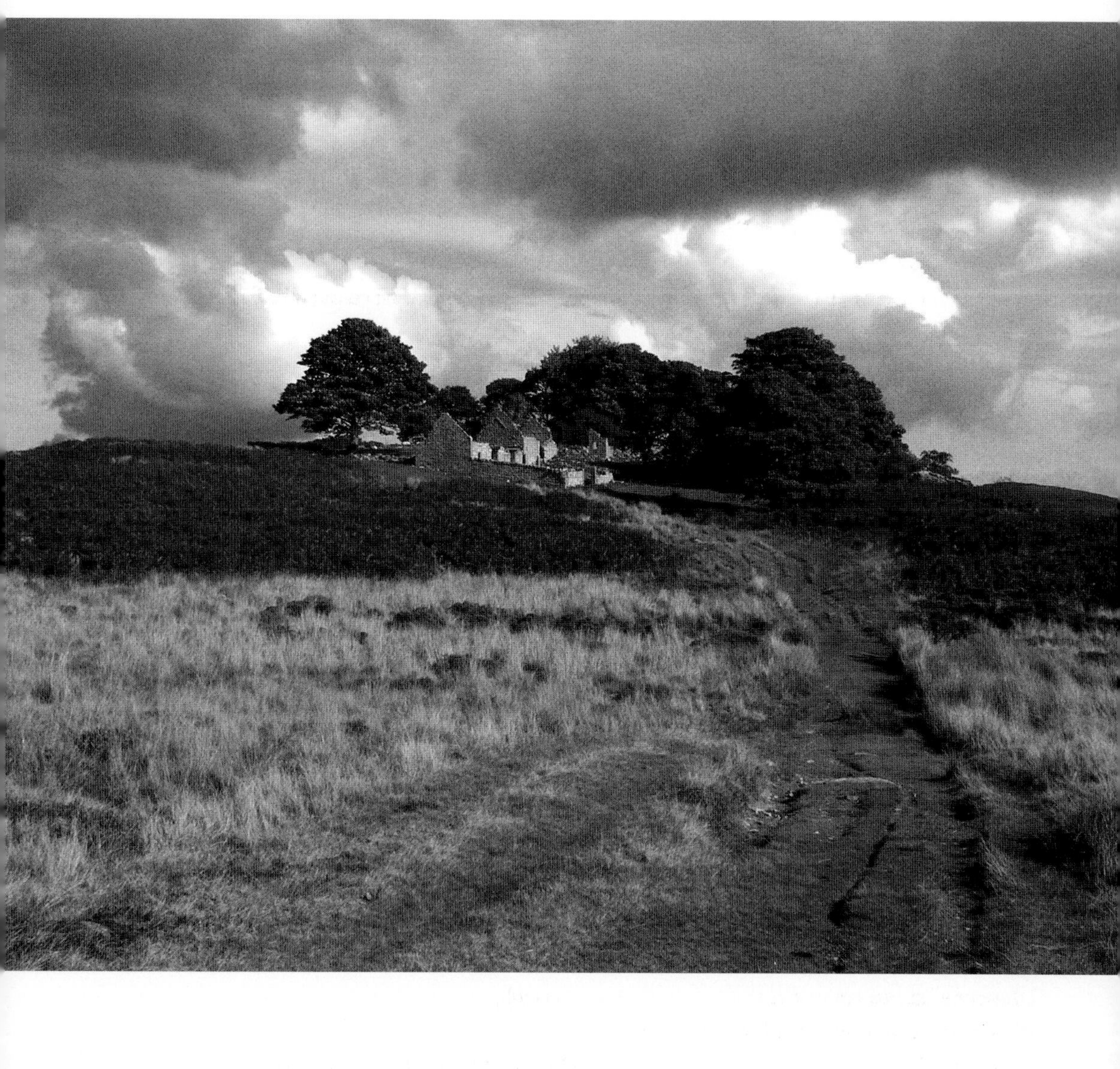

INDEX

The page of text is given with the illustration number is in brackets; colour illustrations are bold

ALSO AVAILABLE FROM THE HISTORY PRESS

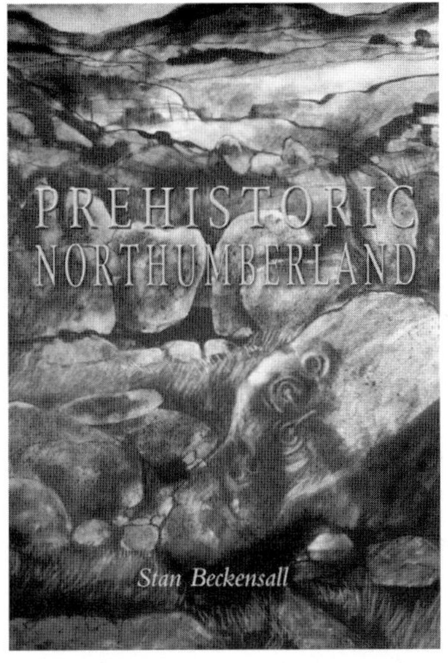

PREHISTORIC NORTHUMBERLAND

Stan Beckensall

'I wholeheartedly recommend *Prehistoric Northumberland* as fascinating informative and beautifully illustrated.'

Independent Archaeology

978-07524-2543-6
RRP £16.99

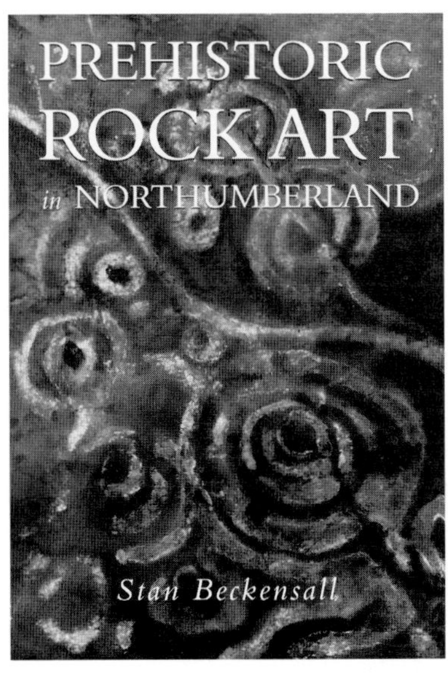

PREHISTORIC ROCK ART IN NORTHUMBERLAND

Stan Beckensall

'This first-rate book gives a comprehensive descriptive account of the rock-art of Norhumberland, richest of the counties in these singular remains.'

Antiquity

978-07524-1945-9
RRP £16.99

www.thehistorypress.co.uk

ALSO AVAILABLE FROM THE HISTORY PRESS

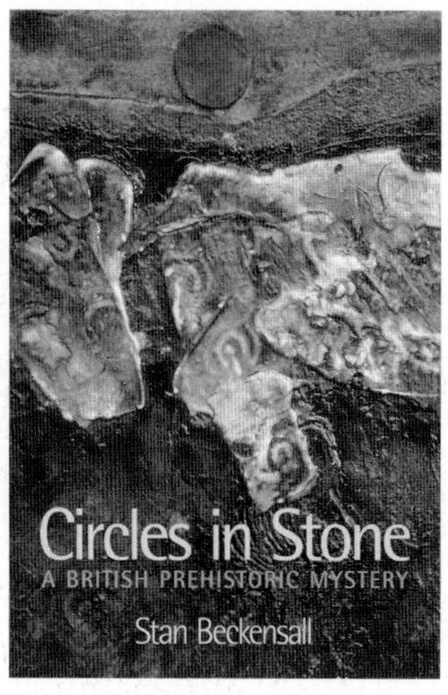

CIRCLES IN STONE
A BRITISH PREHISTORIC MYSTERY

Stan Beckensall

This book looks at the circular designs used throughout the Neolithic and Early Bronze Age in Britain to decorate rock outcrops, boulders, portable stones and monuments, and discusses theories about their origins, use and meaning.

978-07524-4015-6
RRP £18.99

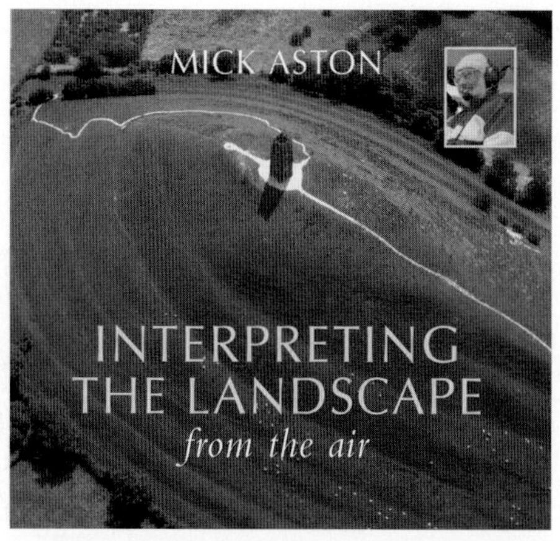

INTERPRETING THE LANDSCAPE FROM THE AIR

Mick Aston

'Mick is a brilliant interpreter of the landscape and here we see him at his best. This book will provide a happy read for all those interested in understanding the landscape.'

Current Archaeology

978-07524-2846-8
RRP £14.99

www.thehistorypress.co.uk